Feminist Perspectives on
Orange Is the New Black

Feminist Perspectives on *Orange Is the New Black*

Thirteen Critical Essays

Edited by
APRIL KALOGEROPOULOS HOUSEHOLDER
and ADRIENNE TRIER-BIENIEK

McFarland & Company, Inc., Publishers
Jefferson, North Carolina

Library of Congress Cataloguing-in-Publication Data

Names: Householder, April Kalogeropoulos, 1972– editor. |
    Trier-Bieniek, Adrienne M., editor.
Title: Feminist perspectives on Orange is the new black : thirteen
    critical essays / edited by April Kalogeropoulos Householder and
    Adrienne Trier-Bieniek.
Description: Jefferson, North Carolina : McFarland & Company, Inc.,
    Publishers, 2016. | Includes bibliographical references and index.
Identifiers: LCCN 2016010991 | ISBN 9781476663920
    (softcover : acid free paper) ∞
Subjects: LCSH: Orange is the new black (Television program) |
    Lesbianism on television. | Stereotypes (Social psychology) on
    television.
Classification: LCC PN1992.77.O735 F46 2016 | DDC 791.45/72—
    dc23
LC record available at https://lccn.loc.gov/2016010991

British Library cataloguing data are available

ISBN (print) 978-1-4766-6392-0
ISBN (ebook) 978-1-4766-2519-5

Cover images © 2016 iStock

Printed in the United States of America

*McFarland & Company, Inc., Publishers
    Box 611, Jefferson, North Carolina 28640
    www.mcfarlandpub.com*

For my son, Athan,
whom everything is for.
—AKH

For Kathy Ransom,
the best law enforcement has to offer and
my own personal cheerleader.
—ATB

Acknowledgments

A special thank you to my co-editor for sharing her expertise and knowledge throughout this process. Thanks to all of the contributors to this book for their hard work and enthusiasm in making this an excellent collection that covers a wide range of important feminist scholarship. I also thank my students, who are always excited to discuss the representational politics of *Orange Is the New Black*, and who teach and empower me every day. And for the strong women behind and in front of the camera, who make a show that has ignited cultural conversations about so many far-reaching issues, and who fiercely challenge the way we see women in television.

—AKH

Thank you to the all the contributors to this text for sharing their expertise and talent. Working with you all has been a privilege and I have learned so much from each of you. These essays are a reflection of outstanding scholarship.

I thank my always feminist partner-in-crime and official book goddess, Patricia Leavy. I also thank Angie Moe, the greatest dissertation chair in the galaxy. Thanks to the usual suspects in my life for their support, my soul-sisters Efua Akoma and Beatrice Yarbrough and their families, Lee Paulsen and family, the Clapper twins, Andy and Dan and their families, the Spertis, the Triers, the Bienieks, Chastity Orrship, Vadzim Sheika and Bethany Kelly. I thank Carrie Buist for always responding to my texts so we can gossip about *Orange Is the New Black*. To Catherine Kelly, thanks for being as big a pop culture junkie as I am. Thanks to my four-legged pals Mara and Charlie for the constant company and to my two-legged husband Tim Bieniek who is just as nerdy and awesome as he was in 1997. Thanks to Rick and Deanne Trier for raising me right.

—ATB

Table of Contents

Acknowledgments   vii

Introduction: Is Orange *the New Black?*
    APRIL KALOGEROPOULOS HOUSEHOLDER *and*
    ADRIENNE TRIER-BIENIEK   1

"Chocolate and vanilla swirl, swi-irl": Race and Lesbian
    Identity Politics
    SARAH E. FRYETT   15

We Will Survive: Race and Gender-Based Trauma as
    Cultural Truth Telling
    KALIMA Y. YOUNG   32

Jenji Kohan's Trojan Horse: Subversive Uses of Whiteness
    KATIE SULLIVAN BARAK   45

"You don't look full ... Asia": The Invisible and Ambiguous
    Bodies of Chang and Soso
    MINJEONG KIM   61

Cleaning Up Your Act: Surveillance, Queer Sex and the
    Imprisoned Body
    YVONNE SWARTZ HAMMOND   77

The Transgender Tipping Point: The Social Death of
    Sophia Burset
    HILARY MALATINO   95

All in the (Prison) Family: Genre Mixing and Queer
    Representation
    KYRA HUNTING   111

Pennsatucky's Teeth and the Persistence of Class
SUSAN SERED   128

Pleasure and Power Behind Bars: Resisting Necropower
with Sexuality
ZOEY K. JONES   140

Anatomy of a Binge: Abject Intimacy and the Televisual Form
ANNE MOORE   157

"You don't feel like a freak anymore": Representing Disability,
Madness and Trauma in Litchfield Penitentiary
LYDIA BROWN   174

Piper Chapman's Flexible Accommodation of Difference
H. RAKES   194

"Can't fix crazy": Confronting Able-Mindedness
SARAH GIBBONS   210

About the Contributors   225

Index   227

Introduction: Is *Orange* the New Black?

APRIL KALOGEROPOULOS HOUSEHOLDER
and ADRIENNE TRIER-BIENIEK

From the classroom to the water cooler, *Orange Is the New Black* (*OITNB*) has been one of the most talked-about shows to emerge from new internet media technology in the 21st century. Nominated for 12 Emmy awards in its first season, *OITNB* has garnered both critical and popular attention for its breakthrough characters, who have pushed the boundaries of how women are represented on television, as well as for Netflix's use of streaming technology, which has produced the cultural phenomenon "binge-watching." Additionally, academic conferences have become overwhelmed with requests to submit papers for panel discussions focused on these themes. In the two years since the series premiere in 2013, *OITNB* has sparked considerable debate in academic communities surrounding its depictions of social class, race, gender, sexual orientation, power, privilege, motherhood, prison, and the criminal justice system. Race, class and ethnicity are featured as prominent narratives, and sexual orientation is a consistent topic, as are people who are transgender. *OITNB* is the first show to present a well-rounded transgender character, Sophia, played by a transgender actress, Laverne Cox, who was featured on *Time* magazine's June 9, 2014, cover as the face of the transgender "tipping point": America's next civil rights frontier. *OITNB* challenges the assumptions of media moguls who argue that television must pander to the 18–35 male demographic, a type of cultural patriarchy that limits women's standpoints and diminishes women's experiences as active consumers and makers of media. Rather, *OITNB* demonstrates how television can appeal to girls and women, signaling a significant shift for programming diversity.

Further, the book on which the show is based has become the "book of the semester" at many colleges and universities. In 2014, the Department of Sociology at UCLA offered a first-year undergraduate seminar titled "Is Orange Really the New Black? Women, Race, and the Carceral State." In the summer of 2013, the University of Minnesota offered an undergraduate course in its Department of Gender, Women, and Sexuality Studies entitled "Gender, Race, and Class: Women's Lives in the United States," which used *OITNB* as a "textbook" to frame issues on race, class, gender, sexuality, the prison-industrial complex, and dis/ability. The course was so successful that it was offered again in the spring of 2015. Blogs written on the show have racked up millions of hits and comments from people all over the world. *OITNB* was renewed for a second season before the first season began, and again for a third season prior to the start of the second. In its third season, it became the most-watched series on Netflix, which has more than 60 million subscribers worldwide (McClelland 2015). To say that *OITNB* has struck a chord within popular culture would be a severe understatement.

Perhaps what makes the show so ripe for analysis is not just its celebration of diversity, but the mixed messages that also dominate many of its narratives. On the eve of the Season 3 premiere, *Rolling Stone* featured a cover story entitled "Caged Heat," a nod to the women-in-prison genre that the show consciously references, featuring actors Taylor Schilling (Piper Chapman) and Laura Prepon (Alex Vause), the white, thin, femme, gay-for-pay leads, bra-less and staring seductively at the reader. The image embodies the main contradictions of the show. It has been both lauded for its original depictions of a diverse, mostly female, ensemble cast, while simultaneously playing up age-old archetypes of women and their sexuality that can be traced back to pulp fiction, 1960s exploitation movies, gender stereotypes in contemporary popular culture, and beyond. A consistent debate is whether *OITNB* celebrates diversity in its multiple and diverse characters, or is a story told through the lens of white privilege, featuring a cast of characters who embody some of the most racist and sexist stereotypes in the history of television.

Despite all of these ongoing conversations, there has been little academic work published on the show. This is especially relevant to the study of gender and pop culture because, in three seasons, *OITNB* has covered more ground for scholarly discussion than most television shows traverse over the course of an entire series. This collection of essays begins to lay the groundwork for an academic dialogue about *OITNB*'s depictions of power and privilege, from an intersectional perspective that considers the overlapping axes of race, class, gender, and sexuality. In this book we show that the success of *OITNB* is based, partly, on its presentation of diverse groups of women who challenge media representations constructed by what bell hooks has called the "white supremacist, capitalist patriarchy," a phrase hooks uses to "remind us of the interlocking systems of domination that define our reality" (hooks 1997).

The Prison Industrial Complex

The United States has the largest prison system in the world, with one out of every nine Americans imprisoned, at a cost of $80 billion per year. In the last 30 years, the number of people incarcerated in the United States quadrupled, from 300,000 to more than two million (Alexander 2011). These trends in increased incarceration rates created a demand for more prison space, and private companies began to invest in building and running prisons, while also advocating for legislation on behalf of the industry. Such private companies, working in tandem with state and federal governments which legislate and enforce unequally across racial and class divides, comprise what Angel Davis has termed the "prison industrial complex" (Davis 2001).

In *OITNB*, the connection between prison as an industry and prison as a form of punishment juxtaposes its characters with one another in complex ways. Characters like the prison executive Natalie "Fig" Figeroa and assistant to the warden Joe Caputo serve as the mouthpiece for the institution. When we meet Fig, the viewer is quick to learn that she is attempting to run a prison based on the rules and regulations set forth by the prison system while also embezzling money from the Department of Corrections. Caputo, while altruistic in some of his intentions, also demonstrates the allure of the prison-industrial complex by entering into contracts with food companies that provide low-cost meals that lack taste and nutrition. The food contracts also take away the women's ability to learn cooking skills, framing these scenes as feminist issues.

OITNB spends a significant amount of its time discussing incarceration rates and laws for drug offenses. Perhaps the single greatest force behind the growth of the prison population and the racial disparities in incarceration rates among blacks and Hispanics has been the national "War on Drugs." According to a 2014 report by Human Rights Watch, "tough-on-crime" laws adopted since the 1980s have filled U.S. prisons with mostly nonviolent offenders. The number of incarcerated drug offenders has increased twelve-fold since the 1980s, when the Reagan Administration introduced federal drug sentencing guidelines that targeted drugs like crack cocaine, prevalent in inner city communities. Mandatory minimum sentences and their relationship to low-level drug offenses becomes a common plot for the series. When we first meet Piper in the pilot episode, we learn that her drug offense was more than a decade old and, because of mandatory minimum laws, she was sentenced to do time rather than receive probation. Nicky's use and sale of drugs landed her at Litchfield, Poussey and Tastee are both serving sentences for minor drug crimes, and Janae was caught selling marijuana on her first run. Drug sentencing disparities target people of color, with African Americans representing 12 percent of the total population of drug users, but 38 percent of those arrested for drug offenses and 59 percent of those in state prison for a drug offense. Five times as many whites are using drugs as African Americans, yet African Americans are sent to prison for drug offenses at ten times the rate of whites. African Americans serve virtually as much time in prison for a drug offense (58.7 months) as whites do for a violent offense (61.7 months) (Sentencing Project). One of the most disturbing realities is that one in three young African Americans will serve time in prison, and in many cities, more than half of all young adult black men are currently incarcerated, or on probation or parole (Alexander 2011). Statistics like these that highlight the racial disparities in the criminal justice system have led civil rights advocate and legal scholar Michelle Alexander to deem this as the new era of Jim Crow, equating these current trends with racial genocide (2011). *OITNB* calls into question the use of mandatory prison sentences for drug-related crime. Given the inequality present in the criminal justice system, *OITNB* seeks to shine a light on how race, class and gender are factors in sentencing disparity.

Gender as a Cultural Construct

To better frame the connection between gender and popular culture, we first need to discuss the concept of gender as a cultural and social construction. In essence, to discuss gender is to break down gender binaries present in everyday life. This is increasingly complex when media and representations of women in popular culture are tossed into the mix. As Judith Butler writes, when considering how gender is defined we must think about the way gender is represented in social structures because "the subjects regulated by such are, by virtue of being subjected to them, formed, defined and reproduced in accordance with the requirement of those structures" (1999, 3). In other words, gender is constructed and reproduced by the media. As Laura Mulvey writes in her seminal work on the male gaze, the place of women in media is as subject to be devoured and reproduced by a patriarchal culture. While our book seeks to challenge perspectives like the male gaze, it is important to recognize the connection between gender as an outcome of social structures, and the way this is replicated in popular culture.

Gender is applied to media or pop culture as an agent of socialization. Popular culture is the images, narratives, and ideas that are regularly found within mainstream culture (Trier-Bieniek and Leavy 2014). Media culture especially is becoming a more mainstream means through which norms, values and attitudes are developed. Rarely will a day go by that we are not exposed to media in some way. As Arend notes, the purpose of a media-driven society is to convince people that they need the products being sold or the lifestyle presented in glossy images, or that they should desire to emulate characters portrayed in film or on television (2014). Additionally, the impact of visual media is particularly present in daily life. Brandt writes, "While the average viewer is most likely unaware of the social construction taking place through television programming, its effects are internalized nonetheless. Indeed, a large part of the success and popularity of television is its ability to anticipate and respond to the cultural concerns and audience desires" (2014, 112).

Yet the sexism found in most media outlets continues to be replicated on television. Rooted in the gender binary, sexism is found in the lack of stories about women's lives, the insistence on defining femininity and masculinity in limiting ways, and the lack of women behind the scenes in the production of media culture, to name a few. When gender is replicated through the eyes of popular culture it often contains dominant narratives about what it means to be male or female through a very narrow lens. This lens then has the ability to reach widely differing communities, regions and lives. "As an agent of socialization, media culture differs from family, religion and other socializing institutions because of its far-reaching grasp or monopoly of the cultural landscape and also because we often elect to spend our leisure time participating in, generally consuming pop culture" (Trier-Bieniek and Leavy 2014, 13). Additionally, as Milstone and Meyer write, "popular-cultural products, or texts, are symbolic because they carry meanings. These meanings are produced through linguistic and visual representations" (2012, 2). Thus, whether we like it or not, popular culture becomes part of our lives and television has the ability to shape what cultural conversations are happening. In *OITNB* this conversation is grounded in feminist concerns that highlight the overlapping intersections of race, class, gender and sexuality.

Intersectional Approaches

Because *OITNB* is situated as a potential game-changer in the representations of gender in popular culture, it becomes necessary to analyze the show through feminist theory. As Butler writes, "For the most part, feminist theory has assumed that there is some existing identity, understood through the category of women, who not only initiates feminist interests and goals within discourse, but constitutes the subject for whom political representation is pursued" (1999, 2). Perhaps the most influential feminist approach to understanding *OITNB* is intersectionality. Intersectionality as a theoretical approach is meant to address systems of inequality and their overlaps (e.g.,

Crenshaw, 1991). In her groundbreaking article, Kimberle Crenshaw focuses specifically on the intersection of race and sex in the lives of black women. Since then, a wide range of work has emerged in critical race, post-colonial, queer, gender and women's studies, utilizing intersectional approaches to understand how interlocking systems of oppression based on categories of race, class, sex, gender, sexuality, nation, ethnicity, coloniality, (dis)ability, etc., shape people's lives and experiences. Essentially, intersectionality views oppression as multi-layered, as one is not simply oppressed based on a single identity alone. Rather, oppression situates the oppressed in different worlds. The media plays a large role in reflecting and constructing these worlds.

Considering the multi-dimensional layers of *OITNB*'s characters, it makes sense to analyze the show using an intersectional approach. *OITNB* has a long list of barrier-breaking TV "firsts" that have been characterized as a form of social activism by the show's creator, Jenji Kohan. *OITNB* is made by, about, and arguably *for* women, as the binge-watching format, sharing the addictive qualities of the soap opera, appeals to women as its central audience. Further, *OITNB* features the first transgender actor (Laverne Cox) to play a transgender character, who maintains a loving and supportive relationship with her wife. It's one of the only shows to feature a bisexual character (Piper) who is matter-of-factly into both men and women, and not "conflicted" about her sexuality. It features a host of diverse female characters including women of color who challenge stereotypes and have depth and narrative development. Its female friendships pass the Bechdel test—characters form deep relationships and talk to one another about things other than men. Older women are given a voice and a sexuality. Class issues are at the surface, and are honestly portrayed, sometimes uncomfortably so. Queer and lesbian characters are not only visible, but sex and gender are complicated, rather than simplified. Sexual and reproductive rights issues are discussed. Characters with physical and mental disabilities are never a source of pity, and their backstories illuminate their personal histories. Trauma is shown as an affront to women's lives on both a personal level and as institutional abuse, and is articulated as a feminist issue. White male guards are exposed as abusive appendages of a corrupt and rapacious prison system, and the prison-industrial complex is at the heart of the show's social critique, positioning the issues in the context of (patriarchal) state power. As Kohan observes, "Our prison-industrial complex is out of control…. It's an embarrassment…. It's something that needs to get talked about, and I'd love to start that conversation. But I can't be didactic about it. I'm here to entertain. This is my activism" (McClelland 2015, 44).

At the same time, the show has been critiqued for its stereotypical depictions of women of color and lesbian/bisexual/transgender women, and its neoliberal pandering to mainstream audiences, who have come to expect explicit sex and violence from non-network TV series. While it has been praised for its unabashed portrayals of sex and sexuality, lesbians are often depicted as sexual predators, and bisexual characters like Piper and Morello are "crazy" and unstable. Others have commented on the show's sexual binaries and its bi-erasure, as it never uses the word "bisexual," and instead refers to Piper as an "ex-lesbian" (Walkley 2013). Biphobia is also evident in Morello, who is over-sexualized, non-monogamous and "gay-for the stay," and lives in a fantasy world influenced by romance novels and women's magazines, where she believes she is engaged to a man whom she is actually stalking. Presenting lesbians as manipulative predators is seen in Alex Vause, who uses her relationship with Piper to manipulate her into the drug smuggling business and later abuses her trust and sells her out in court. Butch women are aggressive and sex-obsessed. Big Boo and Nicky have a competition to see who can sleep with the most inmates—extra points if the conquered is straight. The girl-on-girl misogyny and objectification is evident in Nicky's journal writings, where she keeps a running scorecard: "I collect orgasms." Lesbian sex is routinely portrayed in the vocabulary of made-for-the-male-gaze pornography, and soapy, naked female bodies populate the backdrop of the shower scenes.

These images are particularly problematic when we consider that sexual minorities like transgender adults and LGBT youth are also disproportionately more likely than the general population to come into contact with the criminal justice system. Poverty, homelessness, profiling by law enforcement, and imprisonment are disproportionately experienced by transgender and gender non-conforming people. Many LGBT youth live in homes unwelcoming to their identities. Out of despair and a need for survival, homeless gay and transgender youth are more likely to resort to criminal behaviors, such as selling drugs, theft, or "survival sex" (including sex work), which puts them at risk of arrest and detainment (Hunt and Moodie-Mills 2012). Because of discriminatory practices and limited access to resources, transgender adults are also more likely to engage in criminal activities to be able to pay for housing, health care, and other basic needs. LGBT people are particularly vulnerable to mistreatment in jail and prison by both other inmates and staff. This mistreatment includes solitary confinement (often for their alleged "safety"), mis-gendering inmates who are forced to serve time in all-male or all-female prisons that do not conform to their declared gender identities, physical and sexual violence, verbal abuse, and the denial of medical care and other services, including access to hormone therapies on which their identities depend. According to the National Inmate Survey, in 2011–12, 40 percent of transgender inmates reported sexual victimization compared to four percent of all inmates. Although women are the largest growing prison population in the United States, the majority being women of color—especially black women—

the portrayal of Piper as the only woman able or willing to rise up against the unjust prison system is largely ahistorical (Nair). As Aura Bogado (2013) is right to point out, narratives of women of color "remain deeply powerful, yet each one is framed by a white introduction" and thus whiteness authenticates the black experience on the show. According to Bogado, "Black women in *Orange Is the New Black* are presented as boisterous, aggressive characters who serve—in a rather dehumanizing manner—as comic relief. They fantasize about fried chicken, teach the naive, white protagonist Piper how to fight, and utilize intimidation and scare tactics on other inmates." Suzanne "Crazy Eyes" Warren is a highly intelligent, suburban-raised savant, but she embodies the physical characteristics of the antebellum racial caricature of the pickaninny, complete with "crazy" bulging eyes, a wide mouth, unkempt hair, and a naïve, child-like worldview. She is obsessed with Piper's whiteness as a romantic fetish and calls her "Dandelion" as a term of endearment. Vee can be read as the harsh mammy who is abusive to her own children and upholds the stereotype that all black families are broken and fatherless. The Feminist Griote notes that the focus on Piper and the demonization of black women reinforces the "long racist tradition of white media centering the stories of whites and using people of color as colorful minstrels" (Najumi 2013).

The hyper-sexualization of women of color and their equation with criminality in *OITNB* feeds into an already existent fetishization and pathologization of African American and Latina sexualities. *OITNB* shows Latinas pitted against black women, rather than showing overlapping spaces for solidarity. Like so many Latina TV characters, including Gloria from *Modern Family*, they speak broken English and are unwed mothers who have children by multiple men. Latino men are violent and abusive. Latina women make herbal potions for Santeria rituals, and they control the kitchen, promoting the stereotype of the "hot and spicy" Latina that equates her with cooking. Also, a Latina mother and daughter compete sexually for the attention of a white male prison guard, and one even sends pictures of her vagina to her boyfriend on a contraband phone. In another backstory, we see a Latina mother neglecting her children, and subjecting them to the abuse of her drug-dealing boyfriend. Multiple forms of gender-based oppression are reflected throughout *OITNB*. These contradicting politics of representation form the intersectional feminist questions raised in this collection.

Overview: An Intersectional Feminist Approach to OITNB

Najumi's insightful assessment sets the framework for Sarah E. Fryett's analysis of the intersections of race and lesbian identity on the show. Fryett examines the hegemonic representational practices perpetuated by *OITNB*, specifically in relation to lesbian identification practices. According to Fryett, *OITNB* fetishizes some white lesbian bodies (the ones that conform to a Hollywood ideal of beauty) and relies on age-old stereotypes for others (namely the predatory "butch" lesbian), while consistently denigrating black lesbian bodies (Poussey and Crazy Eyes are rejected and abandoned). Fryett situates *OITNB* within the historical context of representations of lesbians on television, demonstrating where it pushes the boundaries of representation and also where it reifies previous stereotypical depictions. Starting with Vito Russo's assessment of lesbian characters in his seminal text *The Celluloid Closet: Homosexuality in the Movies* (1987) and tracing their history through defining moments such as Ellen Morgan's coming out as the first prime-time lesbian character on *Ellen* (1997), to the all-lesbian cast of *The L Word*, Fryett reminds us of the importance of looking critically at these images. Piper and Alex constitute what Laura Mulvey might call a voyeuristic fantasy of lesbian sexuality that appeals to the heterosexual male gaze, and points to the pornification of the white lesbian body in ways similar to Bette and Tina of *The L Word*.

Exploring accounts of race and gender in popular fiction is the focus of Kalima Y. Young, who addresses the representations of *OITNB* through race and gender-based trauma narratives. Young contends that *OITNB* places its characters in positions of "truth telling" because the narratives about sexual violence are grounded in giving voice to the intersecting factors of race, class, identity and sexuality. Through the lens of individual and cultural trauma, Young discusses how *Orange Is the New Black* is both a spectacle and an exercise in truth telling, a combination that allows the viewer to explore representations of race and gender-based trauma outside of neoliberal survivor frameworks. This essay provides an analysis of trauma, and places *OITNB* in the genealogy of the "breaking the silence" sexual abuse advocacy movement to offer both racial and gendered analysis of trauma while also paying tribute to pop culture as an avenue for narrative-based healing.

Katie Sullivan Barak addresses Jenji Kohan's use of privilege and the subversive implications for Piper as a character with whom Kohan encourages audiences to mis-identify. Barak addresses the ways that Piper's whiteness is presented as neither visible nor neutral or logical, and argues that Piper is the most unlikeable character on the show. Through an analysis of Kohan's statement that Piper was her "Trojan Horse," meaning that the character was meant to be Kohan's foot in the door for a network deal, Barak discusses how the narrative of *OITNB* leaves Piper outside of the center. Barak argues that, as the seasons have played out, Piper's purpose has morphed into a thoroughfare to deconstruct privilege, while the show has become a case study for deconstructing power.

Absent voices in the media is a theme continued by Minjeong Kim. With the exceptions of Margaret Cho's short-lived sitcom *All American Girl* (1994) and ABC's more recent *Fresh Off the Boat* (2015), there has been a dearth of representations for Asian American characters on television. While Kim sees Chang and Soso on *OITNB* as welcome additions, she uses Edward Said's theory of Orientalism to analyze how the show constructs Asian Americans as foreign, inassimilable subjects. Her essay closely examines these two Asian American characters and argues that while it pushes the boundaries of representations of racial and sexual minorities, *OITNB* has failed to do so for Asian Americans. Chang and Soso are not the typical dichotomous Asian female stereotypes—hyper-feminine, geisha-like, submissive lotus blossoms, or belligerent, untrustworthy, sensual dragon ladies—however, Chang's invisibility and Soso's ambiguity fail to fully challenge age-old archetypes that render Asian women as silent, conflatable, and anti-assimilationist.

Yvonne Swartz Hammond discusses how cultural representations of prison shape what we think we know about prison, and how prison sex is another way the media constructs our understanding of inmate life. This "CSI effect" often comes with skewed representations of male prison sex that reveal much about the thresholds of hetero-normative culture, which seems to prefer images of violent male-on-male sex rather than the possibility of mutually consenting relationships. While cultural representations of rape in men's prisons in shows such as *Oz* realize our worst fears about prison sex, namely that this kind of sex is further "punishment" for the criminal, *OITNB* fetishizes lesbian sex by suggesting that sexual relationships in women's prison are born of desire, rather than influenced by positions of power. Healy's policing of Chapman's (homo)sexuality reveals how cultural representations of women's prisons tend to depend on storylines that read like a conventional heterosexual romance, a projection that Swartz Hammond argues is part of a "save the white women" rape fantasy leftover from the Jim Crow South.

The various ways that prison "kills" inmates on a social, emotional, political, and, sometimes, physical level is the subject of Hilary Malatino's essay, which examines the social death of Sophia Burset, played by transgender actor and activist Laverne Cox. What emerges is a dissonance between Sophia's character and the predominant circumstances of actual transgender and gender non-conforming people within the prison-industrial complex. Sophia may go against the prevailing image of the hypersexualized black (trans)woman, but it is at the expense of her sexuality: in the queer space of Litchfield, she is framed as a friend, familiar and attractive, but also unavailable erotically. Desexualized within the prison setting, Sophia faces the ultimate social death when, at the end of Season 3, she is thrown into solitary confinement "for her protection."

Kyra Hunting explores how *OITNB* reimagines the tropes of the women-in-prison genre in novel ways, and uses themes from an emerging genre she calls the "lesbian family program" to draw out the queer, feminist, and revolutionary possibilities of earlier "exploitation" texts. Hunting illustrates the ways in which genre mixing can impact the ideological and representational possibilities of television. She compares three women-in-prison dramas, *Prisoner: Cell Block H* (Australia, 1979–1986), *Bad Girls* (UK, 1999–2006), and *Wentworth* (Australia, 2013-), and four "lesbian family programs," *The L Word* (U.S., 2004–2009), *Sugar Rush* (UK, 2005–2006), *Exes & Ohs* (U.S./Canada, 2007, 2009) and *Lip Service* (UK, 2010–2012), to highlight key features that the two genres share: a strong focus on the lives of women, and a close homosocial environment. She points out the failures of both *OITNB*'s heterosexual romantic couples and heteronormative families, as compared to the affectionate same-sex couples and supportive prison families in the series. In this way, *OITNB* re-works the women-in-prison genre in a feminist direction, as an affirming homonormative text that privileges lesbian representation.

In the midst of a prison culture formally and informally divided by race, Tiffany "Pennsatucky" Doggett embodies an equally powerful yet rarely discussed social divide: class, and an openly ridiculed cultural archetype: white trash. While black and Hispanic women repeatedly shelter their sisters from the worst horrors of prison life, Pennsatucky and Piper end Season 1 with a bloody and nearly deadly fight. Drawing on Marxist theory and firsthand interviews of incarcerated women, Susan Sered utilizes Louis Althusser's concept of "overdetermination" to describe how poor women have internalized definitions of class that come from personal appearances, especially in regard to their teeth. Pennsatucky, the character everyone loves to hate because of her racist, homophobic, Bible-thumping ignorance, is marked by her rotten teeth—a signifier of that supremely unforgivable character trait, not taking care of oneself, a particularly serious flaw in women, who are expected to look attractive. On one side of the class divide are those with normatively attractive bodies, respectable educational achievements and decent jobs. On the other side are those whose poor teeth and other "defects" are read as signs that they are incapable of managing their own lives. Sered shows how gender and class are inextricably linked on the show and in real life, for poor white inmates.

Drawing on the work of Frantz Fanon and Michel Foucault, postcolonial theorist Achille Mbembe, in his article "Necropolitics," defines necropower as the power to dictate who may live and who may die in the context of postcolonial sovereignty. Zoey K. Jones argues that the oppositional sexual politics within the Litchfield necropolitical death world of *OITNB* constitutes a major critique put forth by the show. Although she is quick to point out that the majority of on-screen, pleasurable sexual relationships occur between white women, and that Latina women, in particular, are pathologized as hypersexual, *OITNB* challenges gendered performances and compulsory heterosexuality. In a setting where the female body is objectified and controlled by others, Jones asks the feminist question, "How can women experience pleasure when they do not have control over their own bodies?" While the women of *OITNB* face surveillance, punishment, and the threat of death in their pursuit of intimate physical relationships with one another, they assert their sexuality to affirm that they are very much alive. The transgressive power of pleasure is a major theme in *OITNB* and, as Jones asserts, the mobilization of sexuality is a form of resistance to necropower.

Unlike film, which has historically been associated with the public sphere, television is more intimate, and thus has been characterized as a feminine medium. The gendering of television is not only linked to its "low brow" status in relation to the cinema, but the programming that is aimed at women as television consumers. Daytime programming, especially talk shows and soap operas, occupies an abject position because these genres are considered "feminine": talk-based dramas of family life, gossip about celebrity and popular culture, and the frivolous dramas of interpersonal relationships. Anne Moore argues that instead of distancing itself from the stigma of women's genres as so many "quality television" shows have done, *OITNB* centrally and unapologetically features many of the generic markers of the soap opera—episode-ending cliffhangers, a sprawling cast of characters, multiple overlapping serial plots, and high melodrama. At the same time that it embraces this abject form, the show emphasizes the feminine concerns of intimacy, both on the level of plot and its adoption of the serial tropes that elicit readerly devotion and binge viewing.

Lydia Brown explores how *OITNB*'s first three seasons offer rich possibilities for critically examining representations of disability, madness, and trauma in the popular imagination. The disabled, alongside others at the margins, have long grappled with the image of the "freak" from the circuses and sideshows of the 1800s where handicapped people, gender nonconforming people, and people of color were put on display as a spectacle for the normate gaze. *OITNB* presents its viewers with a multitude of bodies—fat bodies, elderly bodies, physically disabled bodies, neurodivergent bodies—many of which are simultaneously marked by queer, trans, and racialized existence. The show presents itself as a model for media representations of people whose bodies exist outside the bounds of normative beauty and desirability. Brown demonstrates how the *OITNB* writers go to great lengths to suggest humanity and personhood for various characters in the ensemble cast. Yet, she argues, for as long as madness exists primarily as a spectacle for neurotypical entertainment, while reifying dangerously ableist ideas of what psychiatric disability or madness *ought* to look like, it cannot possibly do justice to people with any kind of mental disability. By drawing connections between disability, madness, and trauma, she also suggests possible re-imaginings of pathologizing disability narratives that reject compulsory ablenormativity and instead welcome vulnerability and realness.

The intersectionality of gender, race, and ableness form the crux of H. Rakes' essay, which addresses the concept of "being down" as it relates to flexible accommodation. Rakes makes the case for Chapman as a model character for flexible accommodation while simultaneously being presented as a privileged white person. Even though she is in prison, Chapman finds it necessary to maintain privilege, i.e., to keep a privileged identity, even while she is losing some mental control. The narrative featuring Chapman as the head of an illicit panty-smuggling business invites viewers to critique her power and examine her privilege, which she maintains by becoming a female boss who oppresses other women in a capitalist context of industrial production and greed. A critical engagement with the show, including this type of Marxist-feminist analysis opens a space to question who and what we laugh at in *OITNB*, and why. According to Rakes, white and abled audiences in particular, are encouraged to critically distance themselves from Chapman's centrality via the show's parody of neoliberalism.

The meaning of mental health, particularly the term "crazy," is the focus of Sarah Gibbons' essay. As Gibbons points out, the characters at Litchfield will often label themselves or others crazy. This is seen in insults, self-labeling, and genuine fear that doing time is leading them to go crazy. Gibbons notes that having the luxury of pondering one's own mental health is problematic and related to able-bodiment. Yet she also wrestles with the concept that these concerns, voiced by characters in a fictional setting, present challenges to the dominant ideas of what mental health means. In other words, she examines how the show depicts what being in control mentally, having intelligence, and having agency over one's mental state looks like. Gibbons uses an intersectional approach to dissect the ways *OITNB* juxtaposes anxiety with being able-minded. By combining disability studies and feminist theory, Gibbons notes that questions of women's mental health are often linked to questions of their worth.

All of the issues discussed by these authors contribute to making *OITNB* an extremely watchable show and ripe for academic analysis. In this text we have gathered contributors who take diverse standpoints on the show's impact in order to present a survey of how modern media reflects the intersecting layers of oppression found in the study of gender and pop culture.

REFERENCES

Alexander, Michelle. 2011. *The New Jim Crow: Mass Incarceration in the Age of Colorblindness*. New York: The New Press.
Arend, Patricia. 2014. "Gender and Advertising." In *Gender and Pop Culture: A Text-*

Reader, edited by Adrienne Trier-Bieniek and Patricia Leavy, 53–80. Rotterdam: Sense.

Bogado, Aura. 2013. "White Is the New White." *The Nation*, August 16. http://www.thenation.com/article/white-new-white/.

Brant, Jenn. 2014. "As Seen on T.V.: Gender, Television and Popular Culture." In *Gender and Pop Culture: A Text-Reader*, edited by Adrienne Trier-Bieniek and Patricia Leavy, 103–120. Rotterdam: Sense.

Butler, Judith. 1999. *Gender Trouble*. New York: Routledge.

Crenshaw, Kimberle. "Mapping the Margins: Intersectionality, Identity Politics and Violence Against Women of Color." *Stanford Law Review*, Vol. 43, No. 6 (July 1991), pp. 1241–1299.

Davis, Angela. 2001. *The Prison Industrial Complex* (audio CD). London: AK Press.

hooks, bell. 1997. *bell hooks: Cultural Criticism and Transformation* (DVD). Dir. Sut Jhally. Media Education Foundation.

Hunt, Jerome, and Aisha C. Moodie-Mills. 2012. "The Unfair Criminalization of Gay and Transgender Youth: An Overview of the Experiences of LGBT Youth in the Juvenile Justice System." Center for American Progress, June 29. https://www.americanprogress.org/issues/lgbt/report/2012/06/29/11730/the-unfair-criminalization-of-gay-and-transgender-youth/.

McClelland, Mac. 2015. "'Caged Heat': How Did the Unlikely Stars of '*OITNB*' Revolutionize Television?" *Rolling Stone*, June 12.

Milestone, Katie, and Anneke Meyer. 2012. *Gender and Popular Culture*. Cambridge: Polity.

Najumi, Mohadesa. 2013. "A Critical Analysis of Orange Is the New Black: The Appropriation of Women of Color." *The Feminist Wire*, August 28. http://www.thefeministwire.com/2013/08/a-critical-analysis-of-orange-is-the-new-black-the-appropriation-of-women-of-color/.

The Sentencing Project. sentencingproject.org/.

Trier-Bieniek, Adrienne, and Patricia Leavy. 2014. *Gender and Pop Culture: A Text Reader*. Rotterdam: Sense.

Walkley, A.J. 2013. "Bi-Erasure in *Orange Is the New Black*." Huffpost Gay Voices, August 23. http://www.huffingtonpost.com/aj-walkley/orange-is-the-new-black-bisexuality_b_3799037.html/.

"Chocolate and vanilla swirl, swi-irl"

Race and Lesbian Identity Politics

Sarah E. Fryett

Sam Healy, known to the inmates of Litchfield in the Netflix original drama *Orange Is the New Black* (*OITNB*) as Officer Healy, offhandedly remarks to Piper Chapman: "Lesbians can be very dangerous. It's the testosterone" (S1:E3). Healy adds to this homophobic sentiment late in Season 2 when he says: "Pretty soon men will become irrelevant.... They [lesbians] are making babies out of a tube. Waiting for us [men] to go obsolete" (S2:E12). Though Healy is depicted as both sensitive and idiotic, his comments prompted me to think about the representation of sexual identity, and more specifically, lesbian identity, in the show. Sexual identity—conceptualized here as a broad understanding of one's sexual self-concept, going beyond simply sexual orientation—appears at first glance to embrace diversity and inclusivity. The list ranges from a nun, Sister Jane Ingalls, to Carrie "Big Boo" Black, a butch white lesbian, to Poussey Washington, a thin black lesbian, to Dayanara "Daya" Diaz, a Hispanic inmate in love with prison guard John Bennett. "What a refreshing representation of sexuality and all its various manifestations" was my initial thought. However, sitting down to write that essay lauding the diversity proved futile. While *OITNB* extends some realms of lesbian representation from previous television portrayals—think the thin, white, attractive women of *The L Word*—it remains firmly supportive of alarming stereotypes.

Reviews discussing the eclectic cast of inmates on *OITNB* differ greatly, from praise of the diversity to downright anger, denouncing the stereotypical representations of women of color. Columnist Karen Valby (2013) observes: "Netflix's riveting new show *Orange Is the New Black* has dozens of female characters. They are women of every description—and none of them are stereotypes" (20). My only response to this sentiment is, "Are we watching the same show?" More in line with my perspective, Mohadesa Najumi, in her article on *OITNB* for *The Feminist Wire* (2013), offers a more complex and critical analysis, especially regarding the depiction of women of color. She notes: "Black women … are given a limited and hollow voice," and "the hyper-sexualization of WoC [women of color] feeds into an already existent fetishization and pathologization of African American and Latina sexualities." Najumi's accurate assessment begins to set the framework for my analysis that examines the intersections of race and lesbian identity.

This research seeks to examine the hegemonic representational practices perpetuated by *OITNB*, specifically in relation to lesbian identification practices. Hegemony refers to the ideologically controlled images of the dominant media. My feelings on the show, though, remain complex and at times contradictory. On the one hand, there is an extension of traditional media representations of lesbian bodies. Boo and Poussey, as noted above, Nicky Nichols, a white ex-heroin addict, and Suzanne "Crazy Eyes" Warren, a black inmate, do not fall into the usual portrayals of lesbians: white, thin, and attractive. However, this diversity, on closer examination, is merely superficial. The white lesbian bodies that fall out of the traditional representation, Boo and Nicky, reinforce ideas of lesbians as promiscuous, overly sexual "deviants." The black lesbian bodies are treated in a similar stereotypical fashion; they vacillate between hypersexual and violent to infantilized and de-sexualized. And, you might ask, "What about Piper and Alex?" They maintain the status quo: white, thin, and attractive. Thus, *OITNB* fetishizes some white lesbian bodies and relies on age-old stereotypes for others (namely the predatory "butch" lesbian), while consistently denigrating black lesbian bodies. The purpose of this essay is to illuminate the continued marginalization and erasure of lesbian bodies in order to conceive a practice of oppositional viewing. This practice, conceptualized by bell hooks (1997), "interrogate[s] the gaze of the Other [and] also look[s] back"—naming what is seen and opposing the dominant order (199).

The essay first articulates a frame for thinking through the historical representation of lesbians on television using the work of Steven Capsuto (2000), Stephen Tropiano (2002), and Rodger Streitmatter (2009). These critics help to situate *OITNB* within the historical context of lesbians on television, thereby demonstrating where it pushes the boundaries of representation and also where it reifies previous stereotypical depictions. From there, the essay looks at how these stereotypical representations of gays and lesbians impact our worldview and understanding of sexual identities. To enhance and complicate this conversation, the following theorists are used: bell hooks, Ann Ciasullo, and Laura Mulvey, among many others. These critics, combined with the textual analysis, substantiate a thorough investigation of the intersectionality of race and lesbian visibility, identity, and desire within *OITNB*.

A Brief Overview of Gay and Lesbian (In)Visibility

Outlining the portrayal of gays and lesbians on television locates *OITNB* in its historical trajectory. Vito Russo's seminal text, *The Celluloid Closet: Homosexuality in the Movies* (1987), notes that with the relaxing of the Hays Code in the 1950s representations of homosexuality—which were previously forbidden—slightly increased. The representations, however, demonized homosexuality and included portrayals such as the predatory lesbian: Lauren Bacall as Amy North in *Young Man with a Horn* (1950) and Barbara Stanwyck as Jo Courtney in *Walk on the Wild Side* (1962) (Russo, 1987). Supporting Russo's observation, Steven Capsuto, in *Alternate Channels: The Uncensored Story of Gay and Lesbian Images on Radio and Television* (2000), observes: "Homosexuality remained virtually invisible on television through the mid 1960s, except for a few neurotic and/or violent lesbian roles around 1962" (4). Toward the end of the 1960s, however, television programs started to include depictions of same-sex desire. Capsuto states that these examples were often found in shows catering to urban, college-educated individuals, and they also covered topics such as feminism and the sexual revolution. He continues by noting that during the 1970s, two different scripts for gays on television emerged: the "coming out" script and the "queer monster" script. That is, the gay character was either coming out to a heterosexual cast of individuals or he or she was a ruthless child molester or murderer. As the 1970s wore on, the portrayals of positive gay characters—mainly male gay characters—increased, due in part to the protestations of numerous gay organizations. Capsuto also observes that at this time the majority of depictions were "noble lesbian and gay characters [who] went to court to fight discrimination in a half-dozen shows" (5). This increase of positive images of gays was short lived. Ronald Reagan, with the support of the Reverend Jerry Falwell and the Moral Majority, took office and began a "moral responsibility" campaign. Network sponsors began to withhold contributions and advertising dollars due in part to this "moral" push. The fear and anger surrounding the AIDS epidemic—also emerging at this time—further fueled the lack of gays and lesbians on television and their misrepresentation (Capsuto 2000, 5).

The early 1990s, however, occasioned an increase in lesbian images, but this was short lived, and racial diversity among gay and bisexual characters was minimal. Suzanna Danuta Walters' *All the Rage: The Story of Gay Visibility in America* (2001) perceives this increase but also offers a caveat:

In many ways, this moment provides us with a picture of a society readily embracing the *images* of gay life but still all too reluctant to embrace the *realities* of gay identities and practices in all their messy and challenging confusion. We may be *seen,* now, but I'm not sure we are *known* [10, emphasis in original].

In conjunction with Walters, Stephen Tropiano extends and details this phenomenon in his comprehensive examination of gays and lesbians, *The Prime Time Closet* (2002). While perusing the timeline that opens his text, a distinct lack of lesbian representation is evident. In 1963 *The Eleventh Hour*, an NBC drama about psychiatry, had a patient who was a "paranoid, neurotic stage actress with lesbian tendencies" (ix). The next mention of a featured lesbian occurs in 1974 in an episode of *Police Woman* where three lesbians were murderers. These initial representations embody clear negative portrayals of the "threat" of lesbians. In 1988 the medical series *Heartbeat* contained the first "regular" lesbian couple (x). The next major illustration of lesbians happened in a 1991 episode of *L.A. Law* when C.J., a bisexual lawyer, kisses a heterosexual colleague. The remainder of the timeline includes a kiss here and there, a marriage on *Friends*, but other than that the visibility of lesbians on television remained almost non-existent until *Ellen* and *The L Word* (x).

Finally, in 1997, Ellen Morgan, Ellen DeGeneres' alter ego, came out on her show *Ellen*, bringing about a milestone for lesbian representation on television. Tropiano (2002) notes: "The coming out of both Ellens, DeGeneres and Morgan, opened a new chapter in the history of gays and lesbians on television" (246). As radical as this moment was, critics also noted flaws in the representation. Bonnie J. Dow (2001) contends that the show follows "basic rules of gay and lesbian representation" (132). Those rules include no sexual interaction, treating Ellen's revelation as a "problem" to be dealt with by her heterosexual friends and family, and minuscule representation of any sort of lesbian community (132). Dow does note that the biggest contribution that *Ellen* made was taking us beyond the "one shot" or "one episode" approach (132). In other words, the show offered one of the first sustained lesbian representations. However, Anna McCarthy (2001), responding to ABC president Robert A. Iger's comment that a gay character every week was just "too much for people," contends that "while the network could support queer television as a spectacular media event, it could not sanction a lesbian invasion of serial television's more modest form of history making, the regularly scheduled weeks of televisual flow" (597). While *Ellen* offered a significant breakthrough in a sustained image of a lesbian on television, it was a decidedly brief glimpse. The show was cancelled by ABC shortly after *Ellen*'s coming out episode.

The L Word also offered viewers sustained images and included a variety of different lesbians: Bette and Tina, the interracial and (initially) committed couple, Shane, the semi-androgynous character, Alice, the fun-loving bisexual magazine writer, and Dana, the athletic tennis player, among others. Criticism of the show ranged from applauding its subversive potential to denouncing its reification of heterosexual norms. Critic Constance Reeder, in "Gays & Lesbians, Television Programs, Elections" (2004) observes: "This sort of soft porn has been around for a long time and is more appealing to straight men than to any self-respecting feminist" (51). She also argues that the prevalence of skinny women denies a wider view of the lesbian community (52). Renowned author of *Between Men* (1985) and *Epistemologies of the Closet* (1990), Eve Kosofsky Sedgwick (2004) also chimed in with "Edgy is not the word for the series' relation to reality or political process" (11). Sedgwick does, however, positively nod to the development of a "lesbian ecology" (lesbian community) within the drama—an encouraging addition.

Critics also disagreed on the show's depiction of race and lesbian identity. Jose Esteban Munoz, in "Queer Minstrels for the Straight Eye" (2005), argues: "The race plots that these characters generate keep *The L Word* from slipping into a mode of neoliberalism in which race is sidelined. Indeed, the show often becomes 'the R word,' and that is when it gets good and many queers, of color and not of color, are sutured" (102). This is an overly optimistic reading of the show, though. The diversity was indeed limited—at least in the main characters—to Bette, a very light-skinned biracial lesbian, and her half-sister, Kit, a blues singer with an alcohol addiction. Though many of the main characters engaged in romantic endeavors with a semi racially diverse group of women, the fact remains that for six seasons the white lesbian bodies dominated. Rodger Streitmatter's *From "Perverts" to "Fab Five": The Media's Changing Depiction of Gay Men and Lesbians* (2009) supports this contention: "With regard to how *The L Word* fits into the media's changing depiction of lesbians, the series reinforces many of the messages that previous news stories, films and TV shows sent" (157). These messages are that lesbians are promiscuous, beautiful and light skinned, and cannot commit (157–158). Though *The L Word* clearly pushed new boundaries with the representation of sustained, positive images of lesbians, it also remained firmly entrenched in a variety of stereotypical portrayals, and I argue the same is true for *OITNB*. These portrayals make lesbians palatable; they conform to a Hollywood ideal of beauty but also remain distinctly Other—outside the scope and sanctity of heterosexuality.

Structuring Our Worldview: The Impact of Stereotypes

Why should we examine these stereotypical portrayals? What can we learn from a thorough analysis of these stereotypes? More importantly, what will we do after illuminating them? These questions drive my analysis of *OITNB* because stereotypes inform our worldview, our understanding of people, and our own behavior. Sheng Kuan Chung's essay, "Media Literacy Art Education: Deconstructing Lesbian and Gay Stereotypes in the Media" (2007), begins with the following quote from Croteau and Hoynes:

> Exposure to popular media may be the dominant means by which children, as well as most adults, learn about others and acquire and internalize social norms, values, and beliefs as manifest in the expressions and presentations of the media. Most likely, the media generation learns about social issues like homosexuality not from direct contact with gay people or from their parents, teachers, and peers, but from characters and scenes depicted in films, television programs, fashion magazines, and commercial advertisements [99].

His argument, then, is that our popular media informs our understanding of social norms, and not only does it inform, but it also conditions our beliefs and behaviors. Thus, it is imperative that we critique these representations because the impact is undeniable. Chung's analysis argues for the importance of educating teachers on how to facilitate class discussion about gay issues and stereotypes, but this idea should also be extended beyond students and the classroom to all who engage with these images (103). He follows up with

> Guiding students to identify and investigate lesbian and gay stereotypes in films, television shows/commercials and print advertisements may result in a more accurate understanding of lesbian and gay people and how these stereotypical images may have justified the unequal treatment of lesbian and gay people in society [105].

This analysis identifies and investigates lesbian stereotypes, so that we may begin calling for more positive representations that avoid racist, sexist, and homophobic renderings and that work toward representational parity.

Lesbian Bodies: Pushing Boundaries

OITNB extends the representation of lesbian bodies into new spaces from that of *The L Word*. There are five reoccurring lesbian characters (defined here as someone who is sexually oriented toward women and also identifies as lesbian): Alex Vause, Suzanne "Crazy Eyes" Warren, Nicky Nichols, Poussey Washington, and Carrie "Big Boo" Black. Tricia Miller is also on this list, but she dies of an overdose toward the end of Season 1. There are also two new arrivals in Season 3: Stella Carlin and Maureen Kukidio. A handful of individuals (Lorna Morello and Brook Soso) engage in sex with the reoccurring lesbian characters but do not identify as lesbian and so will remain on the periphery of this investigation. Lastly, Piper Chapman, though initially engaged to Larry and perhaps more in line with the designation of bisexual, leans heavily toward a lesbian identification practice throughout. This list—as it includes black and white lesbians, thin, average, and overweight lesbians, and a handful of socioeconomic backgrounds—offers a more diverse cast than the narrow images of Bette, Tina, Shane, Dana, and Alice from *The L Word*.

Nicky and Big Boo offer two alternative representations, extending beyond what was available in *The L Word*. Nicky, an ex-heroin addict, is a white woman of an average build and height with long, constantly mussed red hair. Similar to Piper, her family is upper middle class, and the flashbacks show a distant and somewhat cold mother figure. Boo, on the other hand, is a short, broad shouldered, overweight white woman with a buzz cut, and many tattoos—a butch. Within her flashbacks, we see a despondent middle class child whose mother was dismayed by Boo's failure to adhere to traditional normative femininity. These two characters, thankfully, offer viewers a broader and more diverse perspective of white lesbians; however, these two alternatives also contain stereotypical portrayals.

Crazy Eyes and Poussey also offer a diversification, though I argue that diversification exists on a superficial level because stereotypes of violence, over-sexualization, and infantilization remain. Crazy Eyes, viewers learn through flashbacks, was raised as an adopted daughter of a white middle class family. She is a black woman of average build, and she suffers from mild mental instability. Poussey, also a black woman, is thin in stature and from a military background. She wears her hair short and can often be viewed in rather baggy clothing. Crazy Eyes and Poussey, combined with Boo and Nicky, challenge the white, middle/upper class depictions created by *The L Word*. Unfortunately, that challenge dissipates upon further scrutiny.

Competition and Promiscuity: Boo and Nicky

The stereotype of lesbian promiscuity is kept firmly intact throughout *OITNB*, and this aspect is no more evident than in the characters of Boo and Nicky. Understanding, of course, that this show is set in a women's prison, the overly sexualized nature of these two women permeates much of the first two seasons. A prime example occurs in S2:E3 when the camera pans into a shower stall, and we see Nicky fingering an unnamed inmate who is making very loud noises of pleasure. After a brief interlude where the camera travels to Crazy Eyes and Vee (a new inmate in Season 2), viewers return to the shower stall with Nicky and another unnamed woman; this is the beginning of a pattern that we see throughout the series. Boo interrupts this shower scene, which foreshadows the next episode where Boo confronts Nicky saying: "Lay off my marks" (S2:E4). The very use of the word "marks"— an object, not a subject—to refer to women suggests a dehumanizing and devaluing. These women are no longer individuals but simply something to be checked off of a list. This example supports Streitmatter's (2009) commentary from above regarding the depictions of lesbians as overly sexual and promiscuous.

This promiscuity continues when Boo and Nicky decide to have a competition to see how many women each can engage in sex. The storyline keeps up for the next few episodes, petering out around mid-season, but it becomes more and more disturbing. Boo and Nicky officially set up a framework for what Nicky will eventually term a "bang-off," with the help of Mei Chang, a Chinese inmate who works in the commissary. The competition, devised with the help of Chang, is made official with rules and regulations and an entire point system (getting a guard being one of the highest). A series of degrading incidents follow that illuminate not only a troubling promiscuity but an out of control lesbian sexuality concerned with scoring as many "marks" as possible. In one example, Piper, in collusion with Boo, attempts to convince Soso, a slightly naïve Asian inmate, to be Boo's prison wife in exchange for the return of a blanket. Soso realizes what is occurring and asks, in a shocked voice: "Were you trying to pimp me out?" (S2:E4). Though this moment is meant to be humorous, it offers a disturbing portrayal of lesbian sexuality. The joke between Boo and Piper—at the expense of Soso—encourages an image of manipulative, lying behavior that harkens back to the predatory lesbian image of the mid twentieth century, as noted in Russo's (1987) examples.

As the competition continues, the image of lesbian sexuality shifts from manipulative and lying to downright demeaning. One incident between Nicky and Soso showcases this aspect. Nicky, in the chapel, is performing oral sex on Soso who, while clearly enjoying the encounter, is also talking non-stop. Nicky shoves Soso's head into her vagina—a gesture of silencing the Other, as Soso is Asian American. Again, this is presumably meant as a comedic moment, but it is a disturbing action of silencing, pointing to deeper issues: sex is meaningless, sex is a game, and women are simply marks. The voice of the Asian character is literally silenced. This all seems reminiscent of something you might see in a film about a frat house—a competition that maintains the narrative of heteronormativity. There are a few more shower scenes, a question from Piper about the competition ("So do they always have to come?"), Nicky trying to seduce Susan Fischer (a new prison guard), and Nicky boasting ("Just bagged a four-pointer," S2:E6). Combined, the entire competition scenario paints an uneasy image of lesbian sexuality as promiscuous and devoid of responsibility and feeling. To be clear, Nicky and Boo are significantly more complex characters than these discussed incidents; however, the troubling narrative of conquest—a heteronormative narrative— is transplanted to the prison and lesbian sexuality.

Rejection and Abandonment: Poussey and Crazy Eyes

In comparison to the white lesbians above, Poussey and Crazy Eyes' stories are laden with rejection, failure, and violence. The renowned cultural critic bell hooks argues, in "Selling Hot Pussy" (1997), "Representations of black female bodies in contemporary popular culture rarely subvert or critique images of black female sexuality which were part of the cultural apparatus of nineteenth-century racism and which still shape perceptions today" (114). In agreement with hooks, I argue that Poussey and Crazy Eyes' depictions continue the traditional narrative of black female sexuality: negated or over-sexualized. *OITNB* perpetuates this narrative within the following stories: Poussey's failed relationship with Franziska, her unrequited attraction to Taystee, Crazy Eyes' unrequired attraction to Piper, and her authoring of an erotica series. Poussey and Crazy Eyes are, as bell hooks terms it, "tragically sexual"—a phrase referring to conventional representations of black women's sexuality—which perpetuates racist ideology and maintains hegemonic sexuality (125).

The representation of Poussey as "tragically sexual" first occurs when we learn about Poussey's backstory. The flashback (S2:E6) begins in Germany with a steamy moment between Poussey and Franziska, the daughter of her father's superior officer. They are resting, partially clothed, in bed, draped over each other. A bit later, we return to the bedroom where they are exploring each other's bodies and speaking loving phrases in German. The lighting is soft and sensual but abruptly shifts when Franziska's father, a commanding German officer, enters. Poussey immediately hides her head in the sheets, and shortly thereafter, she learns, from her father, that they are being transferred back to the States—a direct result of her discovery. In the final moment of this narrative flashback, further bolstering the tragic, Poussey approaches Franziska's father with a gun, declaring: "You don't get to decide what happens to my life" (S2:E6). Fortunately, Poussey's father enters, tightly hugs her, and keeps the gun out of sight. This entire incident reaffirms the stereotype of a "tragic sexuality."

Though discussing a different popular cultural artifact—a film—hooks (1997), again, extends an important critique that supports my reading and sheds light on Poussey's depiction: "The warning for women is different from that given men—we are given messages about the danger of asserting sexual desire. Clearly the message from *Imitation of Life* was that attempting to define oneself as a sexual subject would lead to rejection and abandonment" (125). Poussey, though not rejected by her lover per se, is rejected by Franziska's father and abandoned by Franziska, as the end of the flashback shows Franziska reunited with her father. The depiction of the tragic Poussey continues in the plot line involving Taystee, a fellow black inmate. Throughout Season 2, Poussey develops an attraction to Taystee, but it is clear to viewers that Taystee does not reciprocate the feeling. In one specific moment Poussey tries to kiss Taystee while they are reclining in bed, and Taystee utters: "Sorry, we've been through this. I'm not [gay]. Maybe we could cuddle for a minute" (S2:E4). Poussey is rejected (for what sounds like the second or perhaps third time). Shortly after, Poussey is abandoned by Taystee who finds herself in the clutches of her manipulative adoptive mother Vee.

Rejection and abandonment also permeate the representation of Crazy Eyes, but there is an added element of coded instability and mania. Just as Poussey's like of Taystee is unrequited, Crazy Eyes has a frighteningly similar situation with Piper in Season 1. Crazy Eyes makes a present of jalapeño peppers to Piper, and this begins a series of demonstrations of affection: sharing her ear buds during a film, caressing Piper, and finally an interaction when Piper is jogging. Crazy Eyes comes up to her and says: "Hello, baby. Look at you, getting your sweat on. Smell funky. You're a real woman. A real grown woman. Before I met you, the sun was like yellow grape, but now it's on fire. Why? Because you light a fire inside me." Unable to respond initially, Piper simply stares with a shocked look. Crazy Eyes continues in a sing-song voice: "I wrote it for you. I'm going to call you dandelion. Chocolate and vanilla swirl. Chocolate and vanilla swirl. Swi-irl" (S1:E3). This moment of unsolicited advance reveals Crazy Eyes as lecherous and unintelligent, which perpetuates racist and sexist ideologies. Though hooks (1996) is discussing a decidedly different moment in her analysis of the film *She's Gotta Have It* (1986), her comments are pertinent here: "to black females, and all females, [that] being sexually assertive will lead to rejection and punishment" (233). hooks continues by arguing that even in filmic moments when the director tries to create new, positive images, they often reinforce and perpetuate old stereotypes. Crazy Eyes' portrayal does just that; she is rejected and will soon be abandoned.

Crazy Eyes' depiction continues to spiral downward in many different manifestations throughout Season 2 and Season 3. Tania Modleski, in "Cinema and the Dark Continent" (1997), offers an insight into this representation. She quotes Homi Bhabha who observes: "black skin splits under the racist gaze, displaced into signs of bestiality, genitalia, grotesquerie, which reveal the phobic myth of the undifferentiated whole white skin" (212). Though coming out of Bhabha's text *The Location of Culture* (2004) and revolving around mimicry and colonialism, I contend that this quote is applicable to *OITNB*. Crazy Eyes is more of a caricature than an actual person, and those aspects of the caricature include bestiality, genitalia, and the grotesque. There is no semblance of a whole; she remains fetishized/split into negative stereotypes. She is often shown hitting herself in the head, and when eventually rejected outright by Piper, she, in a manic moment, urinates at the foot of Piper's bed. This bestiality, animal-like behavior and grotesquerie, this monstrousness of Crazy Eyes becomes more pronounced in Season 2, as she loses touch with reality under the influence of Vee. For example, with a look from Vee, in S2:E10, Crazy Eyes attacks Poussey, punching and kicking her most violently. Crazy Eyes also believes for a time that she attacked Red, a Russian inmate, though it was Vee. At the end of the Season 2, she is hysterically crying at Vee's disappearance, and this behavior continues throughout the opening of Season 3: a number of outbursts in the cafeteria, loud nightmares that awaken her bunkmates, and repeated head hitting. Crazy Eyes, harkening back to the image of the pickaninny, with "bulging eyes, unkempt hair, red lips and wide mouths," embodies characteristics of bestiality and grotesquerie, which perpetuate a hegemonic narrative steeped in racism (Pilgrim 2000).

Though there is a slight shift in Crazy Eyes' representation in Season 3, we move into the genitalia aspect of Bhaba's quote. At the encouragement of Berdie Rogers, a new prison counselor, Crazy Eyes begins to write an erotic novel. The book circulates throughout the prison, and many inmates become entranced, asking her for more chapters. The scenes are descriptive of genitalia and detailed sexual encounters. In some sense, this over-the-top portrayal mirrors her obsession with Piper at the beginning of Season 1. In direct contrast to her erotic fiction, viewers learn that Crazy Eyes is sexually inexperienced. A new inmate, Maureen Kukudio, develops a crush on Crazy Eyes. Crazy Eyes agrees to meet Maureen in the closet for a romantic encounter, but when she arrives, she touches the door and decides to keep walking. Her character, throughout the interaction with Maureen, is conceptualized as child-like and inexperienced, which is similar to her persona under the spell of Vee. Crazy Eyes falls into Modleski's (1997) categories in the following quote: "The black woman is seen either as too literally a woman (reduced to her biology and her biological functions) or in crucial ways not really a woman at all" (224). Crazy Eyes' erotica book harkens to the first part of the quote, as it contains an overbundance of sex. She is also not really a woman, though, as evidenced by her obsession with Piper, her violent (animal-like) tendencies, and her sexual inexperience. Crazy Eyes comes to signify the "Other," so that Alex and Piper may become the accepted and ideal.

Idealization and Fetishization: Piper and Alex

Piper and Alex, in contrast to Boo, Nicky, Poussey, and Crazy Eyes, represent acceptable feminine lesbian bodies—white, thin, and traditionally attractive—identity, and desire. The Piper and Alex relationship is an example of the pornification (Dines 2010) of the lesbian body, which is similar to Brian McNair's (2002) notion of pornographication. Dines' book, *Pornland: How Porn Has Hijacked Our Sexuality* (2010), examines the increasing sexualization of American culture by looking at the relationship between the porn industry and mainstream media. In another piece, Dines (2012) argues that pornography within mainstream media creates a "system of images that provides ideological coherence" (514). The Alex and Piper dynamic is part of this system of images, and through their many sexual encounters, they engender moments of festishistic scopophilia (pleasure in viewing), a term coined by Laura Mulvey in "Visual Pleasure and Narrative Cinema" (1975). Her ideas on mid-19th century films are a point of comparison for the depiction of Piper and Alex, who provide a voyeuristic fantasy that at once turns women into objects and also reasserts a heteronormative narrative of the male heterosexual gaze. To extend this argument, I also borrow from Daniel Farr and Nathalie Degrouit (2008) who, discussing *The L Word*, contend: "By and large, these characters demonstrate Caisullo's (2001) concept of the 'consumable lesbian.' These women are created in a manner that allows the mainstream heterosexual audience to regard them firstly as women, and secondly as lesbian" (426). Piper and Alex, along with Bette, Tina, Shane, Alice, and Dana from *The L Word*, continue to propagate this image, an image that is rooted in normative femininity, lack of commitment, and promiscuity.

Piper and Alex, the main characters and dominant romantic interest, are traditionally attractive, white women, which continues the limited representation of lesbian bodies and the trope of one blond/one brunette, as seen in *The L Word* with Bette and Tina. Piper is relatively tall with piercing blue eyes and blonde hair that always, oddly enough, seems recently straightened and fixed to perfection. During many of the flashback sequences, viewers see her in revealing, expensive clothing that clings to her thin frame, and her long, wavy blond locks only enhance this imagery. She is from an upper class East Coast family and well educated. This is abundantly clear, as one of the inmates, Tiffany "Pennsatucky" Doggett, refers to her as "College" in a number of episodes. In comparison, Alex's economic status appears rather lower-socio economic, which we learn in a flashback scene. After being taunted by her school peers for her knock-off sneakers, Alex throws them out of her mother's car window. With the exception of this childhood moment, the majority of flashbacks show her in fancy apartments, traveling the world for the drug smuggling operation, and enjoying drinks at swanky clubs. She is tall and thin with long curly hair and lots of black eye make-up, giving her a mysterious and sensual quality. Piper and Alex perpetuate an ideal of lesbian identity: financially secure and physically attractive in a traditional (white) sense.

The staged sexual encounters that surround these ideal lesbians are many, and they often border on the pornographic. In other words, they are lacking in romance and intimacy, but high on sexual innuendo and a sense of the illicit. As Patricia Duncker (1995) notes: "Heterosexual versions of lesbian desire within pornography, text or image, usually insist on three qualities: commodity, spectacle, and complicity" (7). Piper and Alex's dynamic maintains and supports these ideas of commodity, spectacle, and complicity. For example, in the very first episode of the series, we see this functioning in three flashbacks: Piper performing a stripper dance around Alex's bedroom, removing her clothing tauntingly; lots of sensual fondling with very low lighting; and Alex saying, "I'm going to eat you for dinner." Each of these three flashbacks is accompanied by soft music and a general sense of sexual tension. We, as the viewers, peer voyeuristically into the bedrooms (and eventually shower stalls and chapel at the prison) to see a carefully crafted moment designed, I contend, for a heterosexual male gaze. This gaze continues in many other flashback scenes, but let us look at one more. While attending a burlesque show (S2:E10) in a dimly lit performance space, Piper whispers to Alex: "I want to taste what you taste like." Now, is there anything inherently perturbing about this statement? No, but can you imagine Boo, Nicky, Poussey, or Crazy Eyes saying this and it being the titillating experience that viewers are expected to have with Alex and Piper? Again, the answer is no. What warrants comment is that these highly stylized, heteronormative, designed-for-a-male-gaze scenes are the *only* cinematically condoned lesbian sexual moments within the series.

In conjunction with the above scenes and my argument about the pornification of the lesbian body, I turn to a few scenes in Season 3 that exemplify an equation of sex and violence. This narrative of violence as pleasurable—a narrative found in Hollywood, pornography, novels, and many other spaces—must be critically examined and challenged. The first scene of violence as leading to pleasure and sex occurs when Alex learns that Piper, because she wanted Alex back at Litchfield, informed on her. Alex violently slaps Piper across the face. Instead of backing away or decrying this abusive moment, they begin to wrestle. The music shifts, cueing viewers to a change, and they start having what can only be termed "hate sex." This scene is woven through with disturbing themes of violence. A second scene with the same characteristics occurs a bit later when Alex rudely remarks: "I can't even stand to look at you." The verbal abuse in this scene is followed, once again, by a sexual encounter. These two scenes—bordering on sadomasochistic iconography—reify a pornographic narrative that locates the pleasure of sex within degradation and violence.

Lastly, a decent amount of promiscuity pervades Alex and Piper's dynamic, but it is not the promiscuity of Boo and Nicky; it is a sanctioned, fetishized promiscuity. Three examples come immediately to mind. First, in a flashback of Piper and Alex, viewers discover that Alex's girlfriend, Silvia, interrupted their first sexual encounter. As Piper and Alex are about to have sex, Silvia bursts in yelling: "Get her the fuck out of here" (S2:E10). Second, when Piper and Alex are technically on a break (though they are more often than not on a break), Alex, feeling sad about Piper deciding to return to Larry, turns to Nicky, and they engage in a sexual encounter. Third, in Season 3, one of the new inmates, Stella Carlin, starts to attract Piper's attention and vice versa. There are a number of sexual tension moments, which are followed by a romantic shower scene and a few stolen kisses. All of this happens while Piper and Alex are still technically in a relationship. As Streitmatter (2009) noted above, the representation of *The L Word* lesbians relied on promiscuity, traditional beauty ideals, and an inability to commit, and Piper and Alex continue this tradition five years after the end of *The L Word*.

Conclusion

I argued, at the outset of this essay, that we must embrace hooks' (1997) concept of oppositional viewing because that practice enables looking back, naming, and opposing. Adding to this notion, hooks (1996) poignantly observes: "Since movie culture is one of the primary sites for the reproduction and perpetuation of white supremacist aesthetics, demanding a change in what we see on the screen … is one way to transform the culture we live in" (76). Though she is addressing film, her argument is easily transferable to television programming, and I argue that *OITNB* is a site where white aesthetics triumph. Throughout this essay, I investigated the intersections of race and lesbian identity, implementing a textual analysis of the reoccurring lesbian characters: Nicky, Boo, Poussey, Crazy Eyes, Alex, and Piper.

Future research should broaden the scope to include an analysis of heterosexuality, asexuality, and other present sexualities within *OITNB*. That inquiry must ask, "Is the representation of heterosexuality also problematic? What does sexuality denote within Daya and Bennett's relationship? How can we think elements of control and power? How is the image of sexuality and sexual identity conceptualized among the Hispanic inmates?" That exploration would also need to examine sexuality in the context of the corrections officers and wardens: Officer Healy's relationship with his mail-order Russian wife; Natalie Figueroa and Joe Caputo; Scott O'Neill and Wanda Bell; and, of course, George "Pornstache" Mendez.

Though many routes are yet to be researched, my relationship to the show, even after this analysis, remains complex and contradictory. *OITNB*, unlike previous representations of lesbian identity such as the women of *The*

L Word, offers an image of diversity, extending bodies beyond white, thin, attractive, and middle class. It gives us the notable characters Nicky, Boo, Poussey, and Crazy Eyes. Moreover, it also presents viewers with a sense of a lesbian community, which signals a significant change from limiting 20th century gay and lesbian depiction. There is also a somewhat positive shift from previous prison lesbian narratives. Ann Ciasullo's (2008) comprehensive examination of the women-in-prison narrative suggests that most often the main characters, in these narratives, are "reunited with and guided to goodness by the man in [their] life—a father, a husband, even a priest—swept back into familial and heterosexual bliss" (197). As of the conclusion of Season 3, this is most assuredly not the case, which introduces a positive re-visioning. But I must ask, "How far have these representations of the neurotic, violent, deviant lesbian really come?"

The answer? Not very far, indeed. Nicky and Boo continue to represent lesbian bodies as overly sexual, deviant, and predatory. Poussey's tragic sexual past is evidenced in her abandonment by Franziska and her rejection by Taystee. Crazy Eyes, a caricature, is portrayed as the monstrous Other: violent, unstable, over/under sexualized. Burns and Davis (2009) claim: "Characters from 'diverse' cultural backgrounds are used by the program [*The L Word*] to add depth and interest to plots and storylines about an otherwise very White portrayal of queer living," and the same can be said of *OITNB* (185). Nicky, Boo, Poussey, and Crazy Eyes offer viewers stereotypical images of the "Other"; they are marginalized and denigrated. In contrast, Piper and Alex continue a fetishized and heteronormative history of lesbian representation that is comprised of an ideal image: white, thin, attractive, and middle class. These stereotypical media depictions inform our thoughts, behaviors, and interactions. Therefore, echoing hooks' call, we must demand a change that will transform the culture we live in.

REFERENCES

Attwood, Feona. 2006. "Sexed Up: Theorizing the Sexualization of Culture." *Sexualities* 9:7–94. Accessed August 20, 2015. doi:0.1177/1363460706053336.

Bordo, Susan. 1993. *Unbearable Weight: Feminism, Western Culture, and the Body.* Berkeley: University of California Press.

Burns, Kellie, and Cristyn Davies. 2009. "Producing Cosmopolitan Sexual Citizens on *The L Word.*" *Journal of Lesbian Studies* 13:174–188. Accessed August 7, 2015. doi:0.1080/10894160802695353.

Capsuto, Steven. 2000. *Alternate Channels: The Uncensored Story of Gay and Lesbian Images on Radio and Television.* New York: Ballantine.

Chung, Sheng Kuan. 2007. "Media Literacy Art Education: Deconstructing Lesbian and Gay Stereotypes in the Media." *International Journal of Art & Design Education* 26:98–107.

Ciasullo, Ann. 2008. "Containing 'Deviant' Desire: Lesbianism, Heterosexuality, and the Women-in-Prison Narrative." *The Journal of Popular Culture* 41:195–223.

Collins, Patricia Hill. 1991. *Black Feminist Thought: Knowledge, Consciousness, and the Politics of Empowerment*. New York: Routledge.

Craig, Shelley L., Laren McInroy, Lance T. McCready, and Ramona Alaggia. 2015. "Media: A Catalyst for Resilience in Lesbian, Gay, Bisexual, Transgender, and Queer Youth." *Journal of LGBT Youth* 12:254–275. Accessed August 7, 2015. doi:0.1080/19361653.

Dines, Gail. 2010. *Pornland: How Porn Has Hijacked Our Sexuality*. Boston: Beacon Press.

_____. 2012. "A Feminist Response to Weitzer." *Violence Against Women* 18:512–520. Accessed August 19, 2015. doi:0.1177/1077801212452550.

Dow, Bonnie J. 2001. "*Ellen*, Television and the Politics of Gay and Lesbian Visibility." *Critical Studies in Media Communication* 18:123–140.

Duncker, Patricia. 1995. "'Bonne Excitation, Orgasme Assure': The Representation of Lesbianism in Contemporary French Pornography." *Journal of Gender Studies* 4:5–15.

Farr, Daniel, and Nathalie Degrouit. 2008. "Understand the Queer World of the Lesbian Body: *Using Queer as Folk* and *The L Word* to Address the Construction of the Lesbian Body." *Journal of Lesbian Studies* 12:423–434. Accessed August 7, 2015. doi:080/10894160802278580.

Hall, Stuart. 1997. *Representation: Cultural Representations and Signifying Practices*. London: Sage.

Hedges, Inez. 2014. "Prison Films: An Overview." *Socialism and Democracy* 28:203–207. Accessed August 15, 2015. doi:0.1080/08854300.

Herman, Didi. 2010. "'Bad Girls Changed My Life': Homonormativity in a Women's Prison." *Critical Studies in Media Communication* 20:141–159. Accessed August 18, 2015. doi:0.1080/07393180302779.

hooks, bell. 1996. *Reel to Real: Race, Sex, and Class at the Movies*. New York: Routledge.

_____. 1997. "Selling Hot Pussy: Representations of Black Female Sexuality in the Cultural Marketplace." *Writing on the Body: Female Embodiment and Feminist Theory*, edited by Katie Conboy, Nadia Medina, and Sarah Stanbury, 113–128. New York: Columbia University Press.

Mayne, Judith. 2000. *Framed: Lesbians, Feminists, and Media Culture*. Minneapolis: University of Minneapolis Press.

McCarthy, Anna. 2001. "*Ellen*: Making Queer Television History." *GLQ: A Journal of Lesbian and Gay Studies* 7:593–620. Accessed September 17, 2015.

McNair, Brian. 2002. *Striptease Culture: Sex, Media and the Democratization of Desire*. London: Routledge.

Modleski, Tania. 1997. "Cinema and the Dark Continent: Race and Gender in Popular Films." *Writing on the Body: Female Embodiment and Feminist Theory*, edited by Katie Conboy, Nadia Medina, and Sarah Stanbury, 208–228. New York: Columbia University Press.

Mulvey, Laura. 1975. "Visual Pleasure and Narrative Cinema." *The Norton Anthology of Theory and Criticism*, edited by Vincent B. Leitch, 2181–2192. New York: W. W. Norton, 2001.

Munoz, José Esteban. 2005. "Queer Minstrels for the Straight Eye: Race as Surplus in Gay TV." *Gay and Lesbian Quarterly* 11:101–102.

Najumi, Mohadesa. 2013. "A Critical Analysis of *Orange Is the New Black*: The Appropriation of Women of Color." *The Feminist Wire*. Accessed July 25, 2015. http://www.thefeministwire.com.

Orange Is the New Black. 2013. Directed by Andrew McCarthy. Netflix. Titled Productions, Lionsgate Television.

Paul, Pamela. 2006. *Pornified: How Pornography Is Damaging Our Lives, Our Relationships, and Our Families*. New York: Henry Holt.

Pilgrim, David. 2000. "The Picaninny Caricature." Last modified 2012. http://www. ferris.edu/jimcrow/picaninny/.

Poniewozik, James, and Jeanne McDowell. 1999. "TV's Coming-out Party." *Time* 154:116–119.

Reeder, Constance. 2004. "Gays and Lesbians, Television Programs, Elections." *Off Our Backs* 34:51–52.

Russo, Vito. 1987. *The Celluloid Closet: Homosexuality in the Movies*. New York: Harper and Row.

Sedgwick, Eve Kosofsky. 2004. "*The L Word*: Novelty in Normalcy." *The Chronicle of Higher Education* 10–11.

Streitmatter, Rodger. 2009. *From "Perverts" to "Fab Five": The Media's Changing Depiction of Gay Men and Lesbians*. New York: Routledge.

Tropiano, Stephen. 2002. *The Prime Time Closet: A History of Gays and Lesbians on TV*. New York: Applause Theater & Cinema.

Tukachinsky, Riva, Dana Mastro, and Moran Yarchi. 2015. "Documenting Portrayals of Race/Ethnicity on Primetime Television Over a 20-Year Span and Their Association with National-Level Racial/Ethnic Attitudes." *Journal of Social Issues* 71:17–38. Accessed June 12, 2015. doi:0.1111.

Tyree, Tia. 2011. "African American Stereotypes in Reality Television." *The Howar Journal of Communications* 22:394–413. Accessed June, 16 2015. doi:0.1080/106 46175.

Valby, Karen. 2013. "Caged Heat." *Entertainment Weekly* 1271:20.

Walters, Suzanna Danuta. 2001. *All the Rage: The Story of Gay Visibility in America*. Chicago: University of Chicago Press.

We Will Survive

Race and Gender-Based Trauma as Cultural Truth Telling

Kalima Y. Young

Recent studies reveal the vast majority of women in prison have experienced race and/or gender-based trauma (Smith et al. 2013, 138) but critical explorations of incarcerated women's trauma are rarely investigated in popular culture. Stuart Hall (1996) posits popular culture is "where control over narratives and representations passes into the hands of the established cultural bureaucracies, sometimes without a murmur." If this is the case, *Orange Is the New Black* is a powerful vehicle for codifying representations of women's carceral experiences. This essay suggests the popular television series illustrates multiple theories of trauma grounded in race, class, identity and sexuality. Straddling the line between spectacle and cultural truth telling, *Orange Is the New Black* provides a platform to understand the role of race and gender-based trauma in incarcerated women's lives.

Understanding Race and Gender-Based Trauma

Psychologists, social scientists and feminists have all theorized the concept of race and gender-based trauma. In psychology, trauma theorists believe a singular traumatic event has the ability to shatter an individual's or a group's collective welfare. This framework suggests there are clearly delineated progressions toward "healing" from the traumatic experience. When traumatic events occur, people can be so psychologically affected that the memory of the actual event is repressed (Caruth 1996, 30). This psychological perspective has been applied in the humanities, particularly within literature studies, to investigate the unconscious ways repressed memories of traumatic events seep through cultural texts. Within this context, unearthing and examining repressed memories can aid in restoring the psychological wellbeing of the individual or group. Examples include Holocaust memorials and other public symbols designed for group mourning. Building upon Freud, psychologist Jane Flax (2012) developed the concept of "race and gender-based melancholia," a state of being that is created when people are "unable or unwilling to confront the gaps between an idealized view of [American] history, culture, and subjective organizations and the more complex realities of our wounded present" (12). Within this melancholic state, dominant and subordinate groups remain imprisoned in pathological dynamics of being.

The notion of cultural trauma put forth by social scientists complicates psychology's trauma theory. According to Jeffrey Alexander et al. (2004), "cultural trauma occurs when members of a collective feel they have been subjected to a horrendous event that leaves indelible marks upon their group consciousness, marking their memories forever and changing their future identity in fundamental and irrevocable ways" (1). Trauma is not solely about the group members experiencing each other's pain; it is about the group viewing the traumatic event as fundamental to their collective identity. Collectives decide to "represent social pain as a fundamental threat to their sense of who they are, where they came from and where they want to go" (Alexander et al. 2010, 10). In this model, it is both the group's recognition of the trauma as detrimental to their wellbeing, and the subsequent narrative created around the traumatic occurrence that defines the cultural trauma.

Feminism in the United States has long focused on addressing issues of sexual violence, sex trafficking and intimate partner violence—phenomena referred to as sexual trauma. Sexual trauma is "trauma resulting from sexual abuse, sexual assault, rape or attempted rape, incest, or molestation" (Yuan et al. 2006). U.S. researchers have found that high rates of poverty and multiple levels of victimization make black American women's experiences of sexual trauma very different from white American women's experiences (Yuan et al. 2006). A recent study in *Psychology of Women Quarterly* found that "women in jails had high rates of mental health disorders, with a majority meeting lifetime diagnostic criteria for a serious mental illness (50%), posttraumatic stress disorder (51%), and/or substance use disorder (85%)" (Dehart et al. 2013, 1). Feminist therapists, researchers, scholars and activists have broadened and enriched the field by developing trauma theories that recognize the consequences of power (race, sex, class, ability) differentials in trauma experiences (Webster and Dunn 2005). Combined, psychologists' trauma theory, social scientists' cultural trauma research and feminists' take on power differentials in traumatic experiences articulate a layered concept of race and gender-based trauma. As a cultural text, *Orange Is the New Black* provides a platform to view how race and gender-based trauma manifests in the lives of incarcerated women.

In Season one, Episode 11, entitled "Tall Men with Feelings," the storyline featuring Tricia's overdose death exemplifies collective identity forged by cultural trauma. Piper attempts to host a memorial for Tricia, but no one attends. She later discovers and participates in a spontaneous inmate gathering of mourning and remembrance for Tricia. A hierarchy of power within and between racial and ethnic enclaves is a defining element of community relations and discord in the prison. Nonetheless, the various ethnic and race-based "families" unite with food in Tricia's memory: Chang offers oranges, Gloria brings nachos, and Poussey and Black Cindy deliver alcohol and assorted snacks. The women also commiserate about the injustice of the situation. The inmates' responses to Tricia's death present a significant shift from their understanding of themselves as separate units to having a collective sense of identity as incarcerated women. For a situation to fit the definition of cultural trauma, a collective must see the event as one that leaves a mark on their consciousness, changes their identity and precipitates a seismic shift in the group's power. They understand their powerlessness to influence the workings of the institution that imprisons them. Everyone in the prison has their own enclave and pecking order but Tricia's death upsets these structures of power. This is especially true for Red, as Tricia's death is a precursor to larger ruptures in her status as head of the kitchen. All of the inmates at Tricia's memorial have the same understanding that a conspiratorial death like Tricia's is a possibility for them all and no matter what they do or how much power they have among each other, they cannot control the larger system. They will never sit at the real table of power. Physical, psychological and sexual abuse is an ever-present threat to the inmates, creating an undercurrent of fear and collective cultural trauma.

The story of Tricia's death also evidences race and gender-based melancholia, a concept that speaks to the inability or unwillingness to acknowledge gaps between past trauma and idealized views of the present, locking dominant and subordinate groups into damaging modes of interaction. Many of the inmates have an individual history of trauma that informs their actions in the present; Red's imprisonment is directly related to her experience of sexism and classism, Big Boo is wrestling with her family's rejection of her butch lesbian identity, and Nicky is continually impacted by trauma related to her history of substance abuse. There are rarely any systematic ways to openly acknowledge the role of trauma in these women's lives— including the trauma resulting from Tricia's death. All of the women suspect foul play but none of them have the power to address it as such to the prison administration. The inmates' ongoing struggle to deal with the double consciousness of living with unaddressed trauma while simultaneously presenting a façade of "cool" results in race and gender-based melancholia.

Trauma as Cultural Truth Telling

Visual narrative is a critical device for unveiling memory that has been lost but is still felt. The process of immersing oneself in visual narrative—both identifying with the characters on the screen and objectifying those characters, creates fertile ground to explore unacknowledged trauma. In her classic work *Trauma and Recovery: The Aftermath of Violence from Domestic Abuse to Political Terror*, feminist psychologist Judith Herman argues,

> Atrocities ... refuse to be buried. Equally as powerful as the desire to deny atrocities is the conviction that denial does not work. Folk wisdom is filled with ghosts who refuse to rest in their graves until their stories are told. Murder will out. Remembering and telling the truth about terrible events are prerequisites both for the restoration of the social order and for the healing of individual victims [1].

Orange Is the New Black problematizes "telling" in a myriad of ways. Telling the simple truth often has dire consequences. The story of Soso's attempted overdose in Season 3, Episode 13, "Trust No Bitch," provides a unique example. Over several episodes, we witness Soso's descent into depression, and ultimately Poussey discovers her in the library, unconscious from an overdose of antihistamines. Instead of going to the authorities, Poussey enlists the help of Suzanne and Taystee to secretly nurse Soso through her recovery from her suicide attempt. The women know that the prison mental health system is more abusive than confinement in the Security Housing Unit/Solitary (SHU). Telling the truth in complex situations of inequity can be devastating for those experiencing mental illness, trauma and abuse. For Soso, there is no option for a grand reveal of the truth as a path to healing.

Orange Is the New Black further strips truth telling of its power through Poussey's refusal to fully participate in Officer Healy's Safe Place meetings. She asks, "Did it ever occur to you that we don't wanna get in touch with our feelings? That actually feeling our feelings might make it impossible to survive in here?" This line of reasoning is a clear circumvention of trauma narratives where revealing the truth is the ultimate path to healing for the victim.

Combating Trauma as Spectacle and Dehumanization

Spectacle is created by the endless repetition of uniform narratives and controlling images that render the audience passive. Elizabeth Alexander, in "Reading the Rodney King Video" (2004), contends, "Black bodies in pain for public consumption have been an American national spectacle for centuries. This history moves from public rapes, beatings and lynching to the gladiatorial arenas of basketball and boxing" (77). Within this analysis, Alexander links America's fascination with witnessing black pain across history and across mediums. Saidiya Hartman (1977) further describes the repetitive nature of pain for public consumption as a "convergence of terror and enjoyment" borne out of the spectacle of slavery. She suggests "the fungibility of the commodity [the slave] makes the captive body an abstract and empty vessel vulnerable to the projection of others' feelings, ideas, desires and values; and as property, the dispossessed body of the enslaved is the surrogate for the master's body since it guarantees the disembodied universality and acts as the sign of his power and domination."

Spectacle has been described as "a tool of pacification and de-politicization"(Debord 1994). It separates viewers from the subject matter and strips away the viewers' power to challenge systems, creating scenarios that display "what society can deliver, but not revealing what is possible" (Debord 1994). Spectacle renders the viewer impassive under challenging situations that would otherwise be seen as unconscionable. Spectacle can take a myriad of forms, but is at its most powerful when it is framed within media culture. According to Douglas Kellner and Michael Ryan (1988), media culture acts as a reinforcing agent for the normalization of behaviors, acts as a tool for disseminating information, and is a vehicle for understanding types of individuals and communities. It is a driving force of economic production, creating and determining the global market. Just as media culture has expanded exponentially over time, so has the nature of mass media spectacle. They explain:

> Every form of culture and more and more spheres of social life are permeated by the logic of the spectacle. Movies are bigger and more spectacular than ever, with high-tech special effects expanding the range of cinematic spectacle. Television channels proliferate endlessly with all-day movies, news, political talk, sports, specialty niches, re-runs of the history of television, and whatever else can gain an audience. The rock spectacle reverberates through radio, television, CDs, computer networks, and extravagant concerts. Media culture provides fashion and style models for emulation and promotes a celebrity culture that provides deities and role models [3].

Media culture promotes spectacle, making stories larger than life. If these stories are additionally filled with dehumanizing images, media culture can become a dangerous tool. "Dehumanization is ... the process by which stigmatized groups are placed outside the boundary in which moral values, rules, and considerations of fairness apply" (Goff et al. 2014, 526). As a widespread occurrence, dehumanization has serious consequences. Described as "the most striking violation of our belief in a common humanity: our Enlightenment assumption that we are all essentially one and the same" (Haslam 2006, 3), dehumanization, whether driven by hate or indifference, sets the stage for brutality. Individual identity and community are characteristics of our joint humanity, and when an individual is subject to dehumanizing practices, "victims become a deindividuated mass that lacks the capacity to evoke compassion" (Haslam 2006, 3). From news reports that strip humanity away from those incarcerated, to pornography that objectifies women in support of misogyny, dehumanization is a very strong precursor to violent acts and often is perpetuated through media culture. When paired with the concept of dehumanization, spectacle becomes a powerful technology for erasing victim status from those affected by unconscionable acts. *Orange Is the New Black* intervenes in spectacularization and dehumanization of women in prison by deploying flashbacks to broaden stories of trauma.

One of the most compelling traumatic backstories in the series occurs in Season 1 with Miss Claudette. She is a stern and seemingly dangerous figure in the prison. Rumors about her life outside of Litchfield, fears of her voodoo practice, and suspicions about the violence of the crime she committed shroud her in mystery until Episode 4, "Imaginary Enemies." In flashbacks, we see how Miss Claudette was a young Haitian immigrant who came to the United States to join a housekeeping company. We eventually see her become the manager of the business and learn about her love for Jean Baptiste, the young man who brought her to the States. Flashbacks further reveal Miss Claudette was imprisoned for murdering a client who raped one of her employees. This flashback, told in a matter of fact, straightforward manner, is stripped of all sensationalized elements. Background music is minimized and all of her movements are quiet and restrained— like her persona in prison. She meticulously cleans the client's home, putting away dishes and cutlery. Once the camera finally draws back, we see her client lying on the floor with multiple stab wounds inflicted by Miss Claudette. In showing Miss Claudette's arrival in the United States as a young woman, we see her vulnerability as an immigrant and suspect the many ways she may have been victimized. We see Miss Claudette as a full human being through her story of unrequited love of Jean Baptiste. Flashbacks also reveal how the manager of the housekeeping business is critical and severe and how this cycle continues when Miss Claudette becomes the manager. Miss Claudette has a full interior life complete with a narrative arc, lifting this character out of a stereotypical portrayal of a black incarcerated woman.

According to Patricia Hill Collins, "stereotypes act as controlling images that serve the dual function of normalizing oppression and coercing individuals to act out in ways that support oppressive stereotypes" (1991, 67). Controlling images reduce the stereotyped into objects that can be controlled, and, reinforced by media spectacle, create a box for identity formation that singularly limits the range with which women can express their sexual experiences. Bolstered by sexism that prevents women from defining and owning their sexuality, controlling images obscure stories of sexual abuse, squelch accurate depictions of lesbianism and force women to act out in ways that support the stereotypes of gendered sexuality. Although she is stern and foreboding, Miss Claudette's interior life and her desire for love from Jean Baptiste humanizes her and expands upon her character's development.

Grounding Trauma Narratives

Orange Is the New Black further complicates the spectacle and dehumanization common in trauma narratives by eschewing uniform narratives of female prisoners, instead employing a multi-racial and multi-ethnic cast of characters. This combats common representations of primarily male inmates perpetuated in news and entertainment media. In a recent interview about representations of female prisoners in *Orange Is the New Black*, activist Asha Bandele states, "women are being incarcerated at nearly twice the rate of men. From the 1980s, the female prison population has grown over 800 percent, whereas the male population grew just about 400 percent. Today, some 1 million women are under the supervision of the criminal justice system, with more than 200,000 of them incarcerated" (Soules 2015). Harsh drug sentencing laws, neoliberal surveillance of the poor and untreated mental illnesses contributes to an increase in female prisoner populations. *Orange Is the New Black* deftly turns these statistics about female inmates into fleshed out, human stories.

Several characters have traumatic experiences related to mental illness, substance use, cycles of poverty, and sexual abuse. Their imprisonment is either influenced by or a direct result of these issues. The convergence of mental illness and imprisonment is illuminated in the storyline of Suzanne "Crazy Eyes" Warren, an inmate with a history of mental health issues and episodes of violent behavior. In Season 1, Episode 11, "Tall Men with Feelings," Suzanne reveals that her parents struck a deal with the authorities that she would be incarcerated with the general prison population instead of placed in psychiatric care. In the Season 2 episode "Comic Sans," Jimmy is an elderly inmate suffering from dementia and is estranged from her only daughter. Litchfield abdicates responsibility for Jimmy's elder care by granting her a "compassionate release." Jimmy is taken to the bus station and left there with no support, resources or follow-up case management. Both Suzanne's and Jimmy's stories illustrate the way prisons warehouse the mentally ill and contribute to the homeless, mentally ill population living on the streets.

Many of the characters experience trauma due to their involvement with drugs. *Orange Is the New Black* intervenes in narratives of spectacularized trauma by showing the way the War on Drugs impacts women differently depending on their race, ethnicity and class. Flashbacks into Nicky's life in the episode entitled "Empathy Is a Boner Killer" reveal that she was raised in a wealthy family, but her family's economic status could not shield her from imprisonment for a robbery she committed to fuel her drug addiction. Taystee becomes involved in drug dealing as a way to survive a life of poverty. Leanne becomes addicted to methamphetamines after leaving her Amish faith. Both Alex and Piper are imprisoned due to their involvement with an international drug cartel that preyed upon white, middle class young women as drug mules. Each of these stories shed brighter light on the myriad of ways drug-related laws and sentencing fuel the prison system, a much more nuanced approach than other popular culture depictions of the War on Drugs where typically only poor women or sexually promiscuous women become involved in substance use, abuse and distribution.

In her analysis of the symbolic function of gang rape trials, Kristen Bumiller (2008) argues, "stories about sexual violence are re-narrated for the purpose of locating the threat to society and justifying a punitive response" (37). Her definition of expressive justice, cases where the state is able to develop symbolic messages about the threat of becoming a victim, reveal the ways in which mass media spectacle sets the stage for acceptable sexual victimhood in popular imagination. There is an underlying assumption perpetuated by mass media spectacle that rape primarily happens to white women. Media images of the sexual violation of black women are often only shown in the context of prostitution or domestic abuse perpetuated by black men. On the other hand, white women are depicted as victims of a myriad of sexual abuse scenarios, from domestic violence incidents to stranger rape victimization. As scolding, judgmental and sexist the portrayals of raped white women may be, white female experiences are most often the only ones that are captured, reproduced and advocated against by mainstream media, mainstream feminism and neoliberal punitive practices.

Bumiller's analysis of the Central Park jogger case highlights this understanding of spectacularized race and gender-based violence. She posits the "specter" of the "nearly dead white woman's body" was reproduced by the media and used to create a site of "uncanny strangeness," arousing images of unseen dangers" (2008, 42). The relationship between spectacle and fantasy contributes to a reliance on the state control of criminal populations—often codified as poor people of color. Feminist advocacy against rape has increased crime control measures bolstered by the reliance on the state as the enforcer of "normal" i.e., white, middle class, heteronormative family values.

In Bumiller's chapter about administrative justice, she highlights the different ways women's anti-violence advocacy efforts that helped to develop new avenues of government surveillance. She argues public health workers have been charged with uncovering hidden victims of sexual assault and an expansive network of bureaucratic services have been developed as a response to domestic violence and female rape.

The *Orange Is the New Black* storyline of Dayanara "Daya" Diaz speaks to complicated narratives of sexual violence and surveillance. Daya and her mother Alieda are both imprisoned due to their relationship with Cesar, a drug dealer who is the caretaker of Daya's sisters and brothers while she and Alieda are incarcerated. In Season 1, Daya begins a consensual sexual relationship with Officer John Bennett and becomes pregnant with his child. *Orange Is the New Black* adds a romantic storyline to Daya and Bennett's relationship, bringing into the question the notion of agency. The Prison Rape Elimination Act designates as rape any sexual relationship between a prisoner and a correctional officer, due to the differing power dynamics within prison. (Bill Summary 2003). The complications of rape and consent make for an intriguing trauma narrative—one where Daya is at odds with the system designed to protect her as a prisoner. The stories women tell about sexual trauma complicate lay understanding of trauma theory, agency and resistance, and victim/subject dichotomies. In *Reading Is My Window: Books and the Art of Reading in Women's Prisons* (2010), Megan Sweeney argues: "prisoners' complex engagements with narratives of victimization open important avenues for thinking and talking about victimization and agency in more nuanced, grounded and productive terms" (3). Sweeney theorizes that the way prisoners engage with trauma narratives speaks to their complex personhood; an element of their lives often overlooked by the inequities of the penal system. Similar complexities and inequities are illuminated in Daya's story after her baby girl is born. Cesar is raising the child when the family home is raided and all of the children, including Daya's baby, are taken into the foster care system. The complications of cycles of poverty, state control of poor people of color, questions of agency, and questions of consent create multiple avenues to explore how trauma narratives differ across race, ethnicity and class.

Theorizing Sexual Trauma

Fictional narratives of sexual violence provide a vehicle to theorize sexual trauma. Susan Brownmiller (1975) argues, "our nation's cultural output promotes a climate in which acts of sexual hostility directed against women are not only tolerated but ideologically encouraged" (395). One of the primary ways *Orange Is the New Black* theorizes sexual trauma is through its casual depiction of the way the characters think about, minimize and normalize sexual violence in everyday life, a phenomenon commonly referred to as "rape culture." One telling scene occurs early in Season 2 in the episode entitled "You Also Have a Pizza." Flaca and Maritza casually share stories of their male relatives who inappropriately touch young women in their families. This information is greeted with laughter and knowing glances from other Latina women in the kitchen, speaking to the collective minimizing of sexual violence in families.

Additionally, *Orange Is the New Black* depicts multiple storylines that illuminate a sexual trauma theory that links women's lack of knowledge about their bodies to their vulnerability to sexual violation. In the Season 2 episode entitled "A Whole Other Hole" it becomes apparent that many of the inmates are unaware of the anatomy of their reproductive systems. Sophia, the only transwoman at Litchfield, proceeds to educate the cisgender women about various parts of their anatomy and ways to pleasure themselves. Of interest is the fact that ignorance about female anatomy cut across all racial, class and ethnic lines and the only woman possessing deeper knowledge about female genitalia and female pleasure is transgender. Sophia defined her own womanhood. Her financial desperation to actualize her physical female identity results in her being imprisoned for fraud. The cisgender women in prison had not been encouraged to learn about their bodies nor to appreciate the intricacies of their bodies. Function, smell and erogenous zones are taboo and rarely demystified.

Finally, this sexual trauma theory is tragically illustrated in Season 3's story of Tiffany "Pennsatucky" Doggett. In the episode "A Tittin' and a Hairin'" we learn in flashbacks that Pennsatucky's mother failed to provide her with accurate advice about her body during puberty. Upon having her first period, her mother assures her she is not dying.

> Mama: Don't be scared. All it means is you ain't a little grubber no more. Now you're like a case of pop. You got value. Look, there's some things you gotta know. Now that you're a tittin' and a-hairin', boys are gonna see you different, and pretty soon, they're gonna do you different. Best thing is to go on and let 'em do their business, baby. If you're real lucky, most of 'em be quick, like your daddy. It's like a bee sting, in and out, over before you knew it was happening.
> Pennsatucky: But, Mama, bee stings hurt.
> Mama: Come on now. We're celebrating.

Pennsatucky's mother's faulty advice sets Pennsatucky up for sexual violations as a teenager and then as a prisoner. We see in flashbacks how she traded sex with boys for cases of soda. In the present, Pennsatucky becomes friendly with a new correctional officer named Coates. After several off-the-books outings, Coates proceeds to kiss her without her permission. He later forces her to pick up donut pieces on the ground with her mouth, wielding his authority over her. She does not object, though her body language reveals she is not comfortable with this act. These incidents build until Coates ultimately rapes her in the transportation van. The rape scene foregoes customary spectacularized elements—the camera focuses only on her tearful, expressionless face. In its stark, sudden brutality, the rape scene not only speaks to the withdrawal victims often experience, it also speaks to the truth that most victims of sexual assault know their assailant. It is important to note that depictions of sexual violence have been rare in *Orange Is the New Black*. Many prison television shows such as HBO's *Oz* focus first and foremost on rape scenarios—the threat of rape, the actualization of rape and rape as punishment. Despite some discussions of rape and threats of sexual violation, rape scenarios are rarely trotted out for spectacular consumption in *Orange Is the New Black*. In this way, the series complicates sexual trauma narratives while also illustrating the pervasiveness of rape culture.

Conclusion

A recent study found that the onset of crime and delinquency varied for women depending on their mental health status and trauma exposure. A report released by the Human Rights Project entitled, "The Sexual Abuse to Prison Pipeline: A Girls Story," found that "sexual abuse is one of the primary predictors of a girl's entry into the juvenile justice system" (Saar et al. 2015). The criminalization of victims of sexual abuse contributes to the increase of women in the prison system. The #SayHerName campaign to end racialized violence against women at the hands of the police claims,

> the resurgent racial justice movement in the United States has developed a clear frame to understand the police killings of Black men and boys, theorizing the ways in which they are systematically criminalized and feared across disparate class backgrounds and irrespective of circumstance. Yet Black women who are profiled, beaten, sexually assaulted, and killed by law enforcement officials are conspicuously absent from this frame even when their experiences are identical. When their experiences with police violence are distinct—uniquely informed by race, gender, gender identity, and sexual orientation—Black women remain invisible [Crenshaw et al. 2015, 3].

This is a critical time to explore the linkages between race and gender-based trauma narratives and the criminal justice system. It is a time for revealing the intersections of trauma filtered through race, ethnicity, gender and class. There are more women in U.S. prisons now than ever before in our nation's carceral history. A disproportionate number of these women are black, Latina, poor and queer. The carceral system deploys abusive tactics to punish poor women and control women's bodies, and these issues must be explored for advocacy purposes. Cultural texts are needed to illuminate the role of trauma in lives of incarcerated women. According to Sweeny (2010), "the law revolves around ritualized battles over competing narratives and cultural stories ... women's engagements with narratives of victimization ... serve as a resource for challenging the law's prevailing stories about victimization and agency" (128). Within the representations of race and gender-based trauma narratives, *Orange Is the New Black* complicates our understanding of women's prison experiences and provides a popular culture text to more fully explore these issues. *Orange Is the New Black* also provides women in prison with what Avery Gordon (2008) refers to as "complex personhood" (2), an acknowledgement of the contradictions within us all, the place between recognizing and misrecognizing the self. It is a way to explore victim status and agency, a perfect space for dialogue about race and gender-based trauma.

The women inmates in *Orange Is the New Black* are victims of systems of overlapping traumas related to mental illness, poverty, substance abuse and sexual violence. *Orange Is the New Black* grounds women's trauma narratives in the materiality of women's lives, expanding stories of trauma from their conventional place in popular culture as sensationalized tales of self-help and individual triumph over adversity. It highlights collective identities forged through cultural trauma, acknowledges melancholic states of trauma, and illustrates how trauma precipitates criminal activity.

As a visual text, *Orange Is the New Black* attempts to represent a spectrum of racial, ethnic, class and gendered experiences of trauma. Its multiracial, multi-ethnic and LGBT inclusiveness is rare for a popular text. The series combats uniform narratives of trauma by using flashbacks to provide each character with a full, complex interior lives. Although violence occurs throughout the text, trauma, especially sexual violence, is never used as a primary plot point. By avoiding clear delineations of innocent and guilty characters, *Orange Is the New Black* humanizes its women, pulling them from the brink of controlling images and situating race and gender-based trauma narratives in the complexities of material life.

REFERENCES

Alexander, E. 1994. "'Can You Be Black and Look at This?': Reading the Rodney King Video(s)." *Public Culture* 77–94.

Alexander, Jeffrey C., and Ron Eyerman. 2004. *Cultural Trauma and Collective Identity*. Berkeley: University of California Press.

Brownmiller, Susan. 1975. *Against Our Will: Men, Women and Rape*. New York: Fawcett Columbine.

Bumiller, Kristin. 2008. *In an Abusive State: How Neoliberalism Appropriated the Feminist Movement Against Sexual Violence*. Durham: Duke University Press.

Collins, Patricia. 1991. *Black Feminist Thought: Knowledge, Consciousness, and the Politics of Empowerment*. New York: Routledge.

Crenshaw, Kimberle, and Andrea J. Ritchie. 2015. *Say Her Name: Resisting Police Brutality against Black Women*. New York: African American Policy Forum.
Debord, Guy. 1994. *The Society of the Spectacle*. New York: Zone Books.
Dehart, D., S. Lynch, J. Belknap, P. Dass-Brailsford, and B. Green. 2013. "Life History Models of Female Offending: The Roles of Serious Mental Illness and Trauma in Women's Pathways to Jail." *Psychology of Women Quarterly* 138–151.
Flax, Jane. 2010. *Resonances of Slavery in Race/gender Relations: Shadow at the Heart of American Politics*. New York: Palgrave Macmillan.
Goff, Phillip Atiba, et al. 2014. "The Essence of Innocence: Consequences of Dehumanizing Black Children." *Journal of Personality and Social Psychology* 526–545.
Gordon, Avery. 2008. *Ghostly Matters Haunting and the Sociological Imagination*. Minneapolis: University of Minnesota Press.
Hall, Stuart. 1996. "What Is the 'Black' in Black Popular Culture?" *Stuart Hall: Critical Dialogues in Cultural Studies*. London: Routledge.
Hartman, Saidiya V. 1997. *Scenes of Subjection: Terror, Slavery, and Self-making in Nineteenth-Century America*. New York: Oxford University Press.
Haslam, Nick. 2006. "Dehumanization: An Integrative Review." *Personality and Social Psychology Review* 252–264.
Herman, Judith Lewis. 1997. *Trauma and Recovery: The Aftermath of Violence, from Domestic Abuse to Political Terror*. New York: Basic Books.
Jackson, Cassandra. 2011. *Violence, Visual Culture and the Black Male Body*. New York: Routledge.
Kellner, Douglas, and Michael Ryan. 1988. *Camera Politica: The Politics and Ideology of Contemporary Hollywood Film*. Bloomington: Indiana University Press.
Saar, Malika, and Rebecca Epstein. 2015. "The Sexual Abuse to Prison Pipeline: The Girl's Story." Georgetown Law Press.
Soules, Conor. 2015. "What 'Orange Is The New Black' Gets Right and Wrong About the Criminal Justice System." Indiewire, July 1. Accessed September 21, 2015.
Sweeney, Megan. 2010. *Reading Is My Window: Books and the Art of Reading in Women's Prisons*. Chapel Hill: University of North Carolina Press.
Bill Summary & Status File, S.14435. 2003. The Library of Congress, THOMAS.gov, September 4. Retrieved September 5, 2015.
Webster, Denise C., Erica C. Dunn. 2005. "Feminist Perspectives on Trauma." *The Foundation and Future of Feminist Therapy*. Portland: Hawthorne Literary Press. Web. 22 April 2015.
Yuan, N.P., M.P. Koss, and M. Stone. 2006. *The Psychological Consequences of Sexual Trauma*. Harrisburg, PA: VAWnet. Web. 20 April 2015. www.vawnet.org.

Jenji Kohan's Trojan Horse
Subversive Uses of Whiteness

KATIE SULLIVAN BARAK

There was a moment watching the first few episodes of Netflix's original programming *Orange Is the New Black* (*OITNB*) where I found myself pulled out of the narrative, overwhelmed by the number of women on the show. Sure, it makes sense considering the program is set in a women's prison, but I still experienced a sense of giddiness. On top of that, there was difference represented on-screen: women of color, queer women, older women, women of all shapes and sizes, women from a range of class backgrounds, and their intersectional identities were part of the storyline, too. This moment of elation was cut short, though, when I remembered we were viewing Litchfield Correctional Facility through the eyes of Piper Chapman, a white, femme, upper middle class woman who refers to herself as a WASP. All these diverse stories were being mediated through yet another white lens.

Within the next month, I came across an interview with *OITNB*'s showrunner, Jenji Kohan, on NPR's *Fresh Air* (2013). Kohan explained she is drawn to stories in which disparate folks are slammed together and "forced to deal," a defining characteristic in *OITNB* and *Weeds*, Kohan's 2005–2012 Showtime show. *Fresh Air* host Terry Gross points out another major similarity in Kohan's creations: *Weeds* and *OITNB* both feature white, upper-middle class women as their central characters, both involved in drug crimes. Kohan responds:

> In a lot of ways Piper was my Trojan Horse. You're not going to go into a network and sell a show on really fascinating tales of black women, and Latina women, and old women and criminals. But if you take this White girl, this sort of fish out of water, and you follow her in, you can then expand your world and tell all of those other stories. But it's a hard sell to just go in and try to sell those stories initially. The girl next door, the cool blonde, is a very easy access point,

and it's relatable for a lot of audiences and a lot of networks looking for a certain demographic. It's useful.

A Trojan Horse! In Homer's *Odyssey,* the Trojan Horse is a ruse cooked up by the Greeks after warring for ten years with Troy. They construct a large, hollow wooden horse on wheels, big enough for 30–40 Greek soldiers to fit inside the horse's belly. The Greeks feign retreat and pretend to sail away, leaving the horse in Troy as an offering to Athena. Thinking the war is over, the unsuspecting Trojans wheel the gift inside their walls. That night, the Greeks sneak out of the Trojan Horse, let the other soldiers into the city, and a huge battle ensues. The Trojan Horse got them inside the walls of the city and gave them a strategic advantage that ultimately led to the Greeks defeating the Trojans.

If Piper, the white, upper-middle class, well-educated, straight-appearing female character, was a Trojan Horse, this meant her positioning was intentional … not only intentional, but a strategic move of counterhegemonic storytelling. Imagining this "accessible," "cool blonde" as a clever tool for sneaking diverse stories onto the main stage made sense, albeit sad logic. Opening up the field of representation requires covert actions to get through the initial stages of pitching a show like *OITNB* to any network, even a global distribution platform like Netflix. Despite critics clamoring for more diversity in front of and behind the camera, diversity has to be wrapped up and disguised as a story about a white lady to initially sell to networks and audiences. Popular media still privilege narratives starring, about, and catering to white people.

After acknowledging that Piper's femme whiteness got *OITNB* past the gatekeepers, Kohan tears apart her Trojan Horse. She spends the next three seasons deconstructing the very identities and privileges that brought *OITNB* to the screen. Whiteness is not invisible, nor is Piper's standpoint shown as neutral or logical. She may have initially seemed like the main character or audience's lens into Litchfield, but *OITNB* repositions Piper away from the center. Piper is arguably the most unlikeable character on the show. This essay will examine the ways *OITNB* systematically critiques Piper's privilege and deconstructs her position as a white, upper-middle class, well-educated, femme woman.

A Trojan Horse provides access; it was the Greeks' way through Troy's city gates and *OITNB*'s way "on air." Once it served its purpose, Homer doesn't address what happened to the Trojan Horse. Unlike a wooden horse statue, Piper exists in the self-reflexive world of *OITNB*. Kohan uses Piper as a tool to analyze systems of power. She states:

> We are stuck in our cycles of privilege and poverty, but we can't talk about it; there are classes and there are oppressions and there is racism…. There are a lot of people trying to deal with it, and I'm trying to deal with it too [Willmore 2013].

Netflix has played an important role in this process of "dealing" and Kohan's relationship with the streaming service is unique. When she pitched *OITNB*, Netflix ordered 13 episodes without requiring a pilot. Presumably, her résumé of smart, funny, complicated television shows contributed to their decision. Due to this arrangement, Kohan has unprecedented creative control over the direction *OITNB* takes (McHugh 2015).

It should be noted, Netflix is not like traditional broadcast networks; it is an international, web-based subscription video on demand (SVOD) platform. Sixty-nine million people subscribe globally (Hasting and Wells 2015). Unlike traditional broadcast networks dependent on advertising revenue to pay for content, Netflix, and premium cable channels like HBO and Showtime, evade some of the restrictions attached to a marketer-driven structure. In commercial broadcasting, advertisers look for specific demographics to view their commercials, which means programming must appeal to the people they hope will buy their products. This shapes what kinds of stories are told on TV— their narrative form, the race, gender, class, and sexuality of characters, how much sexual intimacy can be shown, who gets to have sexual intimacy, the amount of violence, and so on. The freedom from advertisers in subscription-based programming yields different kinds of stories and storytelling. Kohan, who already worked without restrictions at Showtime, said of her freedom on Netflix: "It's the Wild West. You can do what you want" (Radish 2013). Despite this, getting *OITNB* through Netflix's door still required a Trojan Horse; the show's emphasis on diverse stories and intersectional representations runs contrary to the focus on whiteness in popular media.

Examining White Privilege through a Feminist Lens

In her 1988 essay, Peggy McIntosh outlines her personal, everyday privilege as a white person and extends the argument to gender privilege in order to highlight the ways racial and gender hierarchies interlock (2011). Using the metaphor of an invisible knapsack filled with unearned "provisions" some individuals are given at birth based on their race, gender, class, ethnicity, ability, etc., McIntosh provides a 48-point list detailing the kinds of "skin privilege" she receives on a daily basis. The list includes things like: I can turn on the television or open to the front page of the paper and see people of my race represented; I can be pretty sure that if I ask to talk to the "person in charge," I will be facing a person of my race; I can expect figurative language and imagery in all of the arts to testify to experiences of my race. McIntosh's list features concrete items and practices as well as structural inequalities. Frequently, these privileges go unseen and whiteness is not considered a racial identity. As a result, conversations about privilege, oppression, and race suffer if this invisibility goes unaddressed.

McIntosh is certainly not the only scholar giving shape to elusive, invisible whiteness in her work. Answering a call put forth by scholars and critics like James Baldwin, W. E. B. Dubois, and Ralph Ellison, some academics in the 1990s drew their attention to whiteness as a social construct creating a burgeoning field of critical white studies (see Morrison 1993; hooks 1992; West 1990; Dyer 1997; Hall 1997; Frankenberg 1993; Hurtado 1996; Flagg 1998). Up to that point, research on race and ethnicity focused almost exclusively on the non-white experience. Valerie M. Babb (1998) sought to define whiteness like other racial categories. She argues:

> More than a classification of physical appearance; it is largely an invented construct blending history, culture, assumptions, and attitudes. From a descent of various European nationals there emerges in the United States the consensus of a single white race that, in principle, elides religious socioeconomic, and gender differences among individual whites to create a hegemonically privileged race category [10].

The push to make whiteness visible occurred across academic fields. Historians questioned who qualified as white and how whiteness came to be the gold standard of race. Literary criticism also reflected the change by challenging the ways written texts reinforced white invisibility. In particular, authors took issue with academia's focus on black cultural representations instead of their white authors, the presumption of a white audience, or the cultural context whiteness imposes thereby qualifying all stories. Instead of allowing it to be the silent, invisible norm, some cultural studies scholars attempted to make whiteness "strange" by analyzing white film characters, paintings, magazine ads, and other visual representations of whiteness.

U.S. film and television reflected the evolving discourse on whiteness. Given the general upheaval of white masculinity, the push for multiculturalism, and the transnational flow of non-white people, there was a general sense of panic traceable throughout American popular culture texts. This period of flux meant hegemonic norms were questioned, putting the status quo in jeopardy. Raka Shome documents a unique trend in 1990s Hollywood films about the U.S. presidency: whiteness is not always invisible (2000). As an important distinction from previous critical white studies, Shome finds that "whiteness often promotes a rhetoric where it begins to construct itself as 'not the norm,' as something particular, full of unique challenges and struggles that need attention" in moments of cultural flux and crisis (368).

This white visibility plays out in narratives of "good" whites and "bad" whites (Shome 2000). Take, for instance, the 1996 film *A Time to Kill*. Matthew McConaughey plays a lawyer defending Samuel L. Jackson, a wronged black man who, in retribution against their crime and the racist legal system, preemptively shoots and kills the two white supremacist men who raped his daughter. McConaughey is the good white lawyer just standing up for what is right. The bad white people range from the white supremacists, Ku Klux Klan members, and white individuals who may not overtly do racist things, but actively discourage McConaughey from standing up for justice. There is certainly allusion to systemic racism, but the more salient narrative is good whites versus bad whites. Shome remarks, "This is an interesting strategy of contemporary whiteness: the identification and acknowledgement of a part of itself as bad, corrupt, oppressive, and needing to be fixed, and a separation of itself from that part by denying identification with it" (396).

Caricatures of "good" and "bad" white people are crude stereotypes. Whiteness is part of a character's representation, but reduced into simple terms, yielding an inaccurate characterization. What they, as well as most media representations, lack is intersectionality. Intersectionality is a helpful analytical tool for exploring the ways power asymmetries limit and expand subjectivities and material conditions, thus contributing to social exclusion and political injustice (Crenshaw 1994). Oppressions are interlinking. Trying to deal with one without looking at the ways it is connected to other forms of inequality ignores the bigger, messier picture of oppression. Race, gender, sexuality, nationality, class, ethnicity, and ability are never experienced individually; these identities occur simultaneously.

Incorporating whiteness into an intersectional framework is not easy. Considering the initial point was to further demonstrate the "double jeopardy" that black women negotiate around race and gender, some theorists and critics argue that the term has been appropriated by white feminism. In this understanding, skin privilege negates the other axes of oppression thus overlooking the interrelated nature of privilege and oppression. This chapter goes broad with its understanding of intersectionality, theoretically considering the coexistence of privileged and oppressed identities in a single body. No position is "unaffected by the contradictory effects of domination" (Levine-Rasky 2011, 244). Including whiteness acknowledges that individuals can be members of multiple dominant groups and members of multiple subordinate groups at the same time. A matrix of domination "contains few pure victims or oppressors" (Collins 1993, 621). Furthermore, identity is "situationally constructed" and context often determines one's position of dominance or subordination (Friedman 1995, 16). By considering identity as a contextually determined, mobile site where domination and privilege interact and change places with subordination and oppression, we can better grasp power differentials at work in personal identities.

This is all well and good for academic theory and every day, real life experiences, but capturing these complex identities in popular culture appears to be very challenging. Mediated representations of realistic, complex human beings have been seemingly incapable of articulating intersectional identities. When characters are presented intersectionally one identity is often prioritized over another. A character's race trumps their class background or their sexuality is deemed more important than their race. Michaela D. E. Meyer examines network television's attempts at representing intersectionality in popular programs like *Bones* (2005-present), *Grey's Anatomy* (2005-present), and *One Tree Hill* (2003–2012). She found that, typically, one character out of the larger ensemble is presented intersectionally, and this character is usually a non–White character (i.e. a queer woman of color). While this inclusion answers the critical call for more representations of diversity and will, in theory, appeal to wider audiences, Meyer notes that the strategic placement of intersectional characters of color does not actually shake up politics of representation. Rather, these characters become points of difference that allow white characters to interact with marginality in "progressive and accepting ways" (Meyer 2009, 248). Furthermore, by lumping issues of race, ethnicity, sexuality, and class into a single character, it "[positions] that character as a token representative for all discourses of cultural struggle" (Meyer 2010, 381). Worse yet, Meyer argues that these characters are visible in that they are present in several network television shows seemingly signifying progressive identity politics, but they are simultaneously invisible because they reinforce the status quo. She states, "They are appealing to everyone because they are essentially no one, culturally erased into a discourse of post-difference where any aspect of identity politics (race, ethnicity, class, sexuality) is essentially and functionally not important in contemporary culture" (2015, 912). Difference is represented in terms of quantity; there is literally more diversity on screen, but that is as far as it goes.

This is not the case on *OITNB*. Showrunner Jenji Kohan is a feminist auteur who steeps the text in social commentary and plays with expectation. If we keep to the Trojan Horse tale, she is King Odysseus of Ithaca: the brains behind the clever scheme to smuggle in something unexpected. At the same time, she sees herself as an entertainer rather than an educator. She proclaims, "I don't set about to say, 'Today we're going to teach people that this is oppressive and wrong.' My first job is to entertain and engage people. I want to be the party starter. And if people start talking about it, then I'm doing my job" (Shaw 2015). The next section will take a closer look at *OITNB* and Piper Chapman. By dissecting Piper's representation, her formal and narrative framing, and the ways she has evolved in the narrative, we can better see how *OITNB* deconstructs their Trojan Horse.

Looking the Trojan Horse in the Mouth: Who Is Piper Chapman?

Piper Chapman (played by Taylor Schilling) is white with straight blonde hair, straight white teeth, and big blue eyes. Piper is an able-bodied, gender-conforming, femme woman. When discussing her family and background, she refers to herself as a WASP (an abbreviation for "White Anglo-Saxon Protestant" that further signifies a woman with wealth and status from the Northeast region of the United States). Considering her intersectionally, this general description shows Piper possesses several axes of privilege. It is her class and education that set her apart the most from the other inmates.

Audiences get a picture of Piper's class through flashbacks to her life before Litchfield. We see evidence of her wealth in these scenes. Her clothes and home are high-end and fashionable. She and her fiancé, Larry, frequently shop at the pricey grocery store, Whole Foods. Piper appears to have been adrift in terms of steady income, which suggests there is family money cushioning her work-free life. Through other interactions and flashbacks, we know she worked as a waitress after completing college at Smith, a private women's liberal arts university. She double-majored in communications and comparative literature (not the most employable of majors unless you remain in the ivory tower of academia). She was involved with a startup company at the beginning of her stay at Litchfield. The plan was to make artisanal bath products in her kitchen with her best friend, Poppy. That career plan is now dead in the water.

Piper's sexuality is not specifically named on the show. Piper does not register as queer or bisexual at first glance because she adheres to a heteronormative gender presentation. While queerness is not normally associated with privilege, the fact that Piper chooses to look feminine means she can pass as straight. From the first episode, audiences know she is engaged to Larry and that she is going to prison because her ex-girlfriend, Alex Vause, named her in court. Although terms like "bisexuality" or "queer" are not used to describe Piper, *OITNB* draws attention to the fluidity of her sexuality in conversations between characters. For instance, Larry and Polly express concern that Piper is locked up with Alex. They ask if she is going to "turn gay" to which Piper responds, "Whoa. That's not happening. And you don't just turn gay. You fall somewhere on a spectrum. Like on a Kinsey scale." There is space on *OITNB* for a multitude of queer identities. Piper's heteronormative performance of femininity means she can choose when and where to reveal her sexuality. At times, she is candid; in a flashback, she tells her best friend Polly, "I like hot girls. I like hot guys. I like hot people. What can I say, I'm shallow." At other points, though, Piper chooses not to disclose her orientation. She understands that other people's presumptions can work for or against her, depending on the situation. The privilege of choice is a point of power.

A Horse of a Different Color: Intersectional Whiteness in Litchfield

On her first day at Litchfield, Morello, another white inmate, is particularly kind to Piper, giving her tissues and a toothbrush. She says, "We look out for our own." Politically-correct Piper cautiously repeats, "Our own?" Morello tells her, "It's tribal, non-racist." While not officially segregated, inmates and administration follow racial divisions within Litchfield; "tribes" determine assigned sleeping quarters, unassigned lunch tables, and representatives on the Women's Advisory Council (WAC). The white inmates consist of Piper, Galina "Red" Reznikov, Tiffany "Pensatucky" Doggett, Alex Vause, Nicole "Nicky" Nichols, Lorna Morello, Carrie "Big Boo" Black, Gina Murphy, Leanne Taylor, Erica "Yoga" Jones, Sister Jane Ingalls, Norma Romano, Stella Carlin, and Tricia Miller (RIP). There are also white women amongst the older inmates nicknamed "Golden Girls." White women and women of color are considered "Golden Girls," too, but the intersectional joke seems to be that old age unites their interests and values more than race.

OITNB makes space in character development for intersectional identities. While the women listed above share skin privilege, not all white (or black or Hispanic or "Golden Girl") characters are the same. Sexuality, class, age, ability, and education overlap, complicating individual experiences in a group united by skin color. The white characters may have more skin privilege than other inmates, but this does not mean they have the same access or unearned assets. Two of the clearest white examples are Pensatucky and Nicky.

OITNB initially pins Pensatucky as Piper's zealous, mentally unstable nemesis. She is unabashedly racist, homophobic, hotheaded, and easily impressionable. Her accent and religious zealotry suggest she is from a rural area. She is petite with freckles and long brown hair. Years of methamphetamine use destroyed her teeth. She is vehemently heterosexual. Early flashbacks focus on Pensatucky's crime: murdering an abortion clinic nurse who cracked wise about Pensatucky's six abortions. These initial flashbacks do not provide context for her character or create sympathy. By the third season, flashbacks reveal more of Pensatucky's upbringing. Her house is rundown, dingy, and small. Her mother abuses the welfare system, further cluing audiences into her class. When Pensatucky starts her period, she receives the following sex talk: "Go on and let them do their business. If you're real lucky, most of them will be quick like your daddy. It's like a bee sting. In and out. Over before you know it's happening." Sexual violence and confusion characterize Pensatucky's life, past and present. Compared to Piper and Nicky, Pensatucky had a very different experience of whiteness.

Nicky had wealth and access as a young white person in New York City. She has an observational, acerbic wit and frequently serves as comic relief. She makes references that suggest a Jewish upbringing, but she does not currently practice. Nicky identifies as a lesbian and, like Pensatucky, makes this clear to the other inmates. Based on her vocabulary ("Sapphic vibes"), cultural references (the Hamptons; Icarus), and astute commentary about the prison system, Nicky comes across as educated, as well as street smart. She frequently points out when Piper forgets her privileged position, which suggests Nicky has a better understanding of or is more sensitive to inequalities connected to race and class than Piper does. The audience knows Nicky is a former junkie and can assume her stay at Litchfield is drug-related, but her crime is not revealed until the third season. *OITNB* frames Nicky's past with a terrible mother-daughter relationship. Nicky attributes her dysfunctional family as the cause for her self-destruction.

Pensatucky, Piper, and Nicky's whiteness lumps them into the same racial category, but these characters do not have the same access to privilege. Even when they do have things in common, this does not make them the same. Piper and Nicky both identify as queer and come from wealth. Nicky and Pensatucky both have problems with addiction. All three of them have lousy mothers. Importantly, there are not "good whites" or "bad whites" on *OITNB*. When characters are intersectional and their backgrounds revealed, they become richer and more complex. Typically, only main characters receive this treatment, with other characters assisting on the journey of growth and self-reflection, but *OITNB* does not reserve this depth for Piper. Inmates have personality-shaping backstories that influences their identities, relationships, and roles in Litchfield.

Decentering Piper: Breaking Down the Trojan Horse

Piper may have been the audience's Trojan Horse into Litchfield, but *OITNB* takes several deliberate steps to decenter her as a main character. She is not the lens through which we understand other characters and she is not a barometer for what is "normal." Piper is just another inmate with her own backstory trying to cope in prison. She is part of the ensemble, not necessarily the star. *OITNB* shakes Piper from the center in a few ways: the opening credit sequence, the use of flashbacks, editing in shots of inmates' reactions, and Piper's evolution through the seasons. These framing devices shape audience's perspectives of Piper by focusing on her whiteness and highlighting her privilege.

From the opening credits, Piper is dislodged from the center of the story. The title sequence for *OITNB* is a montage of extreme close-ups of fifty-two different women's eyes, noses, and lips juxtaposed scenes of prison life set to Regina Spektor's song "You've Got Time." In an interview with *Paste*, showrunner Jenji Kohan stated: "I like an opening credit sequence. It sort of sets up the audience…. I'm also really proud of this opening sequence that we did—all the women in the opening title sequence are former inmates" (Amatangelo 2013). The choice to use real, incarcerated women instead of actresses nods to *OITNB*'s memoir-origins and adds a level of reality. However, this opening was not distributor's first choice. Originally, they wanted to shoot the intro from Piper's perspective, juxtaposing snippets of her yuppie past and prisoner present. Kohan rejected this idea and opted for the current intro because she wanted viewers to know right away that *OITNB* was more than a show about Piper (John 2015). While Piper may be our window into Litchfield, this paratext dislodges her as the focus.

Another formal tool that positions Piper away from the center is the use of flashbacks. Flashbacks are non-linear glimpses into the past. On *OITNB*, audiences get to see personality-shaping events in inmates' lives prior to prison. In addition to present-day drama, each episode focuses on one inmate's personal history in a series of flashbacks. Occasionally, we learn about the crimes committed, but usually jumps in time serve character development.

Importantly, *OITNB*'s use of flashbacks provides audiences a direct line of information about other characters that wholly bypasses Piper. Audiences get to understand characters without Piper's questions or reactions to instigate or qualify their experiences. Through flashback we see Red excluded from a group of attractive Russian mob wives and her intelligence dismissed by her sniveling husband. We see Sophia Burset's transition and the lengths she goes to become a woman. We see Aleida Diaz's struggle to hold on to the admiration of her daughter, Daya, while also letting her go in order to better her chances for a good life. Family, relationships, personalities, and traumas give audiences new perspective on each character. This perspective is separate from Piper. Piper does not have the same information as the audience. She may have been our way into Litchfield, but our experience of this place and the other inmates is not tethered to Piper. Additionally, the information in a flashback does not fuel Piper's narrative.

Formal elements like opening credits and flashbacks are not the only framing devices *OITNB* uses to displace Piper from the center of *OITNB*; narrative progression and reaction shots further destabilize Piper's position. Typically, main characters are voices of reason, likeable to an extent, and the barometer for normalcy. *OITNB* routinely underlines that this is not the case with Piper. In addition to narrative progression, reaction shots show audiences how other characters read Piper: out of touch, entitled, oblivious, and/or monstrous depending on the situation.

In the first season, Piper spins like a top as she adjusts to Litchfield and her role inside. Most of her initial actions are actually reactions as she begins to navigate the Litchfield hierarchy. She relies on privileges granted outside prison walls, which do not always work as she intends. Piper's best skill is manipulation; she exploits guards, administration, and other inmates to get what she wants.

When she initially meets the occasionally racist, always homophobic Counselor Healy, she explains why she is in prison, waffling between nobly accepting her fate and lamenting that the sentence was too harsh or undeserved. For Healy, this white, blonde waif exudes a fragile vulnerability. He responds to her performance by assuming a paternal role: commiserating, comforting, and reassuring. He moves into cautioning Piper about lesbians and gives her strategies for avoiding attention. The audience is in on the fact that she is bisexual or queer, but Healy is not. Her heteronormative, gender-conforming appearance allows her to pass as straight. In another tactical move, she strategically mentions her fiancé, Larry. Healy assumes/projects positive feelings onto Piper because she is white and appears to be a heterosexual woman. Her privilege yields privileges.

Counselor Healy is someone with power at Litchfield; it benefits Piper to have a sympathetic ear with someone who controls access to the outside world. She is not alone in this; the other inmates know which guards respond to tears, and which are strict. These are important tactics for surviving in prison. In addition to influencing people with power and access, inmates often manipulate each other to jostle into a better position. All inmates do this to varying degrees, but some inmates are more manipulative than others. Red, Piper, Pensatucky, and Vee, actively vie for themselves, treating the other inmates as pawns. Incidentally, these characters veer into villainous territory because they often hurt and disregard people on their paths to betterment.

OITNB reveals Piper's capacity for exploitation in early interactions with Suzanne "Crazy Eyes" Warren. Moving away from wide-eyed ignorance, Piper morphs into an active manipulator. Suzanne has a crush on Piper. Piper indirectly and passively rebuffs Suzanne's advances, but Suzanne is undeterred. When Piper has an angry exchange with her ex-girlfriend, Alex, in the lunchroom, Suzanne comes to her defense and asks if Alex is bothering her. Piper gauges the situation, weighs her options, and decides to use Suzanne's romantic fervor to her advantage. She confirms that Alex is bothering her, so Suzanne leaps into action. She yells that Piper is her wife, throws her pie on Alex, and threatens to cut her. After Alex leaves the table and the drama subsides, Piper leans over to Suzanne and whispers that she is not her wife.

In the second season, Piper's manipulations no longer hinge on reactions or opportunities. She makes tactical moves in plain sight; either she no longer cares what other inmates think, or she believes she is the smartest person in the room. For instance, she tries to pimp out new inmate Soso in order to get back a blanket from Big Boo. The audience understands that the blanket has personal meaning to Piper, that it was unfair of the inmates to divvy up her possessions, and that nobody likes Soso, but her plan to trade Soso for a blanket is not justifiable. Soso realizes what is happening and she accuses Piper of being "sick … seriously fucked up." Big Boo laughingly agrees, "You know she's right, Chapman. You're a horrible person."

By the third season, Piper takes her manipulation to bigger and bolder levels. She simultaneously works the system as well as the other inmates. After Litchfield is privatized, Whispers, a Victoria's Secret-like lingerie company, uses prison labor to sew its panties. Piper realizes that one more pair of panties can be sewn from each piece of material. She begins making the extra pairs and sneaking them out of the workshop. This turns into a seedy enterprise. Piper convinces inmates like Flaca, Yoga Jones, and Ruiz to wear the panties so she can sell the soiled underwear to fetishists on the Internet. In exchange, she "pays" the inmates with Ramen flavor packets, while pocketing the sizeable profit (each pair of panties brings in at least $25).

Flaca comes across a unionizing pamphlet meant for the Litchfield guards and becomes the inmates' union rep, demanding "fair pay for skanky pants." Piper asks fellow master manipulator and organized crime aficionado, Red, for advice. Red shows her how to get real money into their commissary accounts and recommends paying them a fair wage. Piper shares this plan with Alex who points out that Piper will be running a prison gang, which Piper receives as a compliment. The inmates accept her negotiations ($8 per pair, continued distribution of flavor packets, and they can request to wear certain styles like thong or boy shorts). She greets them as employees, but before the exchange concludes, she fires Flaca. Flaca protests, and Piper says, "I can do whatever I want … and remember, you will be costing each one of your closest friends hundreds of dollars a month if you so much as open your mouth. So I suggest that you leave quietly." Piper takes on the role of cold, capitalist union-crusher. Piper from Seasons 1 and 2 would never be this out in the open with her double-dealings and exploitation, but by the third season, she lets her calculating, manipulative nature shine.

None of the above examples are presented neutrally. Editing is another framing device used to shape how audiences perceive Piper. Editing acts as a visual language; the order of shots can build tension or create comedy. *OITNB* frequently positions shots of inmates reacting to Piper's wide-eyed innocence and accidental ignorance for comedic effect. Shots of inmates rolling their eyes, exchanging glances, and giggling, shape how the audience understands Piper. In addition, characters react to Piper through dialogue and actions (i.e., Big Boo calling her "horrible"; Pensatucky attacking her).

Highlighting Piper's obliviousness is one tactic *OITNB* employs in unwriting her legitimacy. For instance, Piper never gauges her audience or considers other characters' standpoints. She frequently speaks as if her life is the norm, never stopping to contextualize her privilege. In the first episode, Piper name-drops brands and high-end stores that nobody in Litchfield recognizes. When she moves to explain the reference, you see the other characters disengage. Inmates and guards barely feign interest, yet Piper never takes the hint. In other instances, Piper is painfully unmindful of her privilege. When inmates revive the fortune-telling game MASH (Mansion Apartment Shack House), Daya and Morello tease Piper about living in a mansion. She responds, "Oh, no. It was hardly a mansion." Daya asks her how many bathrooms (Piper: five) and if she had a maid (Piper: no ... a housekeeper) while exchanging bemused and disbelieving glances with Morello. Piper refuses to acknowledge her privilege, instead pouting, "I was very lonely as a child." Piper does not see herself in context and she ignores her prison audience's reactions. This gimmick continues through the seasons.

Another long-standing gag consists of Piper correcting people. Typically, this begins with "You know..." followed by Piper splitting hairs or unnecessarily "educating" her fellow inmates. It is no secret that she is formally educated; inmates call her "College" and seek her out when trying to cut through bureaucratic or legal jargon. But most of the time Piper butts in to pedantically "educate" people. At one point she interrupts a game of Scrabble with Taystee and Tricia to unnecessarily espouse what Robert Frost really meant in "The Road Less Taken." They both look annoyed, but Piper yammers on anyway. Tricia finally says, "I will probably kill her in her sleep tonight."

When trading stories with other inmates and guards it becomes painfully clear that Piper's upbringing, education, and aspirations are completely unrelatable. Viewers are not the only ones learning from inmates' reactions. Piper has brief moments of realization when she sees herself through other characters' eyes. For instance, after returning to Litchfield in Season 2, Piper asks Nicky to verify that everyone was staring at her. Nicky responds, "It's great to see you evolving, Chapman, and getting past the whole 'I'm the star of my own movie and everyone else is too complex.'" Shocked, Piper gasps, "Do I do that?" Piper must be very forgetful because Nicky's summation pretty much condenses Piper's storyline from the first season, yet she is completely unaware that this is who she has been so far at Litchfield.

In a later episode, Piper whines that she gets in trouble for lying and for telling the truth, two tactics she has used to manipulate multiple people and situations in her favor. She claims that she is trying not to hurt people's feelings. Red retorts, "Stop buying into your own horseshit.... Stop trying to mold the real world into the one inside your pointy blonde head." Piper's expression is one of shock, as if she had never thought of herself as manipulative. Red adds, "From what I've seen, to get what you want, while telling everyone how clean you are, you play dirty." Red's summary is accurate, but Piper's reaction suggests this is a new concept for her. After the above two instances occur, Piper takes steps to change, but ends up reverting to the easier routes of exploitation and manipulation.

In the third season, Alex tries to remind Piper that she is different from other inmates. After firing Flaca from the dirty-panty business, Piper gleefully retells the story to Alex, who is disgusted. She says, "That's gross," to which Piper counters, "No, it was bad ass." Alex states, "What you did to Flaca was weird. She's poor. A lot of these girls—they're poor. Of course they were excited about money; they were excited about a dollar an hour job.... I don't like this version of you." Alex's comments are not revelatory, but Piper still needs the reminder that she has wealth and access many of the other women do not. Alex breaks off from the business and breaks up with Piper in one blow. Piper is unfazed and continues to look out only for herself.

Conclusion

Nobody plays the villain in their own story. They are the stars, the main characters. Sometimes there is control, but most of the time it is reaction instead of action. Piper Chapman simultaneously sees herself as a victim as well as someone with agency. She blames Alex for sending her to prison, yet frequently stresses that she chose to break the law. She keeps trampling on other inmates—their feelings, their lives, their relationships—and later apologizing for her wrongdoings as if words can make up for her actions. At times she checks her privilege and in different moments she uses it to her advantage. She plays things up or down depending on the context, traversing domination and subordination. And at other times, there are no moves on the board; she is still in prison without power.

All of this is intentional. Piper Chapman is a study in privilege and *OITNB* a study in power dynamics. Piper may be critiqued the hardest because she has the most privilege to critique, but there are no good white or bad white characters on *OITNB*, just as none of the characters are 100 percent hero or villain. They are messy, humanized, intersectional representations. This too is intentional and indicative of Jenji Kohan's body of work. She is known for playing with stereotypes, challenging cultural norms, and deconstructing American mythology. Kohan elaborates:

> I love flawed characters, male or female, and I only want to talk about flawed
> characters, really, in what I do. I think likability is bullshit—we are complicated

beings, sometimes we're likable and sometimes we're not and sometimes we fuck up radically. I want to live in that gray area, I never want to sit in the black or the white [Willmore 2013].

"Living in the gray" means all the characters on *OITNB* receive a multidimensional treatment. Gender, race, class, ethnicity, ability, age, and sexuality are part of each character's construction. Furthermore, intersectional identities are discussion points in the show as it probes privilege and oppression.

In order for *OITNB* to exist, it needed a white, upper middle class, well-educated, femme character like Piper Chapman to draw in a network as well as an audience. But the show was never only about Piper, and *OITNB* goes to great lengths to destabilize her as the central character. The opening credit sequence, the use of flashbacks, other character's reactions to Piper, and Piper's evolution through the seasons draw attention to Piper's privilege. These techniques highlight the fact that Piper is indeed a Trojan Horse. A Trojan Horse gets you through the gate, but it alone cannot win the war. It is what's inside that matters.

REFERENCES

Amatangelo, Amy. 2013. "Catching up with Jenji Kohan." *Paste.* Accessed October 2, 2015. http://www.pastemagazine.com/articles/2013/07/catching-up-with-jenji-kohan.html.

Babb, Valerie M. 1998. *Whiteness Visible: The Meaning of Whiteness in American Literature and Culture.* New York: New York University Press.

Collins, Patricia Hill. 1993. "Black Feminist Thought in the Matrix of Domination." *Social Theory: The Multicultural and Classic Readings,* edited by C. Lemert. Boulder: Westview Press. 615–626.

Crenshaw, Kimberlé W. 1994. "Intersectionality and Identity Politics: Learning from Violence Against Women of Color." *The Public Nature of Private Violence: The Discovery of Domestic Abuse,* edited by Martha Albertson Fineman and Roxanne Mykitiuk. London: Routledge. 178–193.

Dyer, Richard. 1997. *White: Essays on Race and Culture.* New York: Routledge.

Flagg, Barbara J. 1997. *Was Blind, But Now I See: White Race Consciousness and the Law.* New York: New York University Press.

Frankenberg, Ruth, ed. 1993. *White Women, Race Matters: The Social Construction of Whiteness.* Minneapolis: University of Minnesota Press.

Fresh Air. 2013. "'Orange' Creator Jenji Kohan: 'Piper Was My Trojan Horse.'" Interviewed by Terry Gross. NPR. August 13. http://www.npr.org/templates/transcript/transcript.php?storyId=211639989.

Friedman, Susan S. 1995. "Beyond White and Other: Relationality and Narratives of Race in Feminist Discourse." *Signs* 2:1–49.

Hall, Stuart. 1997. "Old and New Identities, Old and New Ethnicities." In *Culture, Gobalization, and the World System,* edited by Anthony D. King. Minneapolis: University of Minnesota Press. 41–68.

Hasting, Reed, and David Wells. 2015. Netflix Shareholder Report. October 14. Accessed November 1, 2015. http://ir.netflix.com/eventdetail.cfm?eventid=164905.

Homer. 2006. *The Odyssey.* New York: Penguin.

hooks, bell. 1992. "Representations of whiteness in the Black Imagination." In *Black Looks: Race and Representation*. Boston: South End Press. 165–178.

Hurtado, Aida. 1997. *The Color of Privilege: Three Blasphemies on Race and Feminism*. Ann Arbor: University of Michigan Press.

John. 2015. "Who Are the Faces in the *Orange Is the New Black* Opening Credits?" *Starcasm*. June 16. Accessed October 2, 2015. http://starcasm.net/archives/319044.

Levine-Rasky, Cynthia. 2011. "Intersectionality Theory Applied to Whiteness and Middle-Classness." *Social Identities* 17:239–253.

McHugh, Kathleen A. 2015. "Giving Credit to Paratexts and Parafeminism in *Top of the Lake* and *Orange Is the New Black*." *Film Quarterly* 68. Accessed October 2, 2015. http://www.filmquarterly.org/2015/03/giving-credit-to-paratexts-and-para feminism-in-top-of-the-lake-and-orange-is-the-new-black/.

McIntosh, Peggy. 2011. "White Privilege: Unpacking the Invisible Knapsack." In *Women: Images & Realities: A Multicultural Anthology* (5th edition), edited by Suzanne Kelly, Gowri Parameswaran, and Nancy Schniedewind. New York: McGraw-Hill Education. 394–398.

Meyer, Michaela D. E. 2009. "'I'm Just Trying to Find My Way Like Most Kids': Bisexuality, Adolescence and the Drama of *One Tree Hill*." *Sexuality and Culture* 13:337–351.

Meyer, Michaela D. E. 2010. "Representing Bisexuality on Television: The Case for Intersectional Hybrids." *Journal of Bisexuality* 10:366–387.

Meyer, Michaela D. E. 2015. "The 'Other' Woman in Contemporary Television Drama: Analyzing Intersectional Representation on *Bones*." *Sexuality & Culture* 19:900–915.

Morrison, Toni. 1993. *Playing in the Dark: Whiteness and the Literary Imagination*. New York: First Vintage Books.

Radish, Christina. 2013. "Creator Jenji Kohan Talks *Orange Is the New Black*, Her Research into Prison Life, and Graphic Sex Scenes." *Collider*. July 7. Accessed October 2, 2015. http://collider.com/jenji-kohan-orange-is-the-new-black-inter view/.

Shaw, Jessica. 2014. "Orange Is the New Awesome." *Entertainment Weekly*. April 25. Accessed October 2, 2015. http://www.ew.com/article/2014/04/25/orange-new-awesome?iid=sr-linkl.

Shome, Raka. 2000. "Outing Whiteness." *Communication Studies in Media Communication* 17:366–371.

West, Cornel. 1990. "The New Cultural Politics of Difference." *The MIT Press* 53:3–109.

Willmore, Alison. 2013. "'Weeds' Creator Jenji Kohan on Her New Netflix Series *Orange Is the New Black* and Why 'Likability Is Bullsh*t.'" *Indiewire*. July 8. Accessed October 2, 2015. http://www.indiewire.com/article/jenji-kohan-interview-orange-is-the-new-black?page=1.

"You don't look full … Asia"

The Invisible and Ambiguous Bodies of Chang and Soso

Minjeong Kim

In 2005, the film *Crash* (dir. Paul Haggis) was released to critical acclaim. This ensemble film with characters of various races—whites, blacks, Latinos, Persians, and Asians—tells gripping stories about racism in Los Angeles. Those who praised the film contended that it frankly shows that all characters have racist perceptions about others and they "crash" into a situation where they emerge as better selves (Bradshaw 2005; Ebert 2005). Those who were critical of the film argue that the film overlooks "historically sedimented racial formations" by placing all characters and their racism on the same level, and attempts to resolve racial tensions with some dramatic moments of reconcil-iation (Hsu 2006, 146). Still, *Crash* received three Academy awards, including Best Picture. Throughout the awards season where *Crash* was constantly admired and celebrated, I kept thinking about Asian characters in the film—Korean traffickers of Southeast Asians—who never got the moment of redemption, and what this exception meant. Although Asian/American char-acters were part of the cast that maps the diverse ethnoscape of Los Angeles, they were demoted to the roles that only serve the other characters' redemp-tion. It seemed to suggest that Asian Americans were irrelevant to U.S. racial politics—that they are "foreigners" or "aliens."

When *Orange Is the New Black* (*OITNB*) was first released and praised for its racially diverse cast and humanizing portrayals of inmates, I was once again baffled by how the show's only Asian character in the first season, Chang, was portrayed in a cartoonish manner. Even though I, like many viewers of the show, enjoyed the first season, I also had to tolerate the farcical charac-terization of Chang, who spoke in monotone and could not engage in mean-ingful conversations. She did a nonsensical dance that mimicked Hawaiian dance (evoking the memory of William Hung from *American Idol*). Once again, I had to ask what this exclusion meant.

The second season of *OITNB* introduced another Asian American character, Brook Soso, a biracial ciswoman, with more positive and hopeful reception (Stern 2014; Tu 2014). While she is a fresh face and different from other Asian American characters, including Chang, she is often ridiculed for her naivety and quixotic actions. Like in *Crash*, Asian American characters in *OITNB* are included in the racial landscape of the Litchfield Penitentiary, but they are not part of the racial discourses. They represent the Asian race but they do not speak of Asian American identity or politics. The third season provides both Chang and Soso with more substantive roles—Chang with her own flashback episode, and Soso with a dramatic storyline. Nonetheless, Asian American viewers are more critical about their depictions at the end of Season 3 (Builder 2015; Yiin 2015). Despite their expanded story arc, I argue that the idea of American Orientalism that perceives Asian Americans as foreign, inassimilable subjects, is left unchallenged (Kim and Chung 2005).

This essay closely examines the two Asian American characters of *OITNB*, Chang and Soso, and argues how this feminist show that pushes the boundaries of representations of racial and sexual minorities failed to do so (yet) for Asian Americans. Chang's androgyny and Soso's feminist outlook separate them from the typical, dichotomous Asian woman stereotypes—hyper-feminine, geisha-like, submissive Lotus Blossom or belligerent, untrustworthy, and sensual Dragon Lady (Tajima 1989). However, an intersectional perspective allows for a critical analysis that highlights Chang's invisibility and Soso's ambiguity, and their meanings in the media representations of Asian American characters.

Mei Chang

Invisibility

In her 2010 memoir on which the Netflix show is based, *Orange Is the New Black: My Year in a Women's Prison*, Piper Kerman writes:

> [The camp] housed approximately 200 women at any given time, though sometimes it climbed to a nightmarishly cramped 250. About half were Latino (Puerto Rican, Dominican, Colombian), about 24 percent white, 24 percent African-American and Jamaican, and then a very random smattering: one Indian, a couple of Middle Eastern women, a couple of Native Americans, one tiny Chinese woman in her sixties. I always wondered how it felt to be there if you lacked a tribe. It was all so very West Side Story—stick to your own kind, Maria! [66].

Kerman explains how racial segregation was institutionalized in the prison where she served her sentence, and she here hints that there was no "Asian" tribe due to the small number of Asian inmates. The Federal Bureau of Prisons statistics show that as of 2015, Asians account for only 1.5 percent of inmates (www.bop.gov), and her tally does not deviate greatly (although Kerman does mention a Filipina named Joyce with whom she worked at the electric shop, Joyce is not counted here). The character Chang was probably created based on this "tiny Chinese woman in her sixties," but like the Chinese woman in the book, Chang is mostly invisible in the first season.

The number of characters is often an important measure in discussing representational diversity but it is not and cannot be the only measure. According to the GLAAD (Gay and Lesbian Alliance Against Defamation) report on diversity on TV, Asian Pacific Islanders (APIs) make up 4 percent (36 out of 813 characters) of broadcast series regulars, which is a slight underrepresentation since APIs make up 5.6 percent of the total U.S. population. But diversity in media representations is not only about how many people are cast, but also what kind of roles they have (main or supporting or extra); how much they appear (screen time); if they have dynamic storylines; and the purpose of their storylines (Smith et al. 2013). Considering these aspects, it is far-fetched to say that Chang was representative even of 1.5 percent of Asian inmates. In the first season, Chang is introduced in the second episode ("Tit Punch") behind the wired bars of the commissary. We do not see her face and her screen time is less than one minute. Chang also becomes a WAC (Women's Advisory Council) representative of "the others and golden girls" of the camp, indicating she is the main face of "the fourth tribe." However, Chang only appears in five episodes out of thirteen episodes and her screen time is less than five minutes out of approximately 725 minutes (0.6 percent), and she has less scripted time than that. There are no meaningful storylines about her. She is nearly invisible.

Asian Americans' lack of visibility in the U.S. media has manifested in different ways. In early Hollywood, white actors played Asian characters in yellowface, excluding Asian actors (Ito 2014). An exception would be Anna May Wong, the Asian actor who famously embodied Dragon Lady in the first half of the 20th century. Yet, many prominent white actors played in yellowface, including Luise Rainer in *The Good Earth* (1937), Katharine Hepburn in *Dragon Seed* (1944), Marlon Brando in *The Teahouse of the August Moon* (1956), Peter Sellers in *Murder by Death* (1976), and arguably most infamous Mickey Rooney in *Breakfast at Tiffany's* (1961). Even in the 21st century, wearing yellowface—white actors' portrayal of Asian stereotypes mainly for non–Asian viewers or audiences—has not disappeared, stirring controversies. For example, in 2014, the hit television sitcom *How I Met Your Mother* aired the episode titled "Slapsgiving 3: Slappointment in Slapmarra" in which main white cast members Alyson Hannigan, Josh Radnor, and Colbie Smulders portrayed martial arts masters in silk robes, stereotypical Asian accents, and Fu Manchu mustaches (Ma 2014; Sanders 2014). Furthermore, white characters are often representative of Asian cultures (e.g., *Rising Sun* [1993], *The Last Samurai* [2003]) or Asian American stories or characters are whitewashed (e.g., *21* [2008] or *Aloha* [2015]).

Although Chang's invisibility seems to be rectified by the introduction of Soso, the invisibility in the first season, or in the "opening cast," is significant for a television series that may or may not survive beyond the first season. When show producers create a pilot episode to attract a network or develop the first season to solidify its viewership for renewal, they try to appeal to those in Hollywood and the main target audience, who they usually imagine to be white. Therefore, Asian American characters are often excluded because television producers do not consider Asian American stories or viewers as significant (Rodriguez 2014).

Television shows evolve and they can change their course and respond to the viewers' reactions. Asian American (or other minority) characters can be added later as supporting characters and their stories can be more enhanced. Nonetheless, Asian Americans become reservist characters that the producers turn to after establishing the opening case, but character development can be challenging.

American Orientalism

"Hey lesbians. My eyes are squinty, but my ears are fine."
—Chang

The first time the viewers see Chang's face ("WAC Pack"), Chang's look is androgynous with short hair and no makeup. She looks more masculine with facial hair, which can be read as gender queer. But what interrupts that reading is that the facial hair appears to be a mini Fu Manchu mustache. Chang's face is more of a caricature of Orientalist images from the early 20th century.

In *Orientalism* (1972), Edward W. Said argues, "the essence of Orientalism is the ineradicable distinction between Western superiority and Oriental inferiority" (42). Orientalist images and ideologies have sustained Western power in their imperialist enterprises to justify and exert their dominations over Asia. But Orientalism is not a monolithic and constant discourse or a linear construction of ideologies, but heterogeneous and contradictory (Lowe 1991). In the United States, Orientalism has been used to regulate national boundaries and control racial relations in popular culture, literature, and in politics. In the 19th and early 20th century, Orientalist images were used to exclude Asians from entering America. Also, the constant influx of Asian immigrants since the late twentieth century has maintained the identification of Asian Americans with Asians in Asia, perpetuating the "forever foreign" status of Asian Americans (Tuan 1999). Especially in the popular culture, the Orientalist narratives and images of Asians support the idea that Asians cannot assimilate because they are too different racially and culturally. With their slanted eyes, buckteeth (which are often captured in yellowface), and their mysterious, unknown culture, Asians cannot be "Americans." In the context of the Civil Rights era, the assimilation-oriented Model Minority image emerged as the symbolic antithesis of militant political activists. However, the model minority image did not replace the "perpetual foreigner" status of Asian Americans, and they continue to coexist. Also, the myth of "honorary whites" has put down Asian Americans' political agency and obfuscated racial and socioeconomic inequalities that Asian Americans face. Unfortunately, in popular culture, "there might be scarcely little to counteract that dominant force of representation," and some Asian Americans can internalize Orientalism or, in collaboration with those in power, can use, invent, and reinvent Orientalist images (Ma 2000, xiii).

Assimilation itself is a contested concept in various areas—from immigrants' integration to queer theory to activism for gay rights and disability rights (Alba and Nee 2005; Duggan 2004; Sherry 2004). Yet, the idea of "Oriental inassimilability" separates Asians from the ambit of Americans, undermining Asian Americans' social and political citizenship. Many view Chang as an interesting character and root for her with sympathy. They welcome Chang's flashback episode, which enhances diversity. But when the viewers consider Chang's invisibility and isolation as natural and "realistic," they may be blinded from seeing how this character is not that far from stereotypical representations of Asians in the U.S. media (Bonilla-Silva 2003).

Season 3 shows Chang's prison life in greater depth. Chang uses salt to clean her mouth, which is ridiculed by Alex and Piper. Chang also puts her feet in some solutions for a long time, but we do not know why and for what. This strangeness and mysteriousness keeps Orientalism alive, isolating Chang from others. She walks around the camp mostly under people's radar as if she is invisible. She takes food out of the cafeteria but a guard does not even notice her. When she eats her special meals by herself, she looks around the campground where people are interacting with one another. Her eyes are filled with loneliness. Then, we also see her secret place where she defies the prison rules and enjoys her amusements. They vindicate her invisibility as a survivor's hidden resistance. However, her (seemingly self-) exclusion from the general population without her own "tribe" serves to maintain the Orientalist trope that reinforces Asians' inability (or even refusal) to assimilate.

Her backstory is also rather typical. The flashback tells us that younger

Mei Chang moved from China for a marriage arranged by her brother. She is rejected because she is not pretty enough. Mei's brother gets her involved in the family business, which turns out to be criminal operations. Eventually she is placed in a position of power and she orders the suitor who rejected her to be tortured. Orientalist tropes abound. In addition to arranged marriage, Mei's brother's illegal business sells medicinal delicacies like dried sea cucumber, deer antlers, bear bile, and turtle eggs, signifying the Orientalist trope of strangeness, mysteriousness, primitiveness, and unintelligibility. These Orientalist tropes are also used to signal patriarchy: The mysterious delicacies are to cater Asian men customers, with the penis soup or the snake blood believed to enhance men's sexual virility, symbolizing patriarchal power. At first, younger Mei is subjugated to the patriarchal order, which demands her submission and assesses her value based on her looks. Her acne-filled face is the antithesis to the porcelain China doll. When her brother sneers, "she is invisible," he is degrading her. Then, this turns into a feminist fantasy story. Younger Mei becomes a dominant figure in that patriarchal world, overturning the power order. She orders the men to take out the gallbladder of the person who rejected her, "taking out" patriarchal sexuality.

The show thus evokes "feminist orientalism," or, Orientalist tropes that highlight and challenge patriarchal oppression (Zonana 1993). Chang is a feminist heroine with her power over men and her refusal to meet the beauty standard set by patriarchy. Her androgyny and asexuality are her feminist weapons. Yet, even though she is different from highly sexualized Asian women's images, Chang as an Asian is still read as lotus blossom turned Dragon Lady.

The intersectional perspective also cannot overlook the gang association. Award-winning author and journalist, Helen Zia (2000), has summed up Asian stereotypes in 4 Gs: "Gangsters, Gooks, Geishas, and Geeks." Asian gangsters (and gooks) have appeared in numerous Hollywood action films and procedural shows where they are the enemy of righteous white protagonists. As a derivative of the Dragon Lady image, Asian women gangsters also appeared alongside Asian men; they often surprised viewers as nameless shooters with the stark contrast between their petite body (or their gender) and cold-blooded, fatal actions (e.g., *Year of the Dragon* [1985], *Full Metal Jacket* [1987], *Romeo Must Die* [2000]). Younger Mei is not a nameless shooter but a boss. In that sense, *OITNB* deliberately challenges traditional Asian femininity. However, they do so with her "power of invisibility" and through the gang-related storyline, which sustain Orientalist images and tropes.

How about the portrayals of Asian men? As an unapologetic feminist show, *OITNB* critically portrays masculinities, including patriarchal domination, condescension and paternalism, which is important. Yet, from an intersectional perspective, *OITNB* is no different from other shows, as it fails to challenge stereotypical images of racial minorities. Asian American men have been especially marginalized on the small screen. Similar to Asian women, Asian men have been represented in a dichotomous way—either asexual and effeminate, or domineering and violent. They are usually supporting characters without personal storylines, such as lab technicians (e.g., *CSI* and *Dexter*) or psychiatrists (e.g., *Law & Order: SVU*). The hit series, *Lost* (2004–2010), was a turning point for Asian male characters with heterosexual masculinity and romantic storylines. Yet even in this show, Daniel Dae Kim's character began stereotypically as a domineering Asian husband with a gang association. Today, the television landscape includes more positive portrayals of Asian American men, such as Steven Yeun in *The Walking Dead* and John Cho in numerous canceled shows, but it also has Kunal Nayyar's character in *The Big Bang Theory* and Matthew Moy's character in *2 Broke Girls*. Both characters (and Rex Lee's character as a gay personal assistant in *Entourage*) have been criticized for their feminization of Asian men, undermining Asian American men's masculinity compared to white men's. Moy's character is constantly infantilized and made fun of for his small height and penis. When Asian American men are still confined in the prison of stereotypes, the (hitherto) only *OITNB* episode with Asian men sadly joins the long line of gangster Asians that have filled the Hollywood screen for several decades.

What's in the Title?

Chang's flashback episode is titled "Ching Chong Chang." This is supposedly both humorous and provocative, but also extremely offensive. "Ching chong" has often been used to elicit humor from the viewers in contexts involving Asians. In addition to the tastelessness of this racial slur, most people, including some feminists, do not seem to understand how seriously hurtful this slur is to Asian Americans, as shown during the 2014 "#CancelColbert" controversy.

Amid growing controversy over a racially insensitive name of an NFL team, the Washington's Redskins, the popular television character Stephen Colbert on "The Colbert Report" tweeted a suggestion to create "the Ching Chong Ding Dong Foundation for Sensitivity to Orientals or Whatever." When Asian American activist Suey Park started "#CancelColbert" in response to this joke, the scenes that have frequently played out in the virtual world ensued: enormous backlash against the woman activist for not understanding the joke, threats of physical and sexual assaults, and discussions about what should be allowed in satire and comedy. Some feminists also joined this bandwagon. For example, the feminist blog site, *Jezebel*, published a condescending article criticizing Suey Park for starting #CancelColbert, and declared that the word "retard" was much more hurtful than "ching chong" which is an "elementary school playground insult" that is "both boring and hurtful" (Ryan 2014).

In fact, it is not an elementary school playground insult. In 2013, a New Jersey Asian woman received a receipt from CVS photo center where her name appeared as "Lee, Ching Chong" and sued the company (Valiente 2013). This was not the first time this happened. A 2011 Chick-Fil-A receipt for "Ching" and "Chong" and a 2012 Papa John's receipt for "Lady Chink Eyes" have already mobilized local Asian Americans against both companies (*Angry Asian Man*, 2013). However, the public response was not a sympathetic one for the NJ woman who was only viewed as being after a monetary gain. On online sites and in the bloggersphere, many Asians share stories about how they were named, bullied or laughed at with this insult by their teachers, peers, and strangers, and how those insults stay as deeply hurtful memories. Yet, the protest against the term is often belittled and dismissed.

In 2015, the first episode that is dedicated to an Asian character in a critically acclaimed show that emphasizes racial and sexual diversity is titled "Ching Chong Chang." This is the only explicitly racialized, unoriginal episode title, standing in contrast to the other titles that are empowering ("We Can Be Heroes") or irreverent ("Fucksgiving").

Reconciliation? For Whom?

When Pennsatucky calls Chang "Ching Chong Chang," Chang quips, "Fuck you, Cracker." Usually Chang does not take others' insults lying down. Even Vee cannot intimidate Chang. Older Mei is not coy either. When Big Boo hump-dances her, she goes along with it ("WAC Pack"). When Nicky and Big Boo have a "bang-off" (a sex contest), Chang serves as a referee laying out the rules ("Low Self Esteem City"). She jokes about oral sex in front of other people ("Empathy Is a Boner Killer"). These episodic interactions with other inmates are contradictory to Chang's flashback episode, which stresses her invisibility and isolation. Thus, before the flashback episode, Chang was mostly visible as comic relief.

When Piper and Chang run into each other in the bathroom, Chang compliments Piper's body, but Piper shoots her down. Chang crawls back to her shell where she "sees nothing." Then, Piper apologizes about the salt incident, and Chang says, "Thank you, lesbian." When Chang's play is enacted in Berdie's drama class, the other inmates' response is cold (except for Suzanne Warren's). Feeling the lack of sympathy for her, Chang declares, "It's all fake," though people are not convinced. Both the moment of reconciliation and the assuagement could have given Chang an opportunity to connect to others. But no such change occurs. Even though Chang's isolation and loneliness is portrayed in a sympathetic way, I wonder: why do the *OITNB* writers not allow Chang to challenge essentialized racial stereotypes of Asian characters? In the end, it is not just that Chang feels lonely; we are missing another opportunity to create new Asian American stories.

Brook Soso

Soso first appears in the third episode of Season 2 ("Hugs Can Be Deceiving"). She is biracial, more specifically a Scottish-Japanese biracial ciswoman. Soso is a professional activist having worked on various social issues in different settings, from an organic farm to a homeless shelter. She is gregarious but she is also naïve, saying that she thought "the women's prison was all about community and girl power."

Unlike Chang, Soso makes regular appearances with her own storylines. In fact, Soso is Chang's foil in many aspects. Chang is asexual; Soso's sexuality is exoticized. Chang hardly speaks; Soso cannot stop talking. While Chang appears to be rather one-dimensional, Soso goes through a dramatic transformation in two seasons: In Season 2, she organizes a protest and in Season 3, she falls deep into depression. The episode that shows a stark contrast between Chang and Soso is when the prison has a flood ("It Was the Change"). When all inmates are confined in the common room due to the storm, Chang creates a fort around her, separating herself from others, while Soso manages to start a sing along with other inmates. However, like Chang, Soso also appears to be an inassimilable subject that cannot form any meaningful relationships with other inmates.

People laugh at her name. She talks too much. She even irritates Sister Ingalls, a nun who is usually very calm and patient. She smells because she refuses to use deodorant. When she tries to organize a protest for better prison conditions, she appears to be an idealist and gets little support from others. She appears to mirror Piper as a novice inmate, but she just does not seem to know how to blend in. The effect of these characterizations is her isolation from other inmates, despite her desperate attempts to find friends. She is quick to call Piper her friend. She quickly has sex with Nicky. But she is rejected by almost everyone. Yoga Jones was the only person who praises Soso's bravery and joins her protest, but her loyalty was already with Watson. Interestingly, during the hunger strike, Sister Ingalls, whose health debilitated remarkably fast, receives more sympathetic attention than Soso, who vanishes into the background. (Although the *Amadeus*-inspired scene where Sister Ingalls is taken to the infirmary with concerned inmates lined up in the hallway indicates that Sister Ingalls is not a Mozart, a God-chosen genius, but a Salieri who represents mediocracy.) I argue that Soso's inassimilability is attributed to the ambiguity of both her racial and sexual identities.

Racial Ambiguity

In the prison, the inmates are organized by their racial identities. Soso's biracial identity places her in a liminal position, but she is primarily identified by her fellow inmates as "Asian." On Soso's first day, Morello gives Soso toothpaste and soap, which she usually gives only to white inmates. And she adds, "I don't normally bend the rules like this, but you don't look full ... Asia." Big Boo, who immediately has her eye on Soso, calls her "the hot one of the Asian Persuasion" ("A Whole Other Hole"). A Correctional Officer misidentifies her as "Pocahontas" ("Appropriately Sized Pots"), Leanne calls her "Mulan" ("40 Oz. of Furlough"), Pennsatucky calls her "Ching Chong China Doll" ("We Have Manners. We're Polite"). Despite her biracial identity, the viewer is repeatedly reminded of Soso's Asian identity, as she is isolated from others. Also, in a short flashback in Season 3, Soso's mom appears to evoke another Asian stereotype, "tiger mother" who is overly strict and emotionally manipulative with her child to foster high levels of academic achievement. Thus, the exclusion of Soso reinforces the idea that Asian bodies are inassimilable "foreign" bodies."

These initial examples clearly make Soso's racial identity Asian. Due to the assumption that Chang and Soso share a racial identity, Soso and Chang become bunkmates too. However, Chang tells Soso, "You, Scottish," making her a racially ambiguous body. In the camp, Soso wanders around without her own "tribe" like an Asian American token character.

Many Asian American television characters, whether they are in interracial relationships or they are child adoptees (e.g., *Modern Family*, *Trophy Wife*), are often away from Asian American families or communities. When Lucy Lui appeared in a Lifetime mini-series, *Marry Me* (2010) as a social worker searching for the perfect man for marriage, she was the only Asian American character. She was an adoptee with a white mother and her male partners were two white men and a Latino. Her character had racially diverse friends, mostly from the workplace, but no Asian friends.

When Asian families are introduced, they are often stereotypically depicted. For example, in the "Asian F" episode of the popular television show *Glee*, Harry Shum, Jr.'s character clashes with his parents who did not want him to dance but to focus on his studies to become a lawyer or a doctor. The often-depicted conflict between the first-generation Asian parents and the second-generation Asian children presents Asian values as a source of conflicts for the Asian characters. This kind of narrative discursively blames Asians for their racial issues and undermines the racial solidarity of Asian Americans. Also, it gives an illusion that reconciliation over those conflicts can be done through assimilation where Asian identity is no longer an issue. Similarly in *OITNB*, the viewers see a division based on what constitutes

Asian identity between the first-generation immigrant, Chang, and the born-and-raised-in-America Soso. Chang's denial of Soso's Asianness quashes what Soso searches for—her own tribe.

Sexual Ambiguity

"Look, Soso, I know not committing is, like, your thing.
You couldn't commit to saving the world.
You couldn't commit to eating pussy.
You couldn't even commit to being 100% Asian."
—Taylor to Soso

In *OITNB*, most main characters' sexual identity is distinctively clear. Morello, who has had a sexual relationship with Nicky in the beginning of the show, is unequivocal about where her affection is. Also, toward the end of Season 1, Morello breaks off her sexual relationship with Nicky to stay faithful to her imaginary fiancé. Piper's bisexuality follows the pattern of bisexual erasure in the media, meaning that she does not identify herself as bisexual, but her emotional relationships to both Alex and Larry are portrayed with substantial attention. In contrast, Soso's sexual identity is never identified. Upon coming to the prison, she has sex with Nicky. During their sexual encounter, Soso reveals that she only "did this with one other girl" before. Like Morello, she might be "gay for the stay," but her sexual relationship with Nicky soon fizzles and Soso's attention turns to her activism. Then, feeling increasingly lonely, Soso tries to find someone or some group to fit in. She flirts with Nicky but having a "sexual relationship" is not Soso's priority. She laments, "I need a friend," not "I need a girlfriend." Yet, Soso is not necessarily identified as straight either. Struggling with the loneliness, Soso professes to Piper that she should have gotten a prison wife as Piper suggested before. Then, a question is: Is Soso a queer subject?

U.S. television shows have produced a dearth of Asian American lesbian or queer women characters as regular or recurring characters. In 2009, Ming Na played Camille Wray, the first Asian American lesbian television series regular on Syfy's *Stargate Universe*. With Wray as an exception, Asian American queer women characters and their queer subjectivity have often been overshadowed by the historically dominant image as the sexual object of (usually) white men. Kalinda Sharma in *The Good Wife*, played by Archie Panjabi, came out strong as a bisexual character but then had a story line of being abused by her secret white husband. Jamie Chung plays a bisexual character, Mulan, in ABC's *Once Upon a Time*, but her character has yet to be fully developed, especially regarding her romantic/sexual story. Soso is not subject to the typical white man-Asian woman romance but her sexuality is still ambiguous.

Queer subjectivity entails the construction and expression of self, based on same-sex desires and experiences, and there is no legible queer subjectivity with Soso in Season 2. This sexual ambiguity reinforces her inassimilability on *OITNB*, as indicated in Leanne Taylor's outburst above. But, as mentioned before, television shows evolve.

"Assimilable epiphany"

"Blasian is beautiful!"—Poussey

In the very last episode of Season 3, Soso is connected with Poussey, an African American lesbian who has not had a romantic partner for a while. Characters of romantic movies or story arcs experience the epiphanic moment where they realize their "true love" and find a sense of wholeness that was previously lacking (McRuer 2003). When Asian American characters experience the romantic epiphany, especially with non–Asian partners, like when Soso and Poussey smile at each other, the viewers see what I call an "assimilable epiphany" (Kim 2013).

The assimilable epiphany trope has been used in numerous Hollywood films about interracial relationships between white men and Asian women (Marchetti 1994). For example, the film *Thousand Pieces of Gold* (1991), based on the non-fiction novel of the same title written by Ruthanne Lum McCunn, tells a story of a young Chinese woman pioneer, Lalu Nathoy (Rosalind Chao), in late 19th-century Idaho. Lalu arrives in a mining town after being sold by her family. Determined to buy her freedom and return to China, Lalu works hard for years, fending off the affection of a good-hearted white man, Charlie Bemis (Chris Cooper). During the peak of sinophobia among white miners, Polly joins the trail of Chinese men but soon she realizes her love for Charlie and turns around to go "home." Polly's declaration of a life with Charlie as her home means that China is no longer her home, but America is. With simultaneous epiphanies of her love for Charlie and her newfound home, Lalu's sense of wholeness emerges and her "foreignness" dissipates. Lalu transitions from an inassimilable foreigner to an assimilable subject.

Immediately after Soso and Poussey's moment, Soso is also embraced by Taystee and welcomed by the black group. That is, Soso and Poussey's pairing facilitates Soso's transition from a racially and sexually ambiguous body to a queer subject with a sense of belonging. Interestingly, only after the release of Season 3 was Soso acknowledged as an Asian American queer character. One thing to note is that it is a black-Asian pairing; not a white-Asian pairing that has been subject to literary criticism as a symbolic representation of white/West domination over Asian/East (Marchetti 1994). Major Hollywood films and television shows have featured more notable Asian

American-African American couplings than Asian American couples, including Ming-Na and Morris Chestnut in *ER*, Sandra Oh and Isaiah Washington in *Grey's Anatomy*, and John Cho and Gabrielle Union in *Flash Forward*. Black American characters may not symbolize U.S. global power, but, unlike Asians or Latinos, their American identity is not questioned. Thus, the black-Asian pairing has the effect of an assimilable epiphany. Through their romantic connection with the black body that is coded as American, the Asian character is understood as assimilated and the Asian character's cultural identity (thus racial, political identity) is no longer in the way of the character development. Also, the black-Asian coupling offers a sense of democratic multiculturalism. However, as David Palumbo-Liu (1999) argues, interracial relationships are "a spectator sport" and "this positive view of multiracialization masks deeper anxieties over national identity" (110). When Soso's assimilability is achieved through interracial pairing, this projects an illusion of inclusion, or even racial utopia, but it paradoxically leaves the Orientalist inassimilability unchallenged.

Coda

In 2015, ABC introduced *Fresh Off the Boat (FOTB)*, the first sitcom centered on an Asian American family in 20 years since the introduction of Margaret Cho's short-lived *All American Girl*. The show in many ways interrupts the dominant narratives—Asian grandmas rooting for O.J. Simpson (challenging the black-Asian conflict), the reinterpretation of "Tiger Mom" (she tries to spend hours with you because she loves you), and new narratives about assimilation (we are too assimilated!). Eddie Huang, who wrote the memoir on which *FOTB* is based, felt the show did not reflect his life and was domesticated for laughs (Huang 2015). Many Asian viewers expressed nervousness and anxiety before the first broadcasting. To our surprise and relief, the show has been embraced by the Asian American community. The show is distinctive in many ways. Instead of Asia vs. U.S., the show juxtaposes a Chinese-American community where the Huang family used to live and a white-dominated community in Orlando, Florida. The show often shows how the Asian American family looks at their surroundings, not the other way around. Unlike the model minority stereotype, *FOTB* neither hesitates to talk about Asian American identity nor tolerates racism against Asians. Also, they are not shy about sexuality, as demonstrated by the parents' expression of affection to an Asian American gay friend (welcome back, Rex Lee!). Randall Park's new brand of masculinity and fatherhood is like a breath of fresh air. Many are still uncomfortable with Constance Wu's Tiger Mom and Dragon Lady rolled up into one. Personally, I thought Constance Wu's character's "broken gaydar"—she does not recognize gay people—was a creative way to incorporate heteronormativity, but it stopped being funny pretty quickly. Nonetheless, the show set a new bar for Asian American stories. The Huang family is not torn between Asia and America but they are building "Asian America" with their unique voices.

Some Asian American viewers appreciated Soso's story arc in Season 3 involving her depression because mental illness is considered a taboo among Asian American communities (Builder 2015). In some ways, both Chang and Soso are not your typical Asian characters. They are feminist characters. I am especially excited about Soso's potential as one of the few Asian American queer characters on television. I just hope that the show moves beyond drumming Asian stereotypes or showing "how Asians are different." Many of us do not want to simply settle for more Asian American faces on television. We want to see characters with more creative, complex, dynamic, and nuanced stories. We demand them. Because we do not want to set our diversity bar too low.

Acknowledgments

I thank Sungwoo Ahn, Jill Esbenshade, April Kalogeropoulos Householder, Mytoan Nguyen-Akbar, and Petra Rivera-Rideau for their thoughtful comments on previous drafts of this essay.

References

Alba, Richard, and Victor Nee. 2003. *Remaking the American Mainstream: Assimilation and Contemporary Immigration*. Cambridge: Harvard University Press.

Angry Asian Man. 2013. "Customer Sues CVS for 'Ching Chong Lee' on Racist Receipt." April 18. Accessed September 22, 2015. http://consumerist.com/2013/04/18/customer-sues-cvs-for-writing-her-name-as-ching-chong-on-receipt/.

Bonilla-Silva, E. 2003. *Racism Without Racists: Color-blind Racism and the Persistence of Racial Inequality in the United States*. Lanham, MD: Rowman & Littlefield.

Bradshaw, Peter. 2005. *Crash* (film review). *The Guardian*, August 11. Accessed September 24, 2015. http://www.theguardian.com/theguardian/2005/aug/12/1.

Builder, Maxine. 2015. "How 'Orange Is the New Black' Fails Its Asian Characters." Hyphen: Asian America Unabridged, June 30. Accessed September 27, 2015. http://www.hyphenmagazine.com/blog/archive/2015/06/how-orange-new-black-fails-its-asian-characters.

Duggan, Lisa. 2004. *The Twilight of Equality? Neoliberalism, Cultural Politics, and the Attack on Democracy*. New York: Beacon Press.

Ebert, Roger. 2005. *Crash* (film review). RogerEbert.com, May 5. Accessed September 24, 2015. http://www.rogerebert.com/reviews/crash-2005.

Hsu, Hsuan L. 2006. "Racial Privacy, the L.A. Ensemble Film, and Paul Haggis's *Crash*." *Film Criticism* 31(1):132–156.

Huang, Eddie. 2015. "Bamboo-Ceiling TV." Vulture.com, February 4. Accessed September 25, 2015.

Ito, Robert B. 2014. "'A Certain Slant': A Brief History of Hollywood Yellowface." *Bright Lights Film Journal*. Accessed September 22, 2015. http://brightlightsfilm.com/certain-slant-brief-history-hollywood-yellowface/.

Kerman, Piper. 2011. *Orange Is the New Black: My Year in a Woman's Prison*. New York: Spiegel & Grau.

Kim, Minjeong. 2013. "Missing Romance." *Contexts* 12(1):54–56.

Kim, Minjeong, and Angie Y. Chung. 2005. "Consuming Orientalism: Images of Asian/ American Women in Multicultural Advertising." *Qualitative Sociology* 28(1):67–91.

Lowe, Lisa. 1991. *Critical Terrains: French and British Orientalisms*. Ithaca: Cornell University Press.

Ma, Kai. 2014. "Dear, 'How I Met Your Mother': 'Asian' Is Not a Costume." *Time*, January 17. Accessed September 25, 2015. http://time.com/1155/dear-how-i-met-your-mother-asian-is-not-a-costume/.

Ma, Sheng-Mei. 2000. *The Deathly Embrace: Orientalism and Asian American Identity*. Minneapolis: University of Minnesota Press.

Marchetti, Gina. 1993. *Romance and the "Yellow Peril": Race, Sex, and Discursive Strategies in Hollywood Fiction*. Berkeley: University of California Press.

McRuer, Robert. 2006. *Crip Theory: Cultural Signs of Queerness and Disability*. New York: New York University Press.

Palumbo-Liu, David. 1999. *Asian/American: Historical Crossings of a Racial Frontier*. Stanford: Stanford University Press.

Rodriguez, Clara E. 2014. "Latina/os in Primetime Network Television, 2006–2012." Paper presented at the annual Eastern Sociological Society Meeting, Baltimore, February 21.

Ryan, Erin Gloria. 2014. "What We Can Learn From the Embarrassing #CancelColbert Shitstorm" *Jezebel*, March 28. Accessed September 22, 2015. http://jezebel.com/ what-we-can-learn-from-the-embarrassing-cancelcolbert-1553680450.

Said, Edward W. 1972. *Orientalism*. New York: Vintage.

Sanders, Sam. 2014. "Why We've Been Seeing More 'Yellowface' in Recent Months." *NPR: Code Switch*, August 13. Accessed on September 22, 2015. http://www.npr. org/sections/codeswitch/2014/08/13/337184591/why-weve-been-seeing-more-yellowface-in-recent-months

Sherry, Mark. 2004. "Overlaps and Contradictions Between Queer Theory and Disability Studies" *Disability & Society* 19 (7):769–783.

Smith, Stacy L., Marc Choueiti, and Katherine Pieper. 2013. "Race/Ethnicity in 500 Popular Films: Is the Key to Diversifying Cinematic Content held in the Hand of the Black Director?" Media Diversity & Social Change Initiative, University of Southern California.

Stern, Marlow. 2014. "Orange Is the New Black's Kimiko Glenn on Hippie Brook Soso and Chapel Sex with Natasha Lyonne." *The Daily Beast*, June 18. Accessed September 27, 2015. http://www.thedailybeast.com/articles/2014/06/18/orange-is-the-new-black-s-kimiko-glenn-on-hippie-brook-soso-and-chapel-sex-with-natasha-lyonne.html.

Tajima, Renee E. 1989. "Lotus Blossoms Don't Bleed: Images of Asian Women." *Making Waves: An Anthology of Writings by and about Asian American Women,* edited by Asian Women United Of California, 308–317. Boston: Beacon Press.

Tu, Irene. 2014. "OITNB's New Asian Character Could Be Groundbreaking." *The Bold Italic*, June 6. Accessed September 27, 2015. http://www.thebolditalic.com/ articles/5164-oitnbs-new-asian-character-could-be-groundbreaking.

Tuan, Mia. 1999. *Forever Foreigners or Honorary Whites? The Contemporary Asian Ethnic Experience*. New Brunswick: Rutgers University Press.

Valiente, Alexa. 2013. "New Jersey Woman Sues CVS for $1M for Racist Receipt." ABCnews.com, April 18. Accessed September 22, 2015.

Yiin, Wesley. 2015. "Soso and Chang, Prison Bunkmates by Default: Why Won't 'Orange Is the New Black' Expand Its Asian Cast?" www.salon.com, July 3. Accessed http://www.salon.com/2015/07/03/soso_and_chang_prison_bunkmates_by_default_why_wont_orange_is_the_new_black_expand_its_asian_cast/.

Zia, Helen. 2000. *Asian American Dreams: The Emergence of an American People.* New York: Farrar, Straus and Giroux.

Cleaning Up Your Act

Surveillance, Queer Sex
and the Imprisoned Body

YVONNE SWARTZ HAMMOND

Piper Chapman's claim that she has "always loved getting clean" opens Jenji Kohan's Netflix television series *Orange Is the New Black* with just a hint of foreshadowing—because usually you need to get clean because you get "dirty." The statement invokes baptism and the promise of absolution of sin, which is further supported when she says that getting clean is puts her in her "happy place," a place where she snuggles with her fiancé in a bathtub or intimately washes her former girlfriend. Rupturing her cleanliness metaphor, Chapman turns to look at her feet, wrapped in Kotex and duck tape in the open bay shower, shivering while another inmate (admiring her "TV tits") tells her to hurry up. The call and response continues throughout the first episode, comparing and contrasting terms like "marriage" and "strip" from inside and outside prison walls. The didactic qualities of the exposition, paired with Chapman's narrative interruptions, provide for a common perspective; both audiences and Chapman learn what it means to be imprisoned, the minutia of daily life, the new rules and expectations. Her counselor, Mr. Healy, attempts to help by issuing warnings about the way women behave. Women, he says, fight with rumor and gossip. Worse still (in Healy's mind) is the threat of lesbianism, but he emphasizes that she does *not* have to have lesbian sex. No one will mess with her unless she allows it. "This isn't *Oz*," he states. Aware of the cultural representations of prison, Healy's meta-moment goes beyond cautioning Chapman against the dangers of conflating fantasy and reality and begs the question: where *do* we get information about prison life?

For millions of minority and impoverished people, the prison-industrial complex is a familiar institution. But for those unfamiliar with prison or the justice system, popular representations increasingly provide access to what used to be a public institution. For example, the trailer to Will Ferrell's movie *Get Hard* (2015) tells audiences everything they already know about prison. In 2 minutes and 24 seconds, Ferrell assumes that Kevin Hart's character is going to car jack him, that he has obviously been to prison, and that prison is a place where one can expect sexual assault. Hart's wife in the film asks the obvious question: "What reason did you give him to make him assume you went to prison?" And Hart's answer is direct: "I was being black." Hart's recognition of the unequal imprisonment of black men confirms what films have already been telling us. Like *Get Hard*, films such as Frank Darabont's *The Shawshank Redemption* (1994) or Tony Kaye's *American History X* (1998) follow the incarceration of a White man, using a contemporary revision of a black servant narrative (or what Landra Cunninghamm and Cerise Glenn [2009] call the "magical negro") to help white men survive their prison experiences. The salvation of white characters naturalizes the incarcerated black man by granting a "magical" or intuitive knowledge of how to beat the system, forwarding a theme of "social justice." However, as Peter Caster (2008) notes, the fallacy of prison films lies in their endorsement of a legal system that shows prison as a place that is difficult to access "except by black men, who enter far too easily" (xi). The primary difference between older films and Ferrell's *Get Hard* (a title that cannot be disassociated from its allusion to sex) is that unlike Hart, the black men who help the main characters in Darabont's and Kaye's movies will remain right where they "belong"—in jail.

While race is an important way that cultural representations of prisons shape what we think we know or want to know about prison, prison sex is another way films and television navigate our understanding of inmate life. Cultural representations of prison rape in stories about prison, such as *American History X*, Barry Levinson's *Sleepers* (1996), or HBO's *Oz* (1997–2003), contribute to a larger social understanding that prison rape is not just part of incarceration, but what imprisoned persons should expect for having committed a crime. Popular narratives about prison use sex to train our gaze toward the imprisoned body as a non-normative body, an abject body subjected to violent queer sex and queer identities. No show is more guilty of this than Kohan's *OITNB*. During the first episode, Chapman's narrative shifts between life on the outside (where sex appears as an act of expressing love) and life on the inside, where sex is dirty (the assistant warden masturbates after having met her), sometimes painful (another inmate lightly twists her breasts in admiration), always forbidden by prison regulation (relegated to shower stalls or other semi-private spaces), and seemingly pleasurable (as she walks through the bathroom she witnesses two women happily engaged in oral sex).

From these brief images—plenty of naked bodies and lesbian sex—it seems that sex in women's prisons is erotic, desirable, and even fun. Dawn

Cecil (2007) writes that the "most common and damaging of the [representations of female prisoners] are produced by Hollywood," which are "notorious for their highly sexualized images of women" (305). Noted throughout prison literature scholarship is an overt warning that the images of prison in the media become the way we see and define what it means to be an imprisoned woman. The success of prison films and their reinforcement of society's stereotypes about female prisoners as "violent, worthless, sex-crazed monsters totally unworthy of humane treatment" depends on a specific and ongoing connection to an audience willing to watch these types of stories (Clowers 2001, 28). The naked female inmate satisfies a voyeuristic desire for the female body (especially the female body engaged in lesbian sex) that goes beyond fetishization, because the cultural representations of the imprisoned body provide a substitute for real incarcerated persons. In this essay, I argue that queer sex operates as a heuristic for interpreting prison sex through a rhetoric of desire that blurs the margins of consent such that neither consensual, nonconsensual, nor any act in between is responsibly portrayed.

In a 2013 interview, Kohan says that Piper was her "Trojan Horse," used to sell a show with "really fascinating tales of Black women, and Latina women, and old women and criminals" (NPR 2013). She admits that she used the cool, blonde, girl-next-door to access her audiences because she is "relatable for a lot of audiences and a lot of networks [look] for a certain demographic." Similarly, Anna Marie Smith (2015) emphasizes Chapman's role as "interpretive guide" to what she calls the "colonized underworld with whom we, the privileged and largely white audience, can identify; we relate to her well enough to trust her to pull us into the story and to serve as our translator" (276). In spite of Chapman's decreased role in subsequent seasons, the show remains contingent on her presence in Litchfield to provide access to the others. Thus, while Kohan allows audiences to step behind the walls, her narrative once again fails to provide the story of prison from the viewpoint of the majority of those incarcerated.

Scholarship and popular reviews of *OITNB* tend to point out the exchange between the fantasy and reality of incarceration, primarily in terms of race and sex. Some, like Amos Irwin, are apprehensive of the show becoming an authority on women's prisons. Irwin cautions readers to keep in mind what the show misrepresents, and lists four things to remember: most women are incarcerated for low-level drug offenses, have children under eighteen, need counseling and medical help—not prison, and that women's prisons are a relatively new phenomenon (around one hundred years old) with an exponentially growing population. Allison Samuels, a reviewer for *The Daily Beast*, refuses to even watch the show. Her decision is simple: she is not "entertained by shows that feature large numbers of black people exiting, entering or already in prison" (2013). Samuels points out that popular television shows have rarely bothered to feature black faces, but oddly they "never dream of casting any show related to prisons without featuring people of color in prominent roles." In contrast, Kathleen McHugh argues for a more positive view of the show's worldview. In her comparison of *OITNB* to *Top of the Lake*, McHugh narrows her focus to the title sequences, which she argues, provide direct access to the shows' intentions. The sequence of images in the opening credits "emphasize a dynamic and distinctly minoritarian realism" in which are insulated a rare range of social, cultural, aesthetic, and critical feminist discourses (McHugh 2015, 20).

OITNB is less about representing the accuracy of a prison experience, and much more invested in telling us about ourselves—or as Susan Sontag suggests of the pictures of Abu Graib: "The photographs are us" (Sigler 2006, 599). That the show is based on the memoirs of Piper Kerman only serves to underscore the connection to the real. "Representations with claims to the real," according to Caster (2008), "play an important part in defining the shape of what might be understood as the *cultural imagination*, the pages and screens of thought and belief in which people recognize themselves and others" (4). The removal of the carceral body from public view has widened the distance between inmates and privileged society, a gap now filled with media images of what Anne Marie Cusac refers to as "evil" (2009). Former methods of surveillance as a monitor for crime and punishment—public hangings, stocks, debtors cells—all incorporated the public witnessing of punishment and the inducement of shame for violating social codes. The shift from punishment to discipline removed the public, which has effectively removed much of the public from the criminal justice system. The distance between citizen and inmate has also increased the deficiency in our knowledge and information about incarceration and inmate life (see Boudreau 2006, Garland 2010, Foucault 1977 and Wood 2001, 2009). We are more dependent on popular representations to stand in for what we don't know about prison.

While cultural representations of prison rape depend on images of sex as defined by fixed consent, understanding sex in prison depends on exploring the abstracted notions of consent, and just as important, coercion, as it has been coopted by the penal institution for the use of behavior modification. Prison sex is an important way to see the emphasis on the separation between lives on the "inside" versus lives on the "outside." Former inmate Donald Lee argues that part of becoming a true inmate is the practice of homosexuality; it becomes the norm (Kunzel 2008, 96–97). Consequently, part of the "prisonization" is engaging in homosexual sex; it is part of institutionalization. However, Chapman does not need to acquire a new sexual identity to be "prisonized." Instead, her bisexuality suggests that she will easily and enjoyably reenter into a partnership with her former lover who is also imprisoned at Litchfield Penitentiary. And while cultural representations of rape in men's prison realize our worst fears about prison sex, *OITNB* plays off fantasies about lesbian sex by suggesting that sexual relationships in women's prison are born of desire, rather than influenced by positions of power.

What We Tell Ourselves About Ourselves

No representation of prison life is more complex and contingent than prison sex. As Healy demonstrates, society seems to assume the worst: that sex is unwanted and part of the punishment. Yet, while depictions of sexual assault in prison film and television seem to operate as verification of incarceration, the strict split between consent and non-consent in their representations often masks the ways in which the imprisoned are subjected to coercion and power. Department of Justice reports show that imprisoned people are more like to be sexually assaulted by guards and staff (the people with the power) than they are by other inmates. And weaker and vulnerable populations (people without power) are more likely to be assaulted. Healy's early warnings to avoid involvement with the other prisoners not only misrecognize Chapman's sexuality, but also assumes that she needs to fear her bunkmate more than Officer Mendez or Officer Coates. Healy is always looking for sex, and his obsessive desire to eradicate lesbian sex (particularly in the first and second seasons), highlights the relationship between surveillance and sexualization in prison; he tells Chapman: "nothing goes on without [his] knowing." Recognition of authority, and by extension power, is crucial to prison enculturation. Chapman needs to know exactly who is in charge and the extent of that control; her body is no longer her own.

For individuals outside of the prison system, crime and punishment exists only on the television screen in mass-market *Netflix* series' like Kohan's. The implied responsibility requires an interrogation of the pedagogical component of popular culture. Media representations of prison sex are particularly dangerous because they provide the interpretative measures used in courtrooms that determine sentencing, or in political offices that fail to sanction anti-rape measures. A 1994 criminal justice report found that jurors in rape cases often rely on popular conceptions of rape rather than strictly legal definitions (Epstein and Langenbaum 1994, 1318). And portrayals of rape in television aren't uncommon. In their exploration of sex and rape in popular 1996 films, criminal justice scholars Jana Bufkin and Sarah Eschholz (2000) reported that five of thirty sex scenes were rape scenes that presented a "rather homogenous picture" of rape in the United States and a depiction of homosexual sex as a "deviant" act that "only sick child molesters participate in" (1337). Another study, focusing on the impact of crime shows, reveals that jurors assume the truth and relevancy of television forensics. This effect, dubbed the "CSI effect," has raised legitimate concern among judges and attorneys (Call et al. 2013, 52). "In America," states Anne Marie Cusac (2009), "punishment is populist" (6). However, Cusac argues that there is hope: "what punishment has done to television—and what television has done to punishment—is important because television is an agent of cultural change" (211).

Writing about Abu Ghraib, Cusac highlights the most pervasive assumptions about prison: "(1) people who land in jail deserve to be there; (2) criminals are bad people—almost subhuman—who can't be rehabilitated; (3) therefore, punishment can be as harsh as possible; and (4) we don't need or want to know the details" (252). These assumptions are reflected in prison films and television that reinforce our worst fears about prison and prison sex. Assault scenes verify what we think we know about prison; it is a space where criminals are raped in order to be "saved." Arguably the most memorable scene in *American History X* is the rape of Derek Vinyard. Though the film directly explores the complex genesis of indoctrination, the film indirectly works to restore Vinyard to "normal" society. After violently murdering two men who attempted to steal his car, Vinyard is sent to jail for three years. According to the film's primary narrative, Vinyard must learn to see the error of his racist philosophies and repent. His repentance is framed around a shower gang rape performed by the white supremacists, an act that uses rape not just as punishment but also as a means of verifying suffering—rape authenticates the prison experience. Cultural representations of male penitentiaries focus almost exclusively on rape as an expression of desire in prison, in effect criminalizing male-on-male sexuality and denying the possibility of consensual or even loving relationships. Equally troubling, definitions for rape fail to recognize the complexity of prison culture or the act itself. Classic rape scenarios continue to inform a limited understanding of power and consent, and "current legal conceptions are inadequate to the lived experience of the crime of rape" (Anderson 2011, 625). Skewed representations of male prison sex reveal much about thresholds of hetero-normative culture, which seems to prefer images of violent male-on-male sex rather than the possibility of a mutually consenting relationship.

Unlike the violent rape narrative associated with men's prisons, cultural representations of women's prisons tend to depend on a storyline that reads "like a conventional heterosexual romance" (Ciasullo 2008, 197). The narrative trajectory follows a common path: audiences watch an innocent lamb led into a "hellhole" where she must endure the "welcoming ritual" of stripping and showering, face a range of criminals—the perverse matron, the tough-talking sarcastic prostitute; the manipulative, back-stabbing snitch; and, of course, the aggressive prison lesbian—submit to a cruel and sadistic authority with the relatively ineffective protection of the benevolent male employed by the prison—typically a doctor—who intervenes on behalf of the innocent lamb.

Mid-century women's prison films frequently presented prison as an "agent to return women to domesticity," which by extension meant returning imprisoned women to a happy, heterosexual marriage by the end of the film (Morey 1995, 80). Interest in prison sexuality seems to have intensified beginning in the 1950s. Already under observation, prisoners were subjected to numerous invasive and non-invasive studies that attempted to discern direct and indirect signs of homosexuality because "prison life failed to synchronize with dominant notions of sexuality" (Kunzel 2008, 2). Regina Kunzel's work in *Criminal Intimacy* provides some of the most in-depth work about prison sex, tracking the cultural interpretations of prison sex in a discussion framed around modern notions of sexual identity. Prison is a space that lacks the 'normal' notion of time and space, which encourages people to view prisoners' sexuality as contingent and situational.

Concerned about the homosexual spread, mid-century cinematic portrayals of women's prisons followed a didactic formula emphasizing rehabilitation through domesticity, and, of course, heterosexual partnership. Estelle Freedman contends that women's incarceration provided a means for controlling sexuality; crimes like prostitution were an obvious threat to heteronormative culture, but drunkenness, vagrancy, and other "crimes against chastity" demonstrated a lack of domestic skill. In film, women were locked behind the closed doors of "hell" and, to steal a title from popular culture, "scared straight" (Shapiro 1978). The prison lesbian, Freedman (1996) argues, "reveals a complex reconfiguration of the class and racial meanings attached to sexuality in modern America" (397). Films depicted lesbians as criminals and a menace, and more often than not, constructed representations of "African American women prisoners as masculine or aggressive and their white lovers as 'normal' feminine women who would return to heterosexual relations upon release" (399). Decades later, we still find traces of this construction of the sexually aggressive black woman in Suzanne's ("Crazy Eyes") pursuit of Chapman.

Though Healy alludes to our fears about sexual abuse and the aggressive black rapist, he doesn't really need to tell audiences anything about sex in the prison; the show provides plenty of opportunities to see sex. Few episodes in the series lack a lesbian sex scene. Perhaps the most daring attempt to fill an hour with sex is Season 2, Episode 4, "A Whole Other Hole," during which Nicky and Big Boo attempt to out-sex one another. Bolstering *OITNB*'s spectacle-like versions of prison sex are secondary stories about prisoner's pasts revealing physical abuse, betrayal, manipulation, and sexual molestation, which ironically seems to suggest that prison sex is healthier than a heteronormative relationship, or as the backstory of Lorna Morello reveals, heteronormative relationships are a fantasy. The show provides ample evidence of the limitations and failures of heteronormative domesticity: Lorna's empty wedding rituals that turn out to be a stalking fantasy; Dayanara Diaz's affair with her stepfather; Sophie Burset's failing marriage—even Healy's dependence on a mail order bride service reveals the fissures in hetero-narrative. Thus the sex we witness in the show seems to represent a desire for an imagined "freedom" from the demands of heteronormativity.

In addition to images of sexually satisfied women, *OITNB* adds uglier representations of prison, particularly in terms of race and violence. Season one focuses on Chapman's institutionalization, and by the end the transformation seems complete; Chapman as we met her seems to have disappeared. The season ends with Chapman savagely beating Tiffany Dogget ("Pennsatucky"). Season two introduces Vee, a vindictive manipulator, who represents a common racial stereotype: the aggressive, black female criminal and perpetual recidivist. *OITNB* does not just represent our fantasies; it also represents mainstream cultural and political fears about race, homosexuality, and freedom. Vee's presence in the prison helps strengthen racial divides and increases the inmate-on-inmate assault. By Season 3 Kohan really digs deep, abandoning Chapman as the primary narrative, and finally shows us what we really expect from prison: rape.

That rape is a part of the prison experience for men is almost assumed. The narrative of prison rape is so commonplace in contemporary culture that it "has dubbed prisoner rape a joke" (Cronan and Man 2001, 185). Media representations of rape focus on violent rape, but "paradigmatic violent rapes are only a small piece of the sexualization of incarceration" (Ristroph 2006, 149). "Classic" rape scenarios—scenes of painful abuse inflicted upon the new and/or weak inmates—used in male prison narratives dominate media representations. These same prison sex narratives too often depend on sexist and racist imagery that limits our understanding of the actual crime. Weaker, more effeminate men are the victims of rape; black men rape white men. Instead of criminalizing rape, we criminalize the extrinsic factors, such as race or gender. By criminalizing these extrinsic factors, according to Bufkin and Eschholz (2000), representations of rape limit the ability of the viewers to identify with sexual victimization, and therefore, viewers have a greater tendency to blame the victim (1318). Rape operates similarly in *OITNB*: a small, white female—both physically vulnerable and virtually powerless—is overpowered by a white, male guard who takes for granted that she owes him sex. This same storyline is paired with Dogget's developing friendship with Big Boo, whose backstory reveals a lifetime of combatting assumptions about her sexuality and gender. Big Boo becomes Dogget's advocate and mentor, showing her what is means to be a strong woman. Yet, in spite of the positive intentions, the show falls into a familiar pattern—prisoners must be raped in order to be saved, or as Caleb Smith concludes, to save the soul, the convict must die.

OITNB continually relies on juxtapositions in which good intentions mask familiar stereotypes, which allow the show to draw in a certain demographic but maintain a comfortable distance from the "criminal." This is best represented in Chapman's character whose "queerness" (in terms of sexuality and inability to adapt to prison culture) provide an access point for audiences to digest the otherworldliness of prison. The show seems to use her bisexuality as a way of suggesting that Chapman will be open to relationships with women in prison, and therefore, her prison sex experiences will be welcome. This either/or construction eliminates concerns about consent commonly associated with homosexual sex in representations of men's prisons, or older representations of women's prisons. Chapman does not have to worry about lesbians nor does she need to worry about post-prison life since domestic bliss with her fiancé lies just 15 months away. This promise, though lost in subsequent seasons, still grounds the show; Larry's disappearance seems like a loose end rather than a closing of the relationship. More troublesome, however, is the way her sexuality further marginalizes non-normative characters (like Suzanne or even Nicky Nicols) and reinforces the importance of the heteronormative sexuality in Season 1.

Sex and Power

Inmates often hesitate to report sexual abuse and misconduct performed by guards, fearing official or unofficial punishment, or performed by other inmates, fearing community forms of punishment. Much of the first season is focused on Chapman learning the rules and differences between life on the inside and life on the outside. For example, after a snide comment about the food, Chapman receives a bloody-tampon for breakfast. Unaware that she has sinned by insulting Red's cooking, she quickly learns about power. Guards are indifferent to her hunger and suffering, fellow prisoners are scared of similar reprisal—at that moment Red has all the power. Desperate, and still unaccustomed to the new social rules, Chapman turns to Healy. When she asks to be moved to a new facility he immediately assumes it is because of sex—"Did someone try to engage with you sexually?" Healy seems disappointed by her unwillingness to report, and angrily puts away his pen, having been denied the opportunity to police her suxuality. Surveillance by other inmates creates yet another dimension of power and control. Angry with Chapman and Vause, Dogget tells Healy that she has witnessed the two "lesbianing" in the shower, which leads to Chapman being thrown into segregation. Both behavior and definitions for sex in prison impact how inmates relate to one another, and as Dogget demonstrates, the right to determine the limits for queer sex and behavior translates into power.

Despite her experiences with her former girlfriend—experiences that we might assume would prepare Chapman for the shower sex—Chapman's sexual past does not prepare her for sex in prison. Though sex in *OITNB* appears both consensual and erotic, most viewers are equally aware of the converse images in male prisons where the shower is dangerous. Prison sex is not just about desire, but also the influences of space and surveillance. No space is more sexually heightened than prison showers. In the first episode, Chapman walks past an open bay shower where Nicky Nichols is performing oral sex on her lover, Morello. Our notions of public and private spaces shift based on who is watching, and an open bay shower is a perfect example of a fluid public-private space. Prison sex is an important way to see the emphasis on the separation between life on the "inside" versus life on the "outside," and prison society is unique and dictated by a set of codes that needs to be deciphered by the newly incarcerated. After seeing Nichols in the shower, Chapman appears surprised and confused. Nichols later notes with delight that Chapman "got an eye-full in the shower."

Though common sense might suggest that the lack of privacy would reduce the opportunity for sex, the proximity coupled with heightened surveillance further sexualizes the body and increases tension. Historically, prisoners were isolated not only from society, but from one another, to allow them the space and time to reflect on their wrongdoing. As populations increased, the space available for individual isolation decreased and inmates were housed in increasingly closer proximity. This proximity has been blamed for contributing to the availability of prison sex and specifically, rape. Alice Ristroph (2006) believes that overcrowding and stronger surveillance further sexualizes prisoners; there is no privacy in prison (160). The lack of privacy coupled with the layers of power dynamics—relationships between guards and inmates, inmates and inmates, men and women—influence the boundary between consent and coercion.

In *OITNB* the contrast between consent and coercion, or sex as desire versus sex as punishment, is best exemplified in the characters Healy and George "Pornstache" Mendez. As his names suggests, Mendez's character is strongly associated with pornography—he is overly sexualized. Unlike Healy, Mendez does not feel threatened at all by the inmates' sexuality. Instead, he acknowledges the sexual tension resulting from watching the inmates in the guard station and teases rookie guard John Bennett about sexual "possibilities." In one scene, Mendez demands that Sophia Burset, a transgender inmate, come over and smell his McDonald's breakfast sandwich. He asks her if it smells good and if she would like a taste. She asks if he is offering some, and he replies, "You can suck it out of my dick." Her reply that "she doesn't do sausage in her breakfast sandwiches" cleverly avoids further engaging Mendez, and the rejection forces Mendez to rely on his power as a guard to belittle her by asking "what the fuck are you doing in the CO (correction officer) bubble?" Their exchange highlights one of the most important aspects of prison sex—the role power plays in determining the limitations of consent.

Prison sex is frequently represented as an "inevitable aspect of prison life ... understandably born of heterosexual deprivation," but this understanding depends on oversimplified notions of power that fail to recognize the complex situational factors that blur the boundary between yes and no (Kunzel 2008, 5). Mendez is well aware of his position of power and knows that he can use this authority to coerce inmates. After Sophia leaves the guard area, Mendez continues to fetishize what he imagines would be a pleasurable experience with a "cyborg pussy," telling Bennett that "she used to have a dick so she knows what it likes." At this point even Bennett begins to question Mendez's motivations, and Mendez offers a simple, albeit narcissistic, explanation: "All these offenders want a piece of me, Bennett; it's the fucking pheromones man, you get them all locked up like this for a long time and they get this prehistoric yearning for man-stink." Deprived of heterosexual diversion Mendez assumes that the women cannot resist his manliness, which only earlier Sophia rejected. More problematic than Mendez's ego is his quiet whisper to Bennett that though sexual contact is against the rules "some of these bitches would suck it for half a cigarette."

Despite evidence that reveals that staff misconduct occurs more frequently, scholarship exploring prison rape has focused on inmate-on-inmate rape. In 2011–12 the Bureau of Justice (BJS) reported that 4 percent of prisoners experienced one or more incidents of sexual victimization. Rates of reported inmate-on-inmate sexual victimization totaled 2 percent, while rates for staff sexual misconduct were 2.4 percent. Data shows that vulnerable populations—the old, the weak, the young, the effeminate, the overweight or overly thin—experience a higher than average rate of victimization. Though the report shows that other types of victimization ("consensual" or "willing" sexual acts) happen at a much lower rate, the report fails to consider other forms of abuse and coercive acts—from "pimping" services of new and desirable inmates, to unwanted touching or even through their apathetic indifference to misconduct. Furthermore, many guards discourage complaints and indicate that they do not want to be bothered. Some guards perpetuate the violence either through raping inmates themselves, or through "selling" inmates for favors. In *OITNB* Mendez is a well-known smuggler who trades sexual favors for goods (audiences know for sure that Tricia Miller performs oral sex for drugs). Anthony Scacco (1975) writes that there is a disturbing relationship between the guards and inmates regarding rape, including indifference to acts of violence.

Representations of prison facilities in popular culture emphasize the function of rape and sexual abuse as a means to control. Misconduct is rampant in *OITNB*; the guards are as much or more invested in the prison sex as the inmates themselves. Mendez looks at the women as his personal harem; Bennett hopes for the heteronormative true love; Scott O'Neil and Wanda Bell are having sex in the front office—almost every guard is having sex in the prison. One of the exceptions is Healy, who instead of having sex obsessively looks for it. Healy is the best example of a social watchdog. He guards Chapman's sexuality more carefully than he does her physical or mental state. From the first episode, Healy emphasizes a link between Chapman and himself; we're "not like the others," he tells her. On the one hand, this association speaks to race because, of course, there are other prisoners who are not lesbian and don't engage in any lesbian (or other) sexual acts. Healy does not express the same attachment to Nichols or Big Boo, for example. Red is the only other character for whom Healy bends the rules, but only because she acts as a translator between himself and his Russian mail-order bride. Class also plays a part in Healy's desire to imagine a similarity between himself and Chapman. In early episodes, Healy has no connection to Dogget, the leader of the white "gang" despite her clear rejection of homosexuality. Chapman, on the other hand, an upper class, educated, white woman is exactly what Healy wants to believe to be his "people."

As Healy's fantasy deepens, his desire to protect Chapman from lesbianism becomes more obsessive, a projection of the "save the white women" rape fantasy leftover from the Jim Crow South. Healy's efforts to save Chapman reveal an increasingly stronger connection to his perceived lack as a man and a husband. His wife not only doesn't love him, but also does not respect him— at least as far as he recognizes respect. Desperate for a "traditional" marriage, Healy asks Red, a Russian inmate, to intervene and talk to his wife on the phone. He takes language lessons to help his courting efforts. His failures increase his frustration, and he seems to blame the acceptance of queer sexualities as reason for his difficulties. Desperate to stamp out lesbian sex, Healy exploits his power to punish Chapman and others for engaging in any sexual behaviors—even acts as benign as dancing. In subsequent seasons Healy attempts to find validation by starting a therapy group, ironically named *Safe Places*, while cultivating a relationship with Dogget to uncover the hidden "gay agenda." In the second season Healy's relationship with Chapman shifts; he now knows she is a lesbian. Their interactions reveal the multiple and complex ways that power and coercion can be used to control behavior. In one scene Chapman asks for furlough to see her grandmother before she dies. Visibly upset, she knows that Healy will not help her; after all, he stood and watched as Dogget attacked her. Healy enjoys power both as an administrator, a person who can give and take special permissions, jobs, or privileges, and as an individual, prone to petty acts of passive aggression, like calling Chapman's fiancé and telling him that she is having an affair with a her former lover or ignoring a beating. In the end Healy provides the furlough, but only because he believes it will lead Chapman back to heterosexuality.

Healy's relationship to Red is even more complicated than his relationship to Chapman, but similarly exposes a pathological need for dominance and respect. By Season 3 we have seen Red through many hardships: the loss of her kitchen, the cruel tortures inflicted by Vee, an attack that almost killed her, and the closing of her beloved bakery. Furious with her husband's weakness, Red divorces, which, alongside her efforts to help Healy with his wife, seem to inspire her to look at Healy with new interest. Red's character is direct and painfully honest. Though she imagines herself in love with Healy she tells him their paths are not destined to cross. Red's most important contribution is acknowledgement of the systems that keep women powerless. She states: "You take a woman's power away, her work, her family, her currency. You leave her with one coin; the one she was born with. It may be tawdry and demeaning, but if she has to, she will spend it. But you're right, your feelings count to." Red's only power, limited and contingent always on the benevolence of Healy, is her ability to recognize and describe Healy's forms of manipulation. In her statement she shows Healy that his paranoia about his masculinity and his fear of being taken advantage of mask a deeper disconnect; he cannot empathize or identify with women. This is further emphasized when a new counselor comes to work at Litchfield, a black woman with degrees in social work and psychology. The woman is good at her job, which only infuriates Healy. He manipulates her suspension, blaming her for encouraging Suzanne to write pornography. In reality, he is jealous of her ease with the inmates and their relationships with her. Again, he imagines a threat to his masculinity and moves to extinguish the threat.

Healy's use of passive aggressive revenge provides an example of coercive power and shows audiences that relationships in prison are always dictated by complicated and complex power dynamics. Though Healy does not attempt to have a physical relationship with any of the women, he does clearly fantasize about Chapman and Red. Even the most "loving" relationship between prisoner and guard, the relationship between Officer Bennett and Diaz, eventually reveals the structure of power. Daya cannot leave, but Bennett can. Diaz and Officer Bennett, a guard at Litchfield, begin a flirtation that leads to a sexual relationship. Moments of intimacy are frequently interrupted and Bennett must immediately adopt his "guard" voice to discipline Diaz, justifying their proximity. After their initial flirtation leads to sex, Diaz becomes pregnant. Knowing that she does not want an abortion, Diaz faces limited options: tell the officials that she and Bennett have been conducting an affair, the result of which will be Bennett's own incarceration, or find another man to blame. Diaz decides to frame Mendez, who subsequently falls in "love" with Diaz. Diaz's use of Mendez may itself appear manipulative and coercive, after all Diaz's history tells us that she is an accomplished flirt, known cheat, and therefore promiscuous; however, registering her as in control of the relationship between herself and Mendez not only absolves Mendez of responsibility for his actions, but also reifies the tired "she was asking for it" rationale used to justify sexual abuse thinking that any reports that might accuse him of misconduct will be ignored. Diaz's use of Mendez to save her lover Bennett once again places an unfair burden on a vulnerable population, while again confirming that the only hope for power is through what Red calls the "one coin." Though the show wants us to buy into the potential for a romantic relationship in prison, neither audiences nor Diaz can ever forget who is in charge. This becomes more stark with the introduction of Coates.

Officer Coates, a new guard, fails to receive proper training, and relies on Dogget to show him how to be a guard. Belying the stereotype of the untrustworthy inmate, Dogget never tries to escape or break the rules until Coates directs her. They eventually build what seems to be a friendship, until one afternoon Coates throws pieces of bread on the ground and demands that Dogget fetch them like a dog. The scene is tense and clearly sexual, ending with a forced embrace and kiss. Coates insists that Dogget likes him and wants him; Dogget isn't as sure. In one of the most powerful juxtapositions of the show, audiences watch the backstory of Dogget that reveals a childhood lesson about allowing men to just do what they are going to do alongside scenes of Dogget's prostitution and rape. This background plays an important role in justifying Dogget's abuse and rape by Officer Coates; Dogget has always been a tease and a whore. However, unlike the scenes from her adolescence, Dogget's fear of Coates is intensified because she knows she cannot escape. Coates can do whatever he likes to her because, after all, she is only a criminal.

Pedagogy of the Oppressed

If we presume a pedagogical importance inherent in cultural representations, then how do we reconcile the images in *OITNB*? Is the show responsible for telling us about who we are? To whom is *OITNB* really speaking? Healy seems the most likely representation of audience given that he is a white, middle class, heterosexual, Christian male. In an exchange in solitary confinement, Healy and Chapman directly confront the issue through a series of statements that directly confronts Healy's sexual fantasies and misuse of power. Healy tells Chapman that he "tried to be nice to [her] because [he] understand[s] where [she] come[s] from," and Chapman's reply is ugly:

> Wake up Healy. Girls like me? We don't fuck ignorant, pretentious old men with weird lesbian obsessions. We go for tall, hot girls and we fucking love it! So that leaves you on the outside…. You don't get me! Ever!

Before her solitary confinement, Chapman had been living with the notion that prison would not change her, would not affect her plans to marry, or her business with her best friend Polly, but Chapman failed to account for institutional identity and the impact of prisonization, both of which seem to account for her return to Vause. In order to be redeemed, Chapman must recognize her criminal identity, which is not only marked by her queer sexuality, but also her privilege as a wealthy, educated, white woman. Though Kohan's use of Chapman, a woman who knew nothing of crime and punishment, as a tour guide bolsters the shock of the experience, it also subordinates the already marginalized populations she encounters in prison, particularly because it is framed around Chapman's experience. If, as Kohan claims, Chapman is the necessary tour guide, then it seems plausible that the show speaks to and reflects a privileged, white audience because who in the series needs to learn about prison: Chapman's parents, her fiancé, and her friend Polly.

It's crucial that audiences see Chapman's life fall apart, because, at their core, prison narratives need to show audiences what they believe about criminality and prison, primarily that prisoners deserve punishment. To believe that happy sex happens in prison, not only misrepresents what society trusts to be the function of incarceration—punishment, retribution, and possibly redemption—it also misrepresents an environment of coercion and violence. While rape scenes seem to authenticate the prison experience, these scenes are equally guilty of misrepresenting complex power dynamics operating in and outside of prison walls. Paradoxically, prison films expose the brutality of imprisonment, but also provide messages affirming the use of violence to save the criminal. Caster confirms that the fallacy of prison films lies in a redemption narrative that implicitly endorses the legal system even while narrating stories of unjust imprisonment (2008). Criminality, he argues, is a determination of a judge and jury, while criminalization is a matter of "interpellation of being named" (16).

OITNB depends on the naked, assaulted, or sexualized body as a means of authenticating Chapman's experience. Prison sex in popular texts is complicated, contingent, and conflicted, and in the end these narratives rarely if ever, help increase audiences' awareness of the actual conditions of incarceration. The conditions of incarceration are unquestionable for those who know about prison—those who have been incarcerated know the inside well. Their loved ones and those who work for the prison system (from attorneys to prison guards) may not share a singular perspective, but may share a base knowledge of the "inside." These people do not need representations to tell them about prisons. Should any doubt remain about the audience of *OITNB*, in a discussion about popular representations of women's imprisonment, members of a book club at the Federal Women's Facility in Hazelton, West Virginia, unequivocally stated that *OITNB* was both "not real" and "disconnected" from the experience of prison (Ryan 2015). Film and television depictions of incarceration are designed to target audiences without access to life on the inside. What uninformed audiences "know" about prison is based on a vision of the imprisoned body as a sexualized body. The criminal body's rape or sexual assault has become a metonym for prison life revealing a dark conclusion about our popular-culture-based understanding of punishment. As a culture we recognize that dropping the soap is dangerous, and even documentaries like *Scared Straight* or *Locked Up* use editing to emphasize the danger of sexual assault in prison. In directing our attention to sex, *OITNB* maintains a comfortable distance from the real prison issues of class disparity, race, and even to a degree, gender, and instead highlights the "softer-side" of prison.

Sadly, the growth of women in prison has increased exponentially, but in reality, women have always had a place in prison, hidden as domestic workers, or in psychiatric institutions. Angela Davis (2003) sees the character of punishment as "deeply gendered" (61). Sexual abuse, she argues, is too often translated into the "hypersexuality of women prisoners," perpetuating the notion that "female 'deviance' always has a sexual dimension" (68). Though *OITNB* helps address the paucity in the discussion of imprisoned women (in effect acknowledging the role of gender in prison), it does so via a minimum-security prison with characters that are both "friendly" and distanced from Chapman. Chapman's distance from the other inmates as well as her role as storyteller invites audiences to live through her perspective and turn their gaze inward, to look at the inside from the outside. The show reinforces the direction of audiences' gaze, emphasizing that prison is a space where people are looked upon, rather than looked with—from outside in, rather than inside out. Thankfully the show seems to be turning away from Chapman as the primary point of view, which has invited marginalized voices to deepen the show's engagement with contemporary women's social and political issues. In spite of this turn, as outsiders the show maintains a gaze that invites us to become voyeurs, in a sense, fetishizing, like Mendez, the naked female bodies that too frequently become the centerpieces for episodes. Women moaning in pleasure, full pregnant bellies resulting from sex with the irresistible but manipulative guard, the errant female in need of punishment—all of the images from the show directly connect to an eroticism and pornography that has historically defined the genre of women's prison films.

REFERENCES

Aitken, Stuart. 2003. "Composing Identities: Films, Families and Racism." *Journal of Geography* 102, no. 1:2–12.

Alber, Jan. 2011. "Cinematic Carcerality: Prison Metaphors in Film." *The Journal of Popular Culture* 44, no. 2:217–232.

American History X. 1998. Directed by Tony Kaye. Burbank: New Line Home Video, 2000. DVD.

Anderson, Michelle. 2005. "All-American Rape." *St. John's Law Review* 79, no. 3:625–644.

Basketball Diaries. 1995. Directed by Scott Kalvert. New York: Palm Pictures, 1998. DVD.

Boudreau, Kristen. 2006. *Spectacle of Death: Populist Literary Responses to American Capital Cases.* New York: Prometheus.

Bufkin, Jana, and Sarah Eschholz. 2000. "Images of Sex and Rape: A Content Analysis of Popular Film." *Violence Against Women* 6, no. 12:1317–1344.

Call, Corey. 2013. "Seeing Is Believing: The CSI Effect Among Jurors in Malicious Wounding Cases." *Journal of Social, Behavioral, and Health Sciences* 7, no. 1:52–66.

Caster, Peter. 2008. *Prisons, Race and Masculinity in Twentieth-Century U.S. Literature and Film.* Columbus: Ohio State University Press.

Cecil, Dawn. 2007. "Looking Beyond *Caged Heat*: Media Images of Women in Prison." *Feminist Criminology* 2, no. 4:304–326.

Ciasullo, Ann. 2008. "Containing 'Deviant' Desire: Lesbianism, Heterosexuality, and the Women-in-Prison Narrative." *The Journal of Popular Culture* 41, no. 2:195–223.

Clowers, Marsha. 2001. "Dykes, Gangs, and Dangers: Debunking Popular Myths About Maximum-Security Life." *Journal of Criminal Justice and Popular Culture* 9, no. 1:22–30.

Cronan, John, and Christopher Man. 2001. "Forecasting Sexual Abuse in Prison: The Prison Subculture of Masculinity as a Backdrop for 'Deliberate Indifference.'" *The Journal of Criminal Law and Criminology* 92, no. 1/2:127–186.

Cunningham, Landra, and Cerise Glenn. 2009. "The Power of Black Magic: The Magical Negro and White Salvation in Film." *The Journal of Black Studies* 40, no. 2.

Cusac, Anne Marie. 2009. *Cruel and Unusual: The Culture of Punishment in America.* New Haven: Yale University Press.

Davis, Angela. 1998. "Masked Racism: Reflections on the Prison Industrial Complex." *Color Lines: News for Action*, September 10. http://www.colorlines.com/articles/masked-racism-reflections-prison-industrial-complex.

_____. 2003. *Are Prisons Obsolete?* New York: Seven Stories Press.

Epstein, Joel, Esq., and Stacia Langenbahn. 1994. "The Criminal Justice and Community Response to Rape." *U.S. Department of Justice.* Accessed January 15, 2015. https://www.ncjrs.gov/pdffiles1/Digitization/148064NCJRS.pdf.

Faith, Karlene. 1987. "Media, Myths and Masculinization: Images of Women in Prison." *Too Few to Count: Canadian Women in Conflict with the Law.* Edited by Ellen Adelberg and Claudia Currie, 181–219. Vancouver: Press Gang Publishers.

Foucault, Michel. 1977. *Discipline and Punish: The Birth of the Prison.* New York: Random House.

Freedman, Estelle B. 1996. "The Prison Lesbian: Race, Class, and the Construction of the Aggressive Female Homosexual, 1915–1965." *Feminist Studies* 22, no. 2:397–423.

Garland, David. 2010. *The Peculiar Institution: America's Death Penalty in an Age of Abolition.* Cambridge: Harvard University Press.

Get Hard. 2015. Directed by Etan Cohen. Burbank: Warner Home Video, 2015. DVD.

Irwin, Amos. 2015. "How 'Orange Is the New Black' Misrepresents Women's Federal Prison and Why It Matters." *Huffington Post*, June 11. http://www.huffingtonpost.com/amos-irwin/how-orange-is-the-new-black-misrepresents-womens-federal-prison-and-why-it-matters_b_7547334.html.

Kunzel, Regina. 2002. "Situating Sex: Prison Sexual Culture in the Mid-Twentieth-Century United States." *GLQ: A Journal of Lesbian and Gay Studies* 8, no. 3:253–270.

_____. 2008. *Criminal Intimacy: Prison and the Uneven History of Modern American Sexuality.* Chicago: University of Chicago Press.

Kuzina, Matthias. 2001. "The Social Issue Courtroom Drama as an Expression of American Popular Culture." *Journal of Law and Society* 29, no. 1:79–96.

McHugh, Kathleen. 2015. "Giving Credit to Paratexts and Parafeminism in Top of the Lake and Orange in the New Black." *Film Quarterly* 68, no. 3:17–25. Accessed September 27, 2015. http://www.filmquarterly.org/2015/03/giving-credit-to-paratexts-and-parafeminism-in-top-of-the-lake-and-orange-is-the-new-black/.

Morey, Annie. 1995. "'The Judge Called Me an Accessory.'" *Journal of Popular Film & Television* 23, no. 2:80–88.

NPR. 2013. "'Orange' Creator Jenji Kohan: 'Piper Was My Trojan Horse.'" August 13, 2013. http://www.npr.org/2013/08/13/211639989/orange-creator-jenji-kohan-piper-was-my-trojan-horse.

Oz. 1997–2003. Created by Tom Fontana. Performed by Ernie Hudson, J.K. Simmons, and Lee Tergesen. HBO. Television Series.

Ristroph, Alice. 2006. "Prison and Punishment: Sexual Punishments." *Columbia Journal of Gender & Law* 15:139–184.

Ryan, Dr. Katy (representative for the Appalachian Prison Book Project), Hazelton Federal Penitentiary Women's Book Club, Hazelton, WV, 2015, Oral Conversation.

Samuels, Allison. 2013. "I Don't Watch 'Orange Is the New Black.'" *The Daily Beast*, August 19. http://www.thedailybeast.com/articles/2013/08/19/why-i-don-t-watch-orange-is-the-new-black-or-any-shows-with-black-people-in-prison.html.

Sargent, Andrew. 2013. "Representing Prison Rape: Race, Masculinity, and Incarceration in Donald Goines's *White Man's Justice, Black Man's Grief*." *MELUS* 35, no. 3.

Scacco, Anthony. 1975. *Rape in Prison*. Springfield, IL: Charles C. Thomas.

Scared Straight. 1978. Directed by Arnold Shapiro. New York: Docurama, 2003. DVD.

The Shawshank Redemption. 1994. Directed by Frank Darabont. Beverly Hills: Castle Rock Entertainment, 2008. DVD.

Sigler, Mary. 2006. "By the Light of Virtue: Prison Rape and the Corruption of Character." *Iowa Law Review* 91:563–607.

Sleepers. 1996. Directed by Barry Levinson. Burbank: Warner Home Video, 2009. DVD.

Smith, Anna Marie. 2015. "Orange Is the Same White." *New Political Science* 37, no. 2:276–280.

Smith, Caleb. 2009. *The Prison and the American Imagination*. New Haven: Yale University Press.

U.S. Department of Justice. Office of Justice Programs. Office of Justice Programs. August 2007. "Sexual Victimization in State and Federal Prisons Reported by Inmates 2007." *Bureau of Justice Statistics*. NCJ219414. Washington: BJS, August 2007. Accessed December 14, 2011. http://www.bjs.gov/content/pub/pdf/svsfpri07.pdf.

___. August 2007. "Sexual Violence Reported by Correctional Authorities 2006." *Bureau of Justice Statistics*. NCJ218914. Washington: BJS, August 2007. Accessed December 14, 2011. http://www.bjs.gov/content/pub/pdf/svrca06.pdf.

___. May 2013. "Sexual Victimization in State and Federal Prisons Reported by Inmates 2011–12." *Bureau of Justice Statistics*. NCJ241399. Washington: BJS. Accessed January 15, 2015. http://www.bjs.gov/content/pub/pdf/svpjri1112.pdf.

Wlodarz, Joe. 2001. "Rape Fantasies: Hollywood and Homophobia." *Masculinity: Bodies, Movies, Culture*. Edited by Peter Lehman, 67–80. New York: Routledge.

Wood, Amy Louise. 2001. "Lynching Photography and the 'Black Beast Rapist' in Southern White Masculine Imagination." *Masculinity: Bodies, Movies, Culture*. Edited by Peter Lehman, 193–212. New York: Routledge.

___. 2009. *Lynching and Spectacle: Witnessing Racial Violence in America, 1890–1940*. Chapel Hill: University of North Carolina Press.

The Transgender Tipping Point
The Social Death of Sophia Burset

HILARY MALATINO

Laverne Cox, who plays Sophia on the Netflix series *Orange Is the New Black* (*OITNB*), has become perhaps the most prominent transwoman in U.S. pop culture, parlaying her celebrity status into a platform for consciousness-raising and critical engagement of trans issues. This chapter focuses on the dissonance between Sophia's character on *OITNB*—a black transwoman in a woman's prison, receiving hormone therapy, beloved by most other inmates, gradually repairing familial relations from behind prison walls—and the predominant circumstances of actually existing trans and gender non-conforming folks in the prison-industrial complex. These circumstances are shaped by inadequate medical care, placement in facilities that are not gender-confirming, solitary confinement, sexual assault, and harassment. This ensemble of oppressive relations amounts to what Orlando Patterson has termed social death (1982)—a state of being characterized by systematic violence, routine humiliation, and alienation from communities of support, exacerbating what legal scholar and trans activist Dean Spade (2011) has called the "maldistribution of life chances" (126) that already structure the conditions of existence for many trans folk, particularly trans people of color. *OITNB*, in its fabrication of a kinder, gentler prison-industrial complex, serves as a complex mediator for the engagement of trans issues, simultaneously calling attention to certain injustices while painting a much friendlier, more livable image of what navigating the prison-industrial complex is like for trans and gender nonconforming folk. The show subverts certain tropes of transfeminine representation—defying, for instance, representations of transwomen as intentionally deceptive and villainous or wholly victimized—while relying on stereotypes of black feminine strength that serve to minimize the traumatic events Sophia Burset experiences.

95

"For your own good": Segregating the Superwoman

Season 3 of *Orange Is the New Black* is drawing to a close. I've been sitting on my couch for hours, concocting new ways to fold and unfold my limbs, which are starting to ache something serious from being held in this perch. On the television, the vast majority of the inmates at Litchfield Correctional Facility, through a gracefully timed staff strike that coincides with perimeter fence repairs, find themselves able to access the lake that sits on prison property, but on the wrong side of the barbed wire, essentially preventing access for most all of the inmates. Norma Romano—"Magic Norma"—spots this gap in the fence and makes a run for it. The other inmates in the prison yard watch, gradually catching on that Norma is making a break for the lake, and all onlookers eventually join her in her gallop to the shore. What began as a small rivulet of women in brown streaming down to the lake becomes a flood; within minutes, nearly every inmate is in the water, in full prison garb, splashing, swimming, laughing, holding hands. They dub the lake "Freedom Lake." The season ends with a wide-angle shot of these bathing, ecstatic women. The waters of Freedom Lake are quite obviously a spiritual balm; this moment is a cleansing, a christening, a rebirth, a healing of wounds. The inmates, despite all the drama of the previous three seasons, are together experiencing the joy wrought by the gentle freshwater waves, the bright sunlight, the sensation of lightness that floating on one's back and staring at the sky brings. It is a beautiful but tense moment—we assume they will be forcefully returned to the prison momentarily, and—tellingly—not a single woman attempts escape, doubtful they could make a break and not be picked up by correctional officers or the police in short order. It is a moment of severely truncated freedom.

There are a couple of conspicuous absences here, though, and one of them is the character of Sophia Burset—a black trans woman played Laverne Cox. Sophia runs a salon in the prison, and is at Litchfield on account of credit card fraud—she used the misappropriated funds to finance her transition. She has a son named Michael, and remains married to the woman she began a relationship with prior to transition—Crystal. Sophia Burset is one of the first trans women of color we've seen on popular television who has not been relegated to a prop, simple plot device, or hackneyed stereotype. The Gay and Lesbian Alliance Against Defamation (GLAAD) has catalogued a decade of trans representation on television and found that, out of

102 episodes and non-recurring storylines of scripted television that contained transgender characters, 54% of those were categorized as containing negative representations at the time of their airing. An additional 35% were categorized at ranging from "problematic" to "good," while only 12% were considered groundbreaking, fair and accurate [GLAAD 2015].

Their report goes on to highlight that

transgender characters were cast in a "victim" role at least 40% of the time; transgender characters were cast as killers or villains in at least 21% of the catalogued episodes and storylines; the most common profession transgender characters were depicted as having was that of sex workers, which a fifth of all characters were depicted as (20%); [and] anti-transgender slurs, language and dialogue was present in at least 61% of the catalogued episodes and storylines [GLAAD 2015].

The character of Sophia Burset is vastly dissimilar from the types of trans characters so frequently written. She is not presented as victimized, evil, deceptive, or pathological. She isn't a cold-blooded killer, nor is she a sex worker. As a result of this more subtle, humanized depiction, Laverne Cox has been charged with the task of representation and advocacy for trans folk, and for trans women of color in particular. She has also, along the way, become the first full-blown black trans celebrity in the United States.

Where is Sophia, then, while her fellow inmates frolic in the waves, enjoying this small bit of freedom and embodied pleasure? She is in solitary confinement, where she has been placed (ostensibly for her own good) following a group beating motivated quite explicitly by transphobia. Her placement in solitary comes after she approaches Joe Caputo, warden of Litchfield, and demands the firing of correctional officer Sikowitz, who witnessed but failed to intervene in the beating, as well as "crisis and sensitivity training for all the guards." Her demands fall on deaf ears, with Caputo already predisposed to mechanisms that serve to punish the victim. Their conversation begins grudgingly, with Caputo declaring, "I don't need this right now, inmate. I'm developing a fucking ulcer." He grants that he understands her beating was, in essence, a hate crime, and attributes it to a "herd mentality" governed by the notion that "people don't like what they can't understand." His initial solution is to "have the guards keep a closer eye" on her, so that they'll be "ready if anything starts up." Sophia cuts through the doublespeak of this proposition instantly, responding, "So, basically, you're putting me under surveillance?" Caputo contends that there's not much else he can do; Sophia answers this assertion with her demands. Caputo tells her he sympathizes with her, but that she has to be realistic about the recourse to the incident, particularly given the financial stranglehold the recently-privatized prison has been placed wherein they've been charged with the task of maximizing profit. Sophia threatens a lawsuit; Caputo argues that the company that has acquired the prison has teams of lawyers ready to squash her case. Sophia has another recourse, though—going public with the story, drawing bad publicity for the prison as well as its parent corporation, the Management and Corrections Corporation (MCC). She threatens to approach the Post with the headline "She-Male Jail Fail: Balls to the Wall in Tranny Prison Brawl" before telling Caputo to fuck off.

Later in the episode, Sophia approaches an old friend, Sister Jane Ingalls—a political prisoner, a nun arrested for protest at a nuclear facility—for solace and advice. She opens up to Sister Ingalls about the fragility of her inclusion in prison life. "Everybody acts cool most of the time. 'Oh Sophia, hit me with the gossip! What do you think about bangs, Sophia?' You start to feel like one of the girls. But then something turns, and you realize you're still a freak, and you'll never be one of them." Sophia goes on to articulate her rage, her desire for revenge, but Sister Ingalls encourages her to model non-violent resistance, to not give the fellow inmates the satisfaction of seeing her unravel. Sophia is disappointed by the paucity of the Sister's recommendation given the intensity of the situation. Together, they cry—the Sister motivated by empathy, Sophia motivated by hurt and frustration.

As the episode unravels, the corporate higher-ups get word of Sophia's publicity threat; the recommendation is for them to place her in solitary. They rationalize it, mirroring the doublespeak of Caputo's recommendation of surveillance, as being "for her own good," some time alone to get herself together and calm down in the aftermath of her beating while also granting that it is the only possible response given the impossibility of preventing transphobia amongst the prison population.

This episode is one of the first moments throughout the first three seasons where intense transphobic violence occurs, one of the first moments wherein the prison experience of Sophia Burset comes close to approximating the accounts given by imprisoned trans folks of color, who report consistent harassment, high incidences of segregation, sexual and physical violence, and fear of reprisal if they avail themselves of legal assistance to address these issues (National Center for Transgender Equality 2015). Throughout the first three seasons, up until this moment, the Litchfield population—inmates and staff alike, has generally accepted Sophia. She certainly suffers through routinized microaggressions, which typically take the form of misgendering (referring to folks as the gender they were assigned at birth, rather than the gender they actually identify as), prurient and invasive questioning about genitalia, and stereotyping, as well as the docking of her hormones by prison physicians (for fear of liver damage, ostensibly), but these microaggressions are few and far between. These instances work, narratively, to shore up a sense of Sophia as a survivor, tough, discerning; they work in the service of testifying to her character, her fundamental steeliness as well as her fundamental goodness, manifested in her ability to rise above the fray, not lose her temper, not be coerced into sexual exchange with correctional officer Mendez in return for him smuggling in estrogen. We never see Sophia injured, out of control, or allowing her rage, fear, or sorrow to get the better of her.

Sophia is thus figured as the quintessential black superwoman—that figure Michele Wallace (1999) theorized as a "fundamental image" that emerges from the "intricate web of mythology that surrounds the black woman" (154). This image of black femininity that figures black women as possessed of "inordinate strength, with an ability for tolerating an unusual amount of misery and heavy, distasteful work. This woman does not have the same fears, weaknesses, and insecurities as other women, but believes herself to be and is, in fact, stronger emotionally than most men" (154)—but with a twist. Sophia's rearing and socialization as male renders her a kind of super-superwoman; one who has internalized norms of black masculinity and can utilize this reservoir of knowledge in conjunction with her femininity, becoming, indeed, "stronger emotionally than most men." This incorporation of black masculine socialization is in evidence when, on multiple occasions, her wife implores her "man up," and be a better father to her son; we repeatedly see her in the act of fulfilling the footsteps of the absent father—despite the fact that she is the agent behind this absence. The trope of the absent father, and its links to the myth of the black superwoman, is long-standing; what comprises the supposed superhumanity that Michele Wallace critiques is this phenomenon of fulfilling duties and enacting behaviors that are, hegemonically, coded as masculine—hard labor, the disciplining of children, emotional stoicism—in addition to the performance of physical and emotional labor traditionally coded as feminine. Sophia is, in a sense, a super-superwoman; she is charged with the task of filling the shoes of the missing father, which is intensified by her guilt and anxiety over actually being this missing father. While Sophia's character resists many of the stereotypes that accrue to transwomen of color, this resistance relies on a revision of the problematic trope of the black superwoman that has long roots in the popular representation of black femininity.

Untangling Tropes of Transfeminine Representation

Sophia is married, monogamous, not involved in survival sex work or any other outlawed trades, and striving to be a good parent to her one child. These facts alone distance her greatly from the vast majority of popular transfeminine representation, which tend to fall into one of two tropes described by Talia Mae Bettcher: "evil deceivers" or "make believers." That is, trans folk are portrayed as, alternately, deliberately fooling folks into believing they are "real" men and women, or acting "as-if" they were. As Bettcher (2007) explains,

Fundamental to transphobic representations of transpeople as deceivers is an appearance-reality contrast between gender presentation and sexed body. For example, an MTF who is taken to misalign gender presentation with the sexed body can be regarded as "really a boy," appearances notwithstanding. Here, we see identity enforcement embedded within a context of possible deception, revelation, and disclosure. In this framework, gender presentation (attire, in particular) constitutes a gendered appearance, whereas the sexed body constitutes the hidden, sexual reality. Expressions such as "a man who dresses like a woman," "a man who lives as a woman," and even "a woman who is biologically male" all effectively inscribe this distinction [48].

Sophia falls outside these typical transphobic representations. There is no great reveal of her status as trans, à la *The Crying Game* or *Ace Ventura: Pet Detective*. There is no crime with its basis in transphobic responses to supposed deception, as in crime procedurals like *Law and Order: SVU,* or trans biopics like *Boy's Don't Cry,* or *A Girl Like Me: The Gwen Araujo Story*.

The framework of reading and representing trans embodiment along the lines of deception or pretending, according to this "appearance-reality contrast between gender presentation and sexed body," produces a double-bind for trans folks, where they are forced into a position wherein they can "disclose 'who one is' and come out as a pretender or masquerader, or refuse to disclose (be a deceiver) and run the risk of forced disclosure, the effect of which is exposure as a liar" (Bettcher 2007, 50). Much of the drama surrounding popular representations of trans subjects hinges on the tension produced by this double-bind. It isn't surprising that drama is so frequently fabricated from this double-bind, as the existential consequences of it are dire. If one opts for visibility, they risk "having one's life constructed as fictitious; and so failing to have one's own identifications taken seriously; being viewed in a highly condescending way; and being the subject of violence and even murder" (50). However, opting for invisibility—going stealth—carries with it the consequences of "living in constant fear of exposure, extreme violence, and death; disclosure as a deceiver or liar (possibly through forced genital exposure); being the subject of violence and even murder; and being held responsible for this violence" (50).

The path-breaking nature of trans representation on *OITNB* stems from the way the writers have sidestepped this double-bind and, coincidentally, most all of the hackneyed tropes that have historically shaped popular depictions of transfeminine subjects. They don't produce drama from a visibility/invisibility dyad, and they refuse to represent Sophia as a victim. Rather, Sophia is an out transwoman from her moment of introduction and never dissimulates or obscures her past; yet despite this visibility, she is, up until the incident during Season 3 described above, relatively insulated from violence. She is, however, still set apart from the other inmates by virtue of being trans and out, experiencing the phenomenon of having her gender identification not taken quite seriously, her identity construed as a not-fully-authentic form of femininity—not quite pretending or deceiving, but still decidedly exoticized and Othered.

This is, in fact, a holdover from Piper Kerman's memoir (2011). When the character of Sophia—who, in the memoir, is named Vanessa Robinson—is introduced, Kerman writes that "the Camp was abuzz. The he-she is coming up!!!" (181) and goes on to paint a vivid portrait of Vanessa that is rife with exoticization:

> I soon got my first glimpse of Vanessa—all six foot, four inches of blond, coffee-colored, balloon-breasted almost-all-woman that she was. An admiring crowd of young women had gathered around her, and she lapped up the attention. This was no unassuming "shim" unfortunately incarcerated and trying to get along: Vanessa was a full-blown diva. It was as if someone had shot Mariah Carey through a matter-disrupter and plunked her down in our midst [181].

Kerman consistently stresses Vanessa's links to gay male culture, highlighting her participation in the Miss Gay Black America pageant, describing her as "drag-queen funny" (183), and ruminating on the fact that she reminds her of the "gay males and freshly females" she had "known in San Francisco and New York—smart, snappy, witty, curious about the world" (201). Kerman quite obviously lacks a framework for understanding trans subjectivity beyond these insidiously de-authenticating comparisons to gay masculinity and drag culture; while ostensibly well-meaning, she refuses to actually dignify Vanessa Robinson's gender identity, consistently framing it as a pale approximation of authentic womanhood. At another moment in the text, she mentions how unsettled she is by the phenomenon of tattooed makeup—which she spots on several Latina inmates—with this stunningly transphobic sentence: "a significant percentage of the Spanish women had tattooed eyeliner, lipliner, and eyebrows, an effect I found unnerving—I associated it with Meatpacking District transsexual hookers" (110). Kerman has two strategies, it seems, for understanding trans femininity—hyperbolizing or excoriating, both of which function as forms of establishing trans femininity as unlike other modes of feminine embodiment: they are either overdone, larger-than-life, diva-style gender expressions (Vanessa) or done poorly, trashy, and "unnerving" ("Meatpacking District transsexual hookers"). These are classic othering strategies, and both serve to de-authenticate transfeminine gender expressions.

Another de-authenticating strategy for othering trans women hinges on the phenomenon of sexualization. We have been systematically fed hypersexualized images of trans women, typically framed through their involvement in economies of survival sex work. As Traci Abbott (2013) explains, transwomen are

> sexualized and stigmatized due to their role in prostitution and pornography, but even more by popular narratives which sensationalize these stereotypes further ... our cultural fascination with "she-males," a pejorative, but common term for transwomen who retain their male genitalia, highlights how transwomen in particular are fetishized and denigrated as "sexually available and disposable" while dismissing the many reasons transpersons may be unable or unwilling to

surgically change their genitalia, notably the cost of surgery, the limitations of medical intervention, and the age and parental consent requirements for medical treatment [33].

Sophia Burset breaks this representative mold as well. She is not in prison for sex work—has not, in fact, ever engaged in it—but rather comes from a respectable, lower middle class household, held a blue-collar job, struggles to be a good parent. While she did engage in illegal activity to fund her transition—quite like trans folk engaged in survival sex work—her crime doesn't carry with it quite the same risk of sexualized opprobrium or deviance. She enters prison, significantly, post-transition, with all major surgical procedures firmly in her past. Thus, she cannot be made an object of prurient speculation—in the few moments that she finds herself under scrutiny, she shuts that shit down with grace and aplomb.

Furthermore, she remains committed to her wife and family, even as her relationship with Crystal has become pointedly non-sexual. In an early episode, Crystal begs Sophia not to have bottom surgery, to keep her penis intact for her wife. Sophia, quite understandably, refuses. This is one of the only explicitly sexualized moments Sophia's character experiences, and it functions as a death knell for the eroticism in her primary relationship. Sophia's relationship with Crystal upsets the hypersexualized stereotypes that shape popular representations of transwomen, functioning instead as an instance of what Traci Abbott has called the "trans/romance dilemma."

This dilemma occurs in media that seeks to offer "an empathetic view of transpersons that contrasts with the stereotypical parodies and killers found in more traditional narratives in television and film," but ultimately fails to "realistically represent the transgender experience and create empathy for the trans characters because each director tries to avoid the taint of deviant sexuality" (Abbott 2013, 35). We most often see transwomen represented in romantic forays with cisgendered, heterosexual men. Abbott's theorization of the "trans/romance dilemma" focuses on the ways in which sexual interest in transwomen is often represented as a deviation from heterosexuality for these cisgendered male romantic interests. When media focuses on the crisis that attraction to a transwoman prompts in these cis male subjects, there is an obvious problem: "the director's strategies promote the delegitimization of a trans character's gender identity so audiences recategorize it as the biological or birth sex" (35). This is exacerbated by the fact that the actresses cast in roles structured by the "trans/romance dilemma" are often cis women themselves. The audience is strategically encouraged to delegitimate the gender identity of transwomen through both this focus on the moment of sexual crisis in cisgendered male subjects, as well as through the refusal to cast actual transwomen in these roles structured by the dilemma Abbott outlines.

While Sophia's character resists the vagaries of hypersexualization, as well as the most banal iterations of the "trans/romance dilemma," the pendulum swings firmly in the other direction. She is desexualized. Her transition and subsequent imprisonment destroys her erotic intimacy with her wife. On a television show that centers lesbian, bisexual, and queer femininities, Sophia is left radically outside of these circles of intimacy, eroticism, and attraction. Her only significant friendship is, tellingly, with another desexualized inmate—a nun. It is shocking to me that on a television show that so frequently centers the erotic web created between and among the inmates, visitors, and prison staff, Sophia would never become involved—no crushes, no liaisons, no flirtations. It's hard to chalk it up to a simple avoidance of deviant sexuality, as one of the commendable aspects of *OITNB* is its commitment to displaying sexual diversity. Yet it seems that transfeminine sexuality remains an unbreachable frontier for the writers and directors.

We can think of this as an example of what trans activist and porn star Drew DeVeaux has termed the "cotton ceiling." Blogger and National Center for Transgender Equality staffer Natalie Reed (2012) provides a good synopsis of the term, writing that the "cotton ceiling" has to do with

> how trans women are perceived and represented. For example, trans men are often openly regarded as being sexy and hot within queer communities, being the subject of things like calendars and pin-ups and erotica. Trans women, on the other hand, are almost never permitted acknowledgment or representation in such communities as sexual beings. We carry a sort of image of being stuffy, boring, slightly icky, and ultimately eunuch-like things. We're allowed into the parties, but we sit quiet and lonely in the corner. This ends up being a problem not in that we're desperately eager to be sexually objectified (we get enough of that from the straight cis male world), but that this act of conceptualizing us as de-sexed and unfuckable is directly attached to larger systems of oppression, dehumanization and invalidation we face.

The "cotton ceiling"—referring to cotton underwear—is a way of shorthanding the phenomenon of desexualizing transwomen in queer spaces. In *OITNB*, we see the trans/romance dilemma combine with the phenomena of the cotton ceiling. Sophia comes to inhabit a non-sexual space in her marriage on account of her transition—thus violating the formerly heterosexual organization of the relationship, and proving the point that the desirability of trans characters often abdicates to their gender assigned at birth, as in the trans/romance dilemma. However, when she finds herself in the queer space of Litchfield, she is framed as a friend, a familiar, but also as entirely off-the-market, erotically. As she confesses to Sister Ingalls, "you start to feel like one of the girls. But then something turns, and you realize you're still a freak, and you'll never be one of them." Her exclusion from the complicated web of eroticized intimacy that undergirds life at Litchfield is definitively a mechanism of marking her otherness in relation to cis-femininity, a vivid illustration of the cotton ceiling.

I want to imagine, for a moment, a different narrative—one where Crystal's desire for Sophia was not contingent on the presence of a penis, wherein she didn't narrate her desire as something that should trump Sophia's desire for bottom surgery, where she didn't urge Sophia to "keep it" for her. I want to imagine a narrative where, when Sophia enters the world of Litchfield, she is not desexualized, not reduced to playing sage-mother and hand-maiden to cis-women, but is, instead, treated "like one of the girls," included in the intimacies, erotic and otherwise, that cement the homosocial female bonding on the show. I want to imagine a world wherein Sophia Burset is more fully included in the social circuits that comprise life in this fictional prison, this kinder, gentler prison-lite, wherein the realities of life that confront the majority of imprisoned trans folk are decidedly absent. Imagining this other narrative is useful, as a counterpoint to the actual conditions trans folk encounter within the prison-industrial complex.

On the one hand, I've been critiquing the representational politics of Sophia Burset's character for lurching towards desexualization in order to avoid the stereotypical hypersexualization that so often characterizes popular trans representation, arguing that both forms of writing trans characters are methods of othering. However, one of the major issues with *OITNB* is the way it foregrounds the sex lives of the prisoners, offering a mainstream version of lesbian prison-porn. As Noah Gittel (2014) writes, "*Orange Is the New Black* toes a very fine line. It indulges in the lesbian/prison fantasy by depicting beautiful women in various states of undress, while also displaying a winking self-awareness about this titillation, which allows viewers to feel in on the joke about the degrading nature of the sexual material, while also still indulging in it." In doing so, the show reinscribes cis-sexual, white, gender normative beauty ideals; as Gittel argues, one of the main reasons it becomes difficult to read *OITNB* as thoroughly feminist is because "the only featured characters asked to disrobe on *Orange Is the New Black* are those who adhere to our society's rigid and unrealistic definition of female beauty."

It's productive to consider Sophia's relationship to these norms of hypersexualized feminine beauty. Her character is informed by a long tradition of representing transfemininity as good, as desirable, through its attachment to domesticity, modesty, and monogamy: that is, the mores of white bourgeois feminine respectability. Emily Skidmore refers to this representative trope as that of the "good transsexual," and traces its racialized history, detailing how it has shaped popular representations of white transwomen—beginning with Christine Jorgensen and Tamara Rees, both of whom consistently demonstrated their allegiance to white heteronormativity in order to maintain respectability and be perceived as "just like other girls." Skidmore looks back at the tabloid representation of trans women of color and places it in a position of dissonance with the trope of the "good transsexual." Skidmore (2011) argues that "when Latina and African-American transwomen appeared in the media in the mid-twentieth century, they did so as objects of ridicule" (295); this ridicule hinged on their failure to live up to the racialized and classed barometer of respectability that is the trope of the "good transsexual."

Transfeminine distance from this trope was typically marked through hypersexualization, a marked propensity for confrontation, a lack of modesty, or some other refusal of white bourgeois norms of feminine respectability. Thus, it is necessary to consider how Sophia Burset (and Laverne Cox) are positioned in relation to the trope of the "good transsexual." The emphasis on Sophia's domestic life, her ostensible monogamy to a wife who has, inarguably, moved on, and her position as friend, confidante, and wisdom-dispenser to the other women of Litchfield can certainly be read as aspiring to the status of "good transsexual." Indeed, in a public dialogue between bell hooks and Laverne Cox at the New School, hooks calls attention to Cox's negotiation of hegemonic forms of white femininity, as well as her tarrying with the politics of respectability. hooks calls attention to Cox's embrace of "traditional femininity" (hooks and Cox 2014) and discusses the difficult position Cox occupies, as a highly visible trans woman working in entertainment, saying she "has an awareness of the need to decolonize while working within a very colonizing system." Cox discusses her negotiation of the politics of respectability, saying that she's "already black and trans," thus she "can't be too political." She also mentions Janet Mock's commentary on her reticence to discuss race in the public eye. Mock has apparently told Cox, "You speak so elegantly about race but yet you so rarely talk about it publicly"; Cox admits, by way of response, "It scares me to go on national television and use the phrase 'imperialist white supremacist patriarchy.'" This interchange speaks to Cox's extremely self-aware negotiation of the public sphere, her awareness of the limitations that come along with being perceived as a "good transsexual," particularly as a trans woman of color. If she comes across, publicly, as angry, forthrightly sexual, confrontational, intellectual, feminist, or something shy of hyper-feminine, she risks public censure and opprobrium. Sophia Burset, too, navigates similar difficulties within the walls of Litchfield.

Trans Folk, Prison and Social Death

It's important, however, to read Sophia's desexualization as something more than a problematic trope that enables her character to be well-received, popular. There's nothing threatening to heterosexist, white-and-cis-supremacy about watching a black trans woman dish advice and do hair, even though it feels revolutionary to seeing an actual trans woman play one on a series. It's necessary to remember that we're watching a dramedy about the prison-industrial complex, and that this collective fixation on sex and intimacy in prison is enabled by the uniquely light-hearted take on prison life that structures most episodes of *OITNB*. If the viewer is interested in what the actual prison conditions are for trans and gender non-conforming inmates, *OITNB* gives them a skewed perspective, one that softens—to the point of misrepresenting—the issues many trans and gender non-conforming prisoners confront.

My main reason for emphasizing Sophia's desexualization is because I understand it as a harbinger of what's to come for her character—it is a premonitory mechanism of exclusion from the rich textures of daily life in Litchfield. Sophia is presented as additive and adjunct to that everyday existence, as hand-maiden to the cis women of the prison (as if to illustrate this, Laverne Cox's name is left off the roster of actors that runs during the opening credits—despite her being a regular on the show from the first season forward). This adjunctive mode of presentation presages her later, full exclusion from the daily life of the prison—her placement in solitary, for "her own protection." This is a double segregation, a double isolation: her entrance into Litchfield has already severed her, significantly, from communities of support and care located beyond the prison walls; now, she is excised from the minimal support and care she was able to experience from her fellow inmates. This is, in no uncertain terms, an illustration of social death.

Scholar and prison abolitionist Joshua Price understands imprisonment as a form of social death. Social death—a concept coined by Orlando Patterson in his book *Slavery and Social Death*—is constituted by three aspects: subjection to "systematic violence, to generalized humiliating treatment, and to 'natal alienation'" (Price 2015, 5). Natal alienation refers to "severance from ancestors and children," which came—with slavery—in the form of destruction of familial bonds, mechanisms of inheritance, and transmission of heritage. Prison, similar to slavery, erodes these relationships. As Price articulates, "the prison separates people from communities of support, and from their parents and children … natal alienation forces people in prison into a structure of vulnerability, subject to direct and indirect violence and humiliation" (5). The experience of imprisonment, then, bears all of the marks of social death—it serves to isolate people, subject them to systematic violence and generalized humiliating treatment. This is key to grasping the arguments of prison abolitionists who understand prison as an extension of plantation slavery (Davis 2003; Alexander 2012): both institutions are shaped by the phenomenon of social death, and are characterized by the brutal, forced expropriation of labor, the destruction of community, and manifest dehumanization.

If the phenomenon of social death holds true for most prisoners—with, perhaps, the exception of Piper Kerman, whose social world seems to flourish within the confines of Litchfield—it is an experience that is intensified for trans prisoners of color. When considering what constitutes the violence and humiliation that characterizes of social death, it is important to not consider it as solely an interactional, one-on-one phenomenon—i.e., a corrections officer abusing an inmate. Structural violence—such as that which manifests in poor health care and lack of educational opportunities—significantly mold the experience of social death. So does the stigma associated with imprisonment, which informs life upon release, robbing former prisoners of certain rights and contributing to ongoing discrimination—in employment, interpersonal relationships, and through interface with state agencies.

For trans women of color, the experience of imprisonment often intensifies the already-ongoing existential experience of social death. As Beth Richie points out in *Arrested Justice: Black Women, Violence, and America's Prison Nation* (2012),

> The further a women's sexuality, age, class, criminal background, and race are from hegemonic norms, the more likely it is that they will be harmed—and the more likely that their harm will not be taken seriously by their community, by anti-violence programs, or by the general public ... [they] will be left to cope without formal institutional support. And for that, they will be punished. The punishment—the isolation, further stigmatization, or long prison sentence—is made possible by the social climate that constitutes the prison nation [16].

Richie opens *Arrested Justice* by recounting the stories of multiple black women who were sentenced to prison—often receiving radically disproportionate terms—for attempting to individually resist or mitigate circumstances of institutional and interpersonal violence, harm, and neglect. She discusses the case of the New Jersey 4, black, working-class lesbians from New Jersey who, on an evening out in the West Village in New York City, found themselves the target of a homophobic attack—one which began verbally and resulted in physical violence. Richie recounts that, although "eyewitnesses confirm that the young women acted in self-defense against a blatant anti-gay attack," all seven women who were the victims of the attack "were arrested and charged with crimes such as 'gang' assault" (13). Three took plea agreements, and the remaining four "went to trial and were found guilty" (13) for defending themselves against homophobic violence! We see this story again and again with queer, trans, and gender non-conforming folks of color; stories where folks are driven to self-defense on account of a lack of communal and institutional support and the resultant heightened vulnerability to violence, and where they are then prosecuted for the very resistance that is their only recourse.

This experience of consistent maltreatment, communal divestment, and lack of institutional support is corroborated by the life stories of trans prisoners collected in Eric Stanley and Nat Smith's *Captive Genders: Trans Embodiment and the Prison Industrial Complex*. The text is rife with these types of accounts; take the paradigmatic tale told by Candi Raine Sweet in her piece "Being an Incarcerated Trans Person: Shouldn't People Care?" (2011):

> I was born in New York State and deserted by my family. I was really raised by many group homes and residential treatment centers. I have been homeless and I am still currently poor. While in prison, I have been cut by other prisoners for refusing to perform sexual acts for them, and I have been beaten and sexually assaulted (sodomized with the nightstick) by correctional staff. I see first hand the very issues that the system needs to change [185].

In another narrative recounted by Stephen Dillon (2011), we see many of the same issues arise. Dillon writes about R, an imprisoned transwoman that Dillon corresponds with, who "was born into the foster system and passed from family to family" (175), raped by her stepfather at 13, and, "like so many children subjected to sexual violence and extreme poverty, began using drugs, running away, and stealing" (175). While in jail, she was "beaten within an inch of her life by seventeen prisoners and raped by six" (175).

For trans folks, imprisonment often amounts to moving out of the frying pan and into the fire; the stories of female bonding that form the bulk of *OITNB*'s narrative arcs are decidedly absent when we look at the stories of imprisoned trans folk—particularly trans women, who are often placed in men's facilities. The closest we get, in *OITNB*, is Sophia's placement in solitary at the end of Season 3; but even this is framed as a moment she suffers in a dignified manner; we're left feeling as if she's keeping her head up, no matter what, that she is above the trauma of the milieu she finds herself in. This is a hyperbolized narrative of survivorship, and it clouds and misrepresents, through its narrative of exceptional individualism, the real life struggles of trans folk caught up in the prison-industrial complex. Dean Spade, Alexander Lee, and Morgan Bassichis, in the excellent essay "Building an Abolitionist Trans & Queer Movement With Everything We've Got" (2011), make quite clear that "queer and trans people are disproportionately policed, arrested, and imprisoned, and face high rates of violence in state custody from officials as well as other imprisoned or detained people" (19), and this vulnerability to policing, surveillance, and imprisonment stems directly from what Spade, elsewhere, has called the "maldistribution of life chances" (126) that shape the experience of trans and gender non-conforming folk. The ensemble of phenomena that structures the maldistribution of life chances includes "high rates of unemployment, homelessness, and imprisonment," as well as "trans vulnerability to premature death" (Spade, Lee, and Bassichis 2011, 37) on account of poverty, transphobic violence, inadequate or inaccessible health-care, as well as discrimination, harassment, and neglect at the hands of medical professionals.

With the character of Sophia, we are attuned to only the tip of a very large iceberg—while she does encounter transphobic violence, is refused hormones, and placed in solitary confinement for "her own protection," she also maintains the support of a former partner, is employed, has a home to return to, and is imprisoned for credit card fraud that enabled her transition. Most imprisoned trans women have lacked the financial means for the surgical and hormonal procedures Sophia has availed herself of, and this lack of ability to pass—that is, the inability to be stealth, to be read as cisgendered—is often made cause for transphobic violence; many are significantly without a support network of family and friends, and encounter routine institutionalized transphobia in navigating their everyday lives. When the novelty of trans representation in the case of Sophia Burset is celebrated, it is important to recognize the ways in which the transfeminine experience of the prison-industrial complex has been softened, sugar-coated, and made more palatable to mainstream audiences. *OITNB* cajoles the viewer into conceptualizing Sophia as a strong, black woman, able to rise above the intersecting adversities she encounters. Through this framing of her character, the show elides, ignores, and sidesteps the realities of systemic, structural oppression that results in the maldistribution of life chances for trans women of color.

REFERENCES

Abbott, Traci. 2013. "The Trans/Romance Dilemma in *Transamerica* and Other Films." *The Journal of American Culture* 36.1, 32–41.

Alexander, Michelle. 2012. *The New Jim Crow: Mass Incarceration in the Age of Colorblindness.* New York: The New Press.

Bettcher, Talia Mae. 2007. "Evil Deceivers and Make-Believers: On Transphobic Violence and the Politics of Illusion." *Hypatia* 22.3, 43–65.

Davis, Angela. 2003. *Are Prisons Obsolete?* New York: Seven Stories Press.

Dillon, Stephen. 2011. "'The Only Freedom I Can See': Imprisoned Queer Writing and the Politics of the Unimaginable." In *Captive Genders: Trans Embodiment and the Prison Industrial Complex,* edited by Eric Stanley and Nat Smith. 169–184. Edinburgh: AK Press.

Gay and Lesbian Alliance Against Defamation. 2015. "Victims or Villains: Examining Ten Years of Transgender Images on Television." Glaad.org. http://www.glaad.org/publications/victims-or-villains-examining-ten-years-transgender-images-television.

Gittel, Noah. 2014. "The One Thing Keeping 'Orange Is the New Black' from Being the Most Feminist Show on TV." *Arts.Mic.* July 10. http://mic.com/articles/93117/the-one-thing-keeping-orange-is-the-new-black-from-being-the-most-feminist-show-on-television.

hooks, bell, and Laverne Cox. 2014. "bell hooks and Laverne Cox in a Public Dialogue at the New School." YouTube video, 1:36:08, posted by The New School, October 13. https://www.youtube.com/watch?v=9oMmZIJijgY.

Kerman, Piper. 2011. *Orange Is the New Black.* New York: Spiegel & Grau.

National Center for Transgender Equality. 2015. "A Blueprint for Equality: Reducing Incarceration and Ending Abuse in Prisons." Transequality.org. http://transequality.org/sites/default/files/docs/resources/NCTE_Blueprint_2015_Prisons.pdf.

Orange Is the New Black. 2015. "Trust No Bitch." Netflix, June 11.

Patterson, Orlando. 1982. *Slavery and Social Death*. Cambridge: Harvard University Press.

Price, Joshua. 2015. *Prison and Social Death*. New Brunswick: Rutgers University Press.

Reed, Natalie. 2012. "Caught Up in Cotton." *Free Thought Blogs*. April 4. http://free thoughtblogs.com/nataliereed/2012/04/04/caught-up-in-cotton/#ixzz3hCqc TGHs.

Richie, Beth. 2012. *Arrested Justice: Black Women, Violence, and America's Prison Nation*. New York: New York University Press.

Skidmore, Emily. 2011. "Constructing the 'Good Transsexual': Christine Jorgensen, Whiteness, and Heteronormativity in the Mid-Twentieth-Century Press." *Feminist Studies* 37.2, 270–300.

Spade, Dean. 2011. *Normal Life: Administrative Violence, Critical Trans Politics, and the Limits of the Law*. Brooklyn: South End Press.

Spade, Dean, Alexander Lee, and Morgan Bassichis. 2011. "Building an Abolitionist Trans and Queer Movement with Everything We've Got." *Captive Genders: Trans Embodiment and the Prison Industrial Complex*, edited by Eric Stanley and Nat Smith. 15–40. Edinburgh: AK Press.

Sweet, Candi Raine. 2011. "Being an Incarcerated Transperson: Shouldn't People Care?" *Captive Genders: Trans Embodiment and the Prison Industrial Complex*, edited by Eric Stanley and Nat Smith. 185–188. Edinburgh: AK Press.

Wallace, Michelle. 1999. *Black Macho and the Myth of the Superwoman*. London: Verso.

All in the (Prison) Family

Genre Mixing and Queer Representation

KYRA HUNTING

In the last episode of the third season of *Orange Is the New Black* (*OITNB*) Piper's brother, upon seeing her new tattoo, remarks, "Your prison mistress gave you a prison tat. You are turning into a trope" (S: 3 E: 13). Initially, *OITNB* appears to contain some of the oldest tropes of lesbian representation drawn from the "women-in-prison" genre, tropes that have often been pressed into homophobic or exploitative service (Fratini 2008; Shai 2013). However, *OITNB* reimagines these tropes in novel ways, drawing out the queer, feminist, and revolutionary possibilities present in earlier "exploitation" texts identified by scholars (Mayne 2000). It achieves this by building on the more feminist evolution of the women-in-prison genre, seen in *Bad Girls*, while also departing from key genre elements, taking up instead tropes and thematics from an entirely different set of texts that belong to an emerging genre I call the "Lesbian Family Program." Through the combining of key genre elements from the women-in-prison genre with influences from the Lesbian Family Program, *OITNB* is able to expand on the queer elements of the women-in-prison genre and more substantively fulfill its potential for "homonormative" (Herman 2003) representation. Moreover, it illustrates the way in which examining the potential for genre mixing (Mittel 2004) can reveal genre's potential to impact the ideological and representational possibilities of television texts.

In order to identify the patterns among the texts that provide *OITNB*'s genre influences, I compare three women-in-prison dramas, *Prisoner: Cell Block H* (Australia, 1979–1986), *Bad Girls* (UK, 1999–2006) and *Wentworth* (Australia, 2013-), and four "lesbian family programs," *The L-Word* (U.S., 2004–2009), *Sugar Rush* (2005–2006), *Exes & Ohs* (U.S./Canada, 2007, 2009) and *Lip Service* (UK, 2010–2012). Using content analysis, this study tracks lesbian representations and genre attributes, and uses textual analysis to assess the larger narrative and formal dimensions of each series. These series were drawn from four countries to provide a sufficient number of relevant series to look for patterns and to place *OITNB* in a global context, addressing the critique that analysis of lesbian representation has frequently been U.S.-centric (Beirne 2007, 7).

Televisual Context

The inclusion of non–U.S. series in this analysis is also important because of the history of the women-in-prison narrative in which *OITNB* can be situated. *OITNB* is often framed as groundbreaking in the U.S., and it does constitute the first sustained fictional representation of women-in-prison on U.S. television. However, it follows significant women-in-prison series in the U.K. and Australia. The women-in-prison genre on Anglophone television dates to the 1970s with U.K.'s *Within these Walls* (1974–1978), focused on prison staff, and the Australian *Prisoner: Cell Block H* (1979–1986). *Prisoner* can be considered a forerunner to the *OITNB* for its focus on the prisoners' lives both in and outside of the prison and the limited, and often offensive, depiction of lesbian characters. The U.K.'s *Bad Girls* premiered twenty years later in 1999, marking the first television iteration of the genre to place a lesbian character and relationship centrally and positively in the narrative. *OITNB* marks a continuation and revival of the genre alongside Australia's *Wentworth* (2013-), released two months prior to *OITNB*, a modern reworking of *Prisoner*.

While the earliest television women-in-prison dramas were established overseas, America provided the earliest entry into the lesbian family program "proto-genre": the *L-Word* (2004); the first series where the bulk of the main characters were lesbians and where relationships between gay women were central to the plot. The centralizing of lesbian characters and communities continued with *Sugar Rush* (U.K., 2005–2006), following a fifteen year old's tempestuous and lustful relationship with her best friend; *Exes & Ohs* (U.S./Canada, 2007, 2009), and *Lip Service* (U.K., 2010–2012), both about a group of friends pursuing love, lust, and careers. While the stylish homes, bars, and offices of these series may seem far removed from the cells, yard, and cafeteria of Litchfield Penitentiary, the way in which these series construct women's communities, friendships, and romantic relationships are important for understanding *OITNB*.

Both of these genres have been significant touchstones for queer representations (Beirne 2009, 26) and queer audiences (Pratt 2007, 143; Millbank 2004, 177), and *OITNB* shares distinct features of both genres, drawing and departing from each in ways that shape how *OITNB* depicts women at the margins og society. Criminal justice scholar Dawn Cecil, in "Looking Beyond Caged Heat" (2007), criminal justice scholar Dawn Cecil argues that "the media images about women-in-prison are an important source of storytelling and information" because they are rare and most viewers have such little personal knowledge of the experience of women's prisoners (304). A similar case has been made for the significance of gay and lesbian representations, which often have to stand in for personal experience with gay and lesbian individuals (Gross 2001). *OITNB*, with its broad diversity of central lesbian characters in a prison context, thus takes on a double burden of representation. It succeeds, in large part, due to its status as a generically doubled text drawing on ideologies and tropes from both the women-in-prison drama and lesbian family program to aptly depict both a fictionalized prison experience and the lives of lesbian women.

Genre

OITNB is a dual-generic text, belonging simultaneously to the women-in-prison genre and what I am terming the lesbian family program "proto-genre." I use "proto-genre" here to refer to an emerging cluster of texts that share a number of thematic and formal elements and are discursively linked but for which there is not yet a sufficient number of texts to constitute a genre. The generic definition of *OITNB* has been particularly fraught, leading to debate even at the most basic level; exemplified by the conflict over *OITNB*'s genre designation at the Emmys where it competed as a comedy in 2014 and was ruled a drama the following year (Andreeva 2015). In the contention of Netflix Chief Content Officer Ted Saranos that the series "always defied genre" (Andreeva 2015), we see an emphasis on the instability of *OITNB*'s genre designation whose comedic, dramatic and sexual and political elements shift and mingle. While genres may not be stable or inevitable, this does not make them insignificant. Rather, the textual norms, discursive frames, and reception and production practices surrounding a genre can be significant to the ideological dimensions and cultural circulation of the texts.

The reception and production contexts of the women-in-prison and lesbian family genres share important features. The prison genre has been considered significant and problematic for queer viewers and queer representation (Russo 1987), for featuring both "unparalleled queer eroticism and rampant homophobia" (Wlordaz 2005, 70). Contemporary iterations of the genre have garnered significant lesbian fan followings (Millbank 2004) and lesbian family programs have also been touchstones for extensive LGBT fandoms (Pratt 2007, 143). *OITNB* follows in this tradition—garnering particularly close coverage by the lesbian pop culture website AfterEllen.

These series also share the presence of a female creator. Every women-in-prison series following *Prisoner* has a female creator—*Women in Prison* (Katherine Green), *Bad Girls* (Maureen Chadwick and Anna McManus), *Wentworth* (Laura Radulvich)—as do most lesbian family programs—*The L Word* (Ilene Chaiken), *Sugar Rush* (Katie Baxendale), *Exes and Ohs* (Michelle Paradise), and *Lip Service* (Harriet Braun). *OITNB's* Jenji Kohan follows this tradition. This is particularly notable given the relative paucity of female creators, with only 20 percent of all television series of any genre created by women in 2013 (Lauzen 2014, 2). This production context is significant because it suggests that both of these genres are currently spurred by women's voices, and arguably some of the evolutions in the representation of women-in-prison dramas can be attributed to this change.

While women-in-prison and lesbian family programs share attributes, each genre also has distinct traits. Ann Ciasullo (2008) lays out the standard features associated with the women-in-prison narrative including key character types (the naïve protagonist roped into a crime, the lascivious and sadistic guard, aggressive prison lesbian, benevolent male figure) and stock narrative features (shower scenes, catfights, a minor character's death, and often the protagonist's release to reunite with a man) (197). The lesbian family program's core features generally include the following: a group of lesbians including a promiscuous character, a young or emerging lesbian, a stable couple building a family, and a focus on romantic relationships, friendships between queer women, and familial dynamics. This proto-genre often also includes the inclusion of sex scenes, a playful engagement with sex toys and performance, depictions of homophobia, and politicized female communities.

OITNB highlights key features that the two genres share: a strong focus on the lives of women and a close homo-social environment (Pratt 2007, 139). It also takes and eschews elements from both genres in ways that are ideologically significant. For example, the series displaces the features of the sadistic or lascivious prison matron onto male guards and depict male officers who appear to be a "savior" as revealing themselves to be weak or destructive. Most significantly, *OITNB* stands alone amongst women-in-prison series in that it does not feature a single sexually coercive or violent lesbian character. While Big Boo and Nicky can at first appear to fill this role by being sexually "aggressive," pursuing sex voraciously and even competitively, they differ from this traditional predatory "prison lesbian" in crucial ways; neither woman uses the threat of violence to obtain sex, they do not substantially pursue women who are uninterested in homosexual sex , and they do not pair physical intimidation with their advances, avoiding linking sex with terror in prison. Conversely, the series incorporates features from the lesbian family program like regular sex scenes, using familial language (family, mom, daughter) to describe friends, and a diversity of lesbian characters with different attitudes to relationships and sex.

Each of these shifts are ideologically significant. By erasing the cruel female prison guard and the male savior while increasing the presence of familial language, the value of female community is intensified. Disassociating lesbian characters from coercive sex and including consensual sex scenes creates a more positive image of female sexuality. The prison setting allow *OITNB* to address issues of race and class diversity and power that lesbian family programs often lack (Pratt 2007). What becomes apparent here is the way in which *OITNB's* incorporation of features from both genres allows it to address gaps and ideological problems present in the women-in-prison narrative.

The place of the women-in-prison narrative in the queer cannon is a complicated one. It provides some of the earliest prolonged images of lesbian characters (Beirne 2007, 3) and the closed homo-social environment of the prison provides a context for both queer subtext and for lesbian characters. However, these texts were often structured and harnessed for male titillation and the image of the "prison lesbian" as masculine, violent, and sexually aggressive reinforced negative stereotypes. Nonetheless, according to media scholar Andy Medhurst (2009) these texts were embraced by queer audiences who found opportunities for complexity and camp within them in their reception practice and fan engagement (54, 84). For example, Glyn Davis and Gary Needham (2009) note that the theme song of *Prisoner* was remixed and played and in queer clubs and the stars appeared in LGBT venues (84). Despite these limitations, the stock elements of the women-in-prison genre: the closed women's community, absence of men, prison lesbian, and secret relationships provided the raw material for series like *Bad Girls* and *OITNB* to rework the genre in more feminist directions.

Homonormativity in OITNB

These two genres share an investment in tight homosocial communities. While some scholars have critiqued *The L-Word* for its focus on friendships exclusively between lesbians and bisexuals (Lee and Meyer 2007, 235) for others, the depiction of a distinct lesbian community was not only part of its representational value, but facilitated the building of community around it and similar series (Peters 2011, 201; Pratt 2007, 139–140). Both genres allow for a deeper engagement with the challenges of women and the bonds, both platonic and sexual, that they share because of closed homo-social communities, whether chosen and structurally enforced.

This homo-sociality of these series become an important bridge to what Didi Herman (2003) identifies as the homonormative potential of the women-in-prison series. Herman argues that *Bad Girls* is a homonormative text, similar to series like *Queer as Folk* in its construction of "lesbian and gay sexuality" as "both unremarkable and, potentially, desirable" (143) and notes five primary ways "in which *BG's* lesbian lens is highlighted: "diversity of representation, sexual agency, the portrayal of an erotically-charged love story with a happy ending, an insider commonsense, and the representation of family" (148). Problematically, Herman ignores or dismisses some of *Bad Girls* limitations in this respect, in particular the extent to which lesbian relationships are largely sexless either by circumstance (Nikki's girlfriend is a prison official) or in practice (another pair, Denny and Shaz, are never shown having sex). *Wentworth* has similar problems, intensified by the fact that the most significant lesbian character in the the series is depicted as violent and manipulative. While imperfectly enacted in *Bad Girls,* the concept of homonormativity is significant to understanding the way in which a text's structures and thematics can explore lesbian relationships as central and normalized. Homonormativity can also be applied as a salient concept for understanding the lesbian family program, where lesbian characters take primacy and have both sexual and romantic agency.

OITNB builds on the potential observed in *Bad Girls* for a homonormative text, embracing not only the possibility of lesbian relationships and supportive homosocial relationships, but placing them as the driving source of the series. At the most surface level, *OITNB* is marked as a homonormative text at its outset as viewers are invited to enter the world of Litchfield through the character of Piper. At first blush Piper appears to be the archetypal sweet, vulnerable, heterosexual girl who was implicated in a crime not of her own design (Ciasullo 2008, 197) but quickly it becomes clear that Piper is neither sweet or heterosexual, a point driven home in the first episode by the depiction in flashback of sex with her girlfriend at the time, Alex (1.1). While we (literally) enter the prison through heterosexual characters who are, or become, mothers in *Wentworth* and *Bad Girls*, we are explicitly offered a bisexual character as our first point of identification in *OITNB*. Furthermore, the first sex scene of the series that is depicted as satisfying is a same-sex one. Piper previously initiates sex in the pilot with her fiancé Larry, but she stops to cry and describes it unappealingly as "spank bank material" (1.1). As a result we are offered a bisexual woman as not only our key identificatory subject but also as a desiring and desirable subject. It is normal for lesbian family programs to focus initially on a lesbian or bisexual woman's perspective, often emphasized through voice over (*Sugar Rush, Exes and Ohs*), and most also feature a sex scene in their first episode; however, both features are unusual for a women-in-prison drama.

Piper also plays a significant role in suggesting that prison is not only a place that includes lesbian inhabitants and relationships, a feature of *Bad*

Girls and *Wentworth*, but rather that the closed homo-social dynamic allows for the clearer discovery and evolution of lesbian identity and behavior outside of the norms of femininity. In Season 1 Piper confesses to a young visitor from Scared Straight, "I'm scared that I'm not myself in here and I'm scared that I am" (1.10). Here Piper suggests prison functions similarly to the L.A. queer scene in *The L-Word*, a space and community that allows for a character who has adhered to traditional femininity and sexuality (Jenny in *The L-Word*) to explore the more complicated truth of their identities.

Piper is just one way in which *OITNB* expands and deepens the homonormative possibilities of the prison genre. For the remainder of this essay I will consider the key ways in which *OITNB* functions in line with Herman's concept of the homonormative text (2003) and how its combination of genre elements from the women-in-prison and lesbian family programs facilitates its unique representation of queer women and homosocial relationships.

Diversity of Representation

One of the crucial elements for homonormative lesbian representation is to provide a diversity of representations. In earlier periods of lesbian representation, lesbian characters frequently appeared as "token" characters that served the evolution of heterosexual characters and their narratives (Becker 2006, Dow 2001, 131, Lee and Meyer 2007, 236–237). These images ranged from lesbian characters appearing as the perpetrators of violent crimes on crime dramas dating back to *The Asphalt Jungle*'s "The Sniper" (1961) and continuing in present day crime dramas like *Law & Order: SVU* to the more sympathetic coming out of a number of family members (*All in the Family, Mad About You*), exes (*Friends, Chicago Hope*) and friends (*Roseanne, Designing Women, The Golden Girls, 90210*). As a result, a deeper and more complex representation of lesbianism demands not only a central lesbian or bisexual character, but a multiplicity of LGBT characters. This is an area in which *OITNB* succeeds particularly well. Over the course of their first three seasons *Bad Girls* and *Wentworth* have six or fewer significant characters that are depicted as lesbian or bisexual, with some of these characters primarily interested in men. *OITNB*, on the other hand, features eleven lesbian and bisexual characters with a twelfth character, Morello, dis-identifying as lesbian but engaging in same-sex sex. This number is rivaled only by *The L-Word* which features at least 20 narratively significant recurring lesbian characters in the first three seasons. That *OITNB* includes as many or more lesbian characters than the bulk of lesbian family programs is significant because it serves to normalize lesbianism, a point that is underscored by the fact that the majority of the young white inmates in the series are depicted as lesbian or bisexual.

The remaining white characters are mostly either sympathetic but much older, or part of a group of young but unsympathetic white meth-addicts led by the initially intensely homophobic Pennsatucky, both groups are desexualized. By depicting lesbian characters as numerous and spread throughout the different racially divided subgroups in the prison, *OITNB* presents a variety of lesbian experiences and "types." *The L-Word* has been critiqued for the privileging of whiteness, middle/upper class uniformity, and femme-performance in its depiction (Douglas 2007; Pratt 2007), a critique that is somewhat addressed as its ensemble cast grew. The large number of lesbian characters in *OITNB* help to diversify its representation, with characters ranging from the self-identified butch Boo to the eye liner-donning femme Alex. There are lesbian characters of every race on the series, except for Latina women; and while the lesbian characters tend to come from more upper or middle class backgrounds than the bulk of the prisoners, class diversity is depicted. The prison context of the series facilitates this in a way that is somewhat difficult in lesbian family programs, because the structure of prison affords a logical context for women from extremely different backgrounds to meet one another.

This multiplicity is impacted by intersectionality in *OITNB* where lesbian characters are often separated from one another through the prison's social structure that groups inmates by age and race. This is particularly significant because it allows the series to simultaneously provide images of lesbian community without the implication that sexuality alone is sufficient to bond people. This presents a challenge for many series. Lesbian family programs like *The L-Word* have been critiqued for their focus on a nearly exclusively lesbian community that does not provide many images of interactions with heterosexuals (Lee and Meyer 2007, 24) while *Bad Girls* has been lauded for having its lesbian inmates exist in non-intersecting social spheres (Herman 2003, 149). However, elsewhere the extent to which lesbian characters traditionally have not existed as part of a lesbian community, true of *Wentworth* and *Bad Girls*, has long been a critique of lesbian representation (Dow 2001, 131). *OITNB* manages to leverage its groups of lesbian characters to enact both dynamics. Piper initially finds her place in a group of primarily lesbian and bisexual women in her white dorm, while simultaneously having nothing but dislike for Soso and extremely little to do with Poussey, an African American lesbian whose best friend is the heterosexual Taystee and who has little patience for queer Suzanne. In this way, *OITNB* is able to combine the size of their lesbian ensemble, consistent with lesbian family programs, with the unique social dynamic of prison to achieve both images of lesbian community and a rejection of the "heteronormative assumption that all lesbians have some connection" (Herman 2003, 149).

This diversity is significant because it allows *OITNB* to avoid the idealized "respectable" lesbian and the stereotypically dangerous "prison lesbian" extremes that emerge in other women-in-prison dramas. *Bad Girls* evidences this dichotomy with politically engaged business owner Nikki on one end of the scale, and violent, mentally unstable and sexually predatory "Mad Tessa," on the other. *Wentorth* has a similar dynamic with Franky, who, while not idealized and a sometimes violent drug dealer—is smart, literate and strategic, contrasted with sexually predatory and wantonly violent "Juicy Lucy."

The throwback stereotypes of Tessa and Lucy, who evoke the aggression and unwanted sexual advances of Franky in *Prisoner*, are somewhat tempered by primarily directing their unwanted advances on characters that have been shown or implied to engage in consensual sex with another women making it clear that it is their advances, not lesbian sex itself, that is undesirable. However, the threat of violently coercive sex is disturbing and rendered frighteningly dangerous because these characters are infected with HIV and Hepatitis C, respectively, drawing on older homophobic associations of lesbianism and contagion (Butler 2005, 142, Ciasullo 2008, 203).

Franky and Nikki's status is problematically achieved largely through the politics of respectability garnered in part from their preference for romance and collaboration with prison officials rather then other prisoners. *OITNB* resists the politics of respectability by dismantling the initial appearance of Piper as an emblem of middle class respectability and by placing her attempts to deploy this image at the root of some of her problems. In *OITNB*, lesbian characters do not exist statically on a scale of respectability nor do they conform to the idea of "user-friendly lesbian" (Dow 2001) who is celibate, feminine, and non-threatening. Rather, these characters are shown to be able to play with and strategically use the politics of respectability, exemplified by Poussey and Taystee playfully putting on upper class mannerisms for their entertainment.

This rejection of respectability is particularly significant in relationship to the ways in which lesbian characters are often proposed as the moral center in *OITNB*. This is an important element of homonormativity because using a lesbian character as the voice of reason or moral center encourages identification with that character and presents them as a positive feature of the larger community. This aligns it with the lesbian family program where, since the bulk of characters are lesbian or bisexual, they are also the voice of reason or moral center in almost every scenario.

That Nikki presents a strong moral center in the prison in *Bad Girls* is an important element of the series' homonormativity for Herman (2003, 144) normalizing and valorizing lesbian representation. But this feature is unevenly deployed in the women-in-prison genre, given that the moral center of *Wentworth* is made up of heterosexual characters who are also mothers, and in *Bad Girls* Nikki is the only lesbian character functioning as a moral center and she shares that role with other older women who are heterosexual.

OITNB diffuses the role of the moral center at different times across the series. Piper often takes up this role when speaking to the administration and initially appears to position herself in this role. However, we can see that just as Piper can function as a moral center and advocate for prison reform, she can also act unethically and selfishly; allowing another prisoner to go to solitary for her mistake and actively taking steps to put or keep ex-lovers Alex (2.13) and Stella (3.13) in prison both as revenge and to satisfy her own needs (3.13). Often it is not Piper, marked by the politics of respectability, who is the moral center for the group of white women but drug addict and promiscuous Nicky—whose appearance and lascivious language has rough edges but who consistently provides the most rational advice to other inmates. In the group of African American women, Poussey shares the role of the voice of reason with her heterosexual best friend Taystee. When Vee comes to the prison in Season 2 and tries to take control of the group of African American women and become top dog of the prison, it is Poussey who stands alone to resist her. Poussey and Nicky are both depicted as imperfect, particularly when they fall pray to their respective alcoholism and drug abuse, and can become decentered from this role shifting the moral center.

This structure, where lesbian characters function as moral centers in some contexts and are led astray in others, and where the moral center shifts from character to character, is consistent with the lesbian family program. While *Bad Girls* and *Wentworth* tend to frame their lesbian characters as either productive or disruptive, lesbian family programs and *OITNB* resist this classification. Rather, these series share the moral center role amongst lesbian characters, and occasionally heterosexual characters, de-centering it in a way that undermines simplistic notions of good/bad characters. In these series, lesbian characters articulate crucial moral values for their community, while enacting a morality that is complex and contextual, illustrating that characters do not have to be "model minorities" to be likable.

Sex, Violence and Family Ties

One of the clearest ways in which *OITNB* departs from the other women-in-prison series, aligning itself with the lesbian family program, is the way it organizes interpersonal relationships and power structures within the prison. While all the series depict close interpersonal friendships and romantic and sexual relationships, each balances the significance of violence, sexuality, and familial relationships in their depiction of how the prison operates and the ways in which characters resolve issues within the prison.

Violence is overwhelmingly more common in *Wentworth* and *Bad Girls* than it is in *OITNB*. While there are memorable moments of violence in

Orange Is the New Black they are rare and momentous, marking an important shift in a character or relationship. Conversely, in *Wentworth* and *Bad Girls* violence is not momentous but mundane; it is part of how the prison normally operates and from the first episode is a central and regular feature of the plot. *Wentworth's* first two episodes include a prison riot, a stabbing, and an inmate intentionally burned in a steam press. *Bad Girls'* first four episodes follow a young woman who is badly beaten, threatened and driven to suicide. By contrast, *OITNB's* first four episode's incidences of violence are: a mother who briefly slaps her daughter in the face, and brief wrestling between two inmates (without real potential for injury) over access to something in the break room. In *Wentworth* and *Bad Girls* violence is an important way in which the women address grievances and exert power and the prison is depicted as a place of regular violence. This is consistent across the series; 68 percent of *Wentworth* episodes feature violence inside of the prison and 64 percent of *Bad Girl* episodes feature violence committed by one prisoner against another, more feature prisoner/guard violence, and this violence is often extreme, even lethal. However, only 28 percent of *Orange Is the New Black* episodes feature violence of any kind and this number drops to 18 percent if we exclude light violence not intended to do real harm—for example a prison food fight or when Daya's mother slaps her for getting arrested.

In *OITNB* violence is more frequently depicted outside of the prison then inside of it. Inside the prison serious violence takes two forms: violence that is an outgrowth of homophobia, memorably an extremely violent fight between Piper and Pennsatucky that is the culmination of ongoing conflict spurred by Pennsatucky's homophobia (1.13) or transphobia (3.12) and a sequence of violent actions in Season 2 spurred by a new prisoner, Vee, whose bringing of violence to the prison is depicted as such a violation of the normal dynamic of the prison that the women cross cultural lines to facilitate her expulsion from the prison community. Both of these instances reinforce Litchfield as a homonormative and positively homosocial place, with violence as a violation of the prison community's norm rather than essential to its operation. This is particularly notable given the depiction of both violence and rape committed outside of the prison's walls by prison guards, intimate partners, and business partners. It is individuals, primarily men, outside of the prison and hiding behind the power offered them as prison officials that are the primary source of violence and threat. *OITNB* highlights the brutality women face outside the prison rather then defining the prison itself as a place of violence, the strategy of *Bad Girls* and *Wentworth*. *OITNB's* reduction of the role of violence in the women-in-prison genre also is a rejection of the stereotypical association of lesbianism and violence (Lee and Meyer 2007, 237). The crimes of many of the lesbians in *Wentworth* (assault, rape) and *Bad Girls* (murder, manslaughter, arson) are violent; the lesbian characters in *OITNB* crimes are all non-violent (drugs, theft, fraud). Those inmates in *OITNB* who are violent are invariably heterosexual; divorcing violent criminality from its stereotypical association with lesbianism.

Rather than violence, Litchfield appears to operate through bartering, withholding of access to desired objects and spaces, and through tight friendship groups, "prison families," and sexual relationships that facilitate sharing within groups and negotiations with other groups. As a result, violence is not the form of physical activity that drives the series; rather physical affection (both platonic and romantic) and sex scenes are far more common and significant for *OITNB*. The presence of explicitly depicted, and narratively rich, sex scenes is a key factor that distinguishes *OITNB* from other women-in-prison series. While *Wentworth* and *Bad Girls* "normalize" lesbian sex by depicting it, they only do so rarely; only 11.7 percent of *Wentworth* episodes show or clearly imply same-sex sex and *Bad Girls* depicted it only once. *OITNB* regularly depicts same-sex sex scenes, including them in 36 percent of episodes, successfully making this sex visible and "everyday" (McCarthy 2001, 609). Sex scenes serve a variety of purposes in the series, marking shifts in relationships, providing humor, and even forming a multi-episode story arc focused on a sexual competition between Boo and Nicky (2.5–2.6). *OITNB*'s regular depiction of same-sex sex and its use of it as significant to the narrative is consistent with lesbian family program's *The L-Word, Lip Service* and *Exes and Ohs* which all have similarly explicit and narratively significant sex scenes in over half the episodes of the series.

Arguably, the representation of same-sex sexual interaction is political in and of itself but in the context of *OITNB* it is at times presented as explicit resistance. The first time we observe Piper and Alex have sex in "real-time," it is expressly framed as an act of defiance. After being placed in solitary simply for dancing with Alex, when Piper is released she goes directly to find Alex and leads her to the chapel to have sex (1.9). This is a powerful and multi-layered moment. Piper's expression of defiance for her mistreatment and her act of freedom is to embrace her desire for Alex in a space, the chapel, that is both a normal space for sex in the prison but can also be considered subversive, a violation of the cultural taboos she represents in her "nice blonde lady" persona. This moment also speaks to the way in which same-sex sex reorganizes the spaces of prison. Recounting the restroom sex scenes of *The L-word*, Catherine Jonet and Laura Williams observe that "lesbian desire also reconfigures heteronormative spaces, such as public restrooms" (156). Because there is no private space in the context of the prison sex in *OITNB* takes this disorganizing potential of sex further, reframing almost any space—the library, bathroom stalls, the chapel—as a space for lesbian desire. Further, in a prison context same-sex sex is given additional value because it represents a kind of escape from coercion and confinement.

Sex and sexuality are also used in a way to reimagine the prison dynamic. In *OITNB* physical affection between inmates is common and is used as gestures of support, comfort, and to express friendship and desire. It is not uncommon for physical affection to deliver information to other characters and viewers and it often follows or replaces violence. While violence is harmful in other series, *OITNB* focuses on "light violence" (slapping someone across the face) between two people who care about each other and quickly evolves into affection like hugging, indicating a strengthened relationship (2.12). Sex also often stands in where violence may be expected. A particularly telling example comes early on where a screwdriver goes missing, leading the guards to fear that it will be used as a weapon. The construction of the narrative encourages the viewer to believe that Boo will use it against her ex-girlfriend who is getting out, only to discover that her true purpose for it is as a sex toy (1.4). Sex and violence are sometimes linked, for example angry at one another Alex and Piper have extensive angry rough sex (3.2, 3.3), but it is consensual and desirable for both partners. This mirrors *The L-Word*, in which Bette and Tina engage in violence-inflected sex (1.14), a trend in lesbian family programs where sex is used for self discovery and problem solving. *OITNB* presents sex as an alternative to violence as a potential solution to conflict and by reimagining objects that are framed as weapons by the patriarchal voice of the prison as tools for pleasure.

Homosocial Families and Heteronormative Failure

This emphasis on physical affection and intimacy takes its most frequent form in platonic gestures; a hug, a squeeze of the hand, holding them as they cry. That this is the primary physical gesture in *OITNB*, over and above violence, is important because it supports the significance of familial intimate relationships as the core of the series. I have defined *The L-Word*, *Lip Service*, etc., as lesbian family programs, because they take on many of the features of the traditional family drama but focus not on a biological family but on women who create a family of choice (Weston 1991). While choice may not be a fair descriptive for *OITNB* where women literally are assigned to live with other women, *OITNB* shares the focus on the non-biological family as an important source of support and guidance.

Herman (2003) argues that this feature exists in other women-in-prison series, stating that "*BG* constructs an environment ... where the community of women inmates function as a real family, providing the warmth, support and ... mothering that the prisoners have not experienced on the outside" (152). I argue that in *Bad Girl* and *Wentworth* this potential is undercut because of the emphasis on violence and power struggles that lead women to more frequently re-organize their allegiances than on *OITNB*. These series also cycle in and out characters more frequently and rarely evoke the language of family. *OITNB* on the other hand, shared with *The L-Word* and *Lip Service* the persistent utilization of the language of family. Familial organization is formalized in Litchfield, each racial group has a "mom" who looks out for and controls the other women in her group and the women often refer to each other as family, at times extending to their future lives outside (3.2). The persistent use of this language is notable because it functions as an insistence on the legitimacy of these families. While there is no doubt that other women-in-prison series have equally significant homo-social relationships (in *Bad Girls* one inmate stays in jail to be with her dying friend [2.8] while another returns to jail because she feels her friend cannot be without her [3.4]) they are unique to these women. *OITNB* differs in that it presents these constructed families as central to the organization of the prison itself and a pivotal part of these women's lives within it.

These families are often depicted as *better* than biological families. That Daya often prefers her prison mom over her biological mother, who is inside with her, is a powerful factor in the privileging of homo-normativity in the series. Heterosexual nuclear families are primarily shown as damaged, destructive, and even abusive, with the most positive examples (Piper's) simply being cold and judgmental. While most women-in-prison series valorize maternity, depicting pregnancy and motherhood as redemptive (as is the case with Zondra in *Bad Girls*) or validating her moral stance, mothers are particularly problematic figures in *OITNB*. While many appear to try their best for their children, they are depicted as unable to provide the support and understanding that is possible in the prison families. That there are no fathers in these familial units can be understood as particularly disruptive to the heteronormative ideal.

Herman (2003) suggests that these types of representations also undermine heteronormativity by making heterosexuality "largely unappealing problematic" (153). This is a common thread across all the series included in the study. Physically or sexually abusive heterosexual relationships are depicted in *OITNB*, *Bad Girls* and *Wentworth*, and past sexual abuse looms large in *The L-Word*. While the figure of the "prison lesbian" threatening coercive sex is removed in *OITNB*, *OITNB* (like *Bad Girls*) features guards who barter for sex and rape prisoners. When heterosexual relationships appear to be with kind men, we see that even these "good men" often cheat or abandon their partners when difficulties arise. While Piper enters prison with an apparently satisfying heterosexual relationship, he quickly appears to be both unfaithful and perfectly willing to use her for his own ends without regard to its affect on her and her life in the prison.

While the unreliable and threatening image of male partners undermines the romanticization of heterosexuality in these series, female sexuality is also depicted as problematic in a heterosexual context. A key case in *OITNB* is the character of Morello who is initially shown in a sexually satisfying and emotionally supportive same-sex relationship with Nicky that she ends because of her fiancé (1.5) Morello appears to be an icon of heteronormativity, with an obsession with her femme appearance and her wedding. However, we later discover that her "fiancé" is actually a man whom she stalked after he rejected her after one date; spying on him, threatening his fiancé, and even putting a bomb under his car. Far from an idealized romance, her heterosexual relationship is purely fantasy and leads to violent and criminal behavior. This stands in stark contrast to the comparatively healthy lesbian relationship with Nicky that she rejected.

While all these series share a suspicion of heteronormative relationships and nuclear families, *OITNB* persistently undermines the possibility of such relationships being successful for women-in-prison. *Bad Girls* and *Wentworth* each temper their negative images of heterosexuality with a heterosexual couple (an inmate and prison handyman in *Bad Girls* and two inmates in *Wentworth*) that is loving and romanticized. Moreover both these couples are productive, leading to pregnancies within the first three seasons. *OITNB*, on the other hand, like *The L-Word, Lip Service* and *Exes and Ohs,* does not depict any stable heterosexual couples, with the exception of one pair of guards whose relationship appears positive but is only seen in brief glimpses.

The depiction of heteronormative romance and families as unsatisfying and deeply flawed is significant paired with the affectionate and supportive prison families and the same-sex scenes in the series. By comparison, lesbian relationships appear as not only possible and normal but as potentially desirable. At one point *OITNB*'s Red and Gloria joke about the possibility of becoming gay (3.6) given its clear advantages, in the prison context. While this possibility is brushed aside as impossible it remains an important moment for the way in which it highlights the "prison lesbian" as reworked and reimagined in *OITNB* as not only desiring but *desirable*, both as a subject and a status.

Conclusion

Most episodes of *Orange Is the New Black, The L-Word* and *Wentworth* contain or begin with flashbacks. This shared formal convention is important because they draw attention to the fact that the characters have a *history* and that both criminality and sexuality do not exist in a vacuum. *OITNB* also does not exist in a vacuum; it fits into an important history of both lesbian representation and representations of women-in-prison. I have argued here that the history of the women-in-prison genre is a troubled one providing both queer possibilities and homophobic images.

However, *OITNB* is not solely a member of the women-in-prison genre, and I have demonstrated here that its incorporation of features from the lesbian family program has allowed it to build-on and transcend both genres to complicate and improve images of lesbian characters and relationships, to create a text that privileges and normalizes lesbian sexuality and homonormative relationships. These representations cannot just be understood as an improvement on the women-in-prison drama. Rather, as fellow inmate Cindy winks at when she refers to Piper as "The L Word" (3.13), this text also fits into the history of lesbian family programs and draws from and expands on its themes and ideological investments.

When Piper appears in prison it is as a "nice blonde lady" with a passion for homemade soap, whole foods, and her fiancé. This surface appearance is broken down as the series evolves and we discover that Piper is far more sinister, complex, and queer than that. Similarly, we need to peel back the surface appearance of *Orange Is the New Black* to discover its complex generic resonances and the deeper representational possibilities it's double-genre attributes facilitate behind and beyond the bars.

References

Andreeva, Nellie. 2015. "Emmys: 'Orange Is the New Black' to Run as Drama, Ineligible for Comedy Race." *Deadline Hollywood.* http://deadline.com/2015/03/orange-is-the-new-black-run-drama-ineligible-as-comedy-emmys-1201395807/.

Becker, Ron. 2006. *Gay TV and Straight America.* New Brunswick: Rutgers University Press.

Beirne, Rebecca. 2007. "Introduction: A Critical Introduction to Queer Women on Television." In *Televising Queer Women: A Reader*, edited by Rebecca Beirne. New York: Palgrave MacMillan.

Beirne, Rebecca. 2009. "Screening the Dykes of Oz: Lesbian Representation on Australian Television." *Journal of Lesbian Studies* 13(1):25–34.

Butler, Judith. 2005. "Contagious Word: Paranoia and 'Homosexuality' in the Military." *Queer Theory*, edited by Iaian Morland and Annabelle Willox, 142–157. New York: Palgrave Macmillan.

Cecil, Dawn K. 2007. "Looking Beyond *Caged Heat*: Media Images of Women in Prison." *Feminist Criminology* 2(4):304–326.

Ciasullo, Ann. 2008. "Containing "Deviant" Desire: Lesbianism, Heterosexuality, and the Women-in-Prison Narrative." *The Journal of Popular Culture* 41(2):195–223.

Douglas, Erin. 2007. "Pink Heels, Dildos, and Erotic Play: The (Re)Making of Fem(me)ininity in Showtime's *The L Word." Televising Queer Women: A Reader*, edited by Rebecca Beirne. New York: Palgrave MacMillan.

Dow, Bonnie. "Ellen, Television, and the Politics of Gay and Lesbian Visibility." *Critical Studies in Media Communication* 18(2):123–140.

Fratini, Dawn. 2008. "Caged Heat and the Women-In-Prison Genre" *Critical Commons.* http://www.criticalcommons.org/Members/DawnFratini/clips/caged-heat-and-the-women-in-prison-genre.

Gross, Larry. 2002. *Up From Invisibility: Lesbians, Gay Men, and the Media in America.* New York: Columbia University Press.

Herman, Didi. 2003. "'*Bad Girls* Changed My Life': Homonormativity in a Women's Prison Drama." *Critical Studies in Media Communication* 20(2):141–159.

Jonet, M. Catherine, and Laura Anh Williams. "'Everything Else Is the Same': Configurations of *the L Word.*" *Televising Queer Women: A Reader*, edited by Rebecca Beirne. New York: Palgrave MacMillan.

Lauzen, Martha M. 2014. *Boxed In: Employment of Behind-the-Scenes and On-Screen Women in 2013–14 Prime-Time Television.* San Diego: Center for the Study of Women in Television & Film. http://womenintvfilm.sdsu.edu/files/2013–14_Boxed_In_Report.pdf.

Lee, Pei-Wen, and Michaela D.E. Meyer. 2010. "'We All Have Feeling for Our Girlfriends': Progressive (?) Representations of Lesbian Lives on *The L Word.*" *Sexuality & Culture* 14:234–250.

Mayne, Judith. 2000. *Framed: Lesbians, Feminists, and Media Culture.* Minneapolis: University of Minnesota Press.

McCarthy, Anna. 2001. "Ellen Making Queer Television History." *GLQ: A Journal of Lesbian and Gay Studies* 7(4):593–620.

Medhurst, Andy. 2009. "One Queen and His Screen: Lesbian and Gay Television." *Queer TV: Theories, Histories, Politics*, edited by Glynn Davis and Gary Needham, 79–87. New York: Routledge.

Millbank, Jenni. 2004. "It's About *This*: Lesbians, Prison Desire." *Social & Legal Studies* 13(2):155–190.

Mittel, Jason. 2004. *Genre and Television: From Cop Shows to Cartoons in American Culture.* New York: Routledge.

Peters, Wendy. 2011. "Pink Dollars, White Collars: *Queer As Folk*, Valuable Viewers, and the Price of Gay TV." *Critical Studies in Media Communication* 28(3):193–212.

Pratt, Marnie. 2007. "'This Is the Way We Live … and Love!': Feeding on and Still Hungering for Lesbian Representation in *The L Word.*" *Televising Queer Women: A Reader*, edited by Rebecca Beirne. New York: Palgrave MacMillan.

Shai, Oren. 2013. "The Women in Prison Film: From Reform to Revolution." *Bright Lights.* http://brightlightsfilm.com/the-women-in-prison-film-from-reform-to-revolution-1922–1974/#.VeZB57SIV_Z.

Weston, Kath. 1997. *Families We Choose: Lesbians, Gays, Kinship.* New York: Columbia University Press.

Pennsatucky's Teeth
and the Persistence of Class

SUSAN SERED

If the beautiful, educated and articulate Piper is the protagonist of *Orange Is the New Black* (*OITNB*), then Tiffany "Pennsatucky" Doggett—ignorant, often incoherent and toothless (her most prominent physical feature)—plays the role of antagonist. Tiffany wound up in prison after going to a women's clinic for her fifth abortion. When a nurse made a condescending, classist remark ("Number five, huh? We should give you a punch card. Give you the sixth one free"), Tiffany grabbed a shotgun—which she just happened to have handy in her car—and shot her. Surprised to find herself embraced by the right-to-life movement as a hero (she certainly did not set out to take a political stance when she shot the nurse), she spends most of Season 1 as a wanna-be religious leader whose cluelessness is a constant punch line. She isn't cute or funny or even an "Andy Griffith" font of homespun southern wisdom. In the midst of a prison culture formally and informally divided by race, Tiffany embodies an equally powerful yet rarely discussed social divide—class, and an openly ridiculed cultural archetype—white trash.

In the context of *OITNB*, race generally trumps class for the black and Hispanic women. Class does not divide the black or the Hispanic women into sub-groups. They are "black" or "Hispanic"—not rich or poor. Middle class Poussey and Suzanne talk literature and philosophy with ghetto-raised Taystee, who worked at a fast food joint following a childhood spent in institutions and group homes. Middle class Gloria, who owned her own business on the outside, works and socializes with Flaca, whose mother barely scrapes by as a piecework seamstress working out of their tiny apartment.

The white women, in contrast, are sharply divided along class lines. Pennsatucky, though white, has nothing in common with most of the other white women: Machiavellian Alex, gender savvy Nicky, hip Sister Jane, peacenik Yoga Jones, or even Russian entrepreneur Red, all of whom are presented as smart, literate women who are capable of scheming to improve their lot in life. Pennsatucky doesn't even fit in with Morello, a well-groomed woman with a working-class accent who lives in a fantasy world of romance and Hollywood magazines. Most telling, while black and Hispanic women repeatedly shelter their sisters from the worst horrors of prison life, Pennsatucky and Piper end Season 1 with a bloody and nearly lethal fight.

In the beginning of Season 2 Pennsatucky acquires dentures, necessary but not sufficient for transition to middle class status. By Season 3 she's been tamed and no longer provokes fights with Piper. But even the acquisition of teeth—that ultimate marker of class in America—can't change a cracker sow into a silk purse.

Intersectionality and Overdetermination

Drawing on Marxist theory, philosopher Louis Althusser (1962) developed the concept of "overdetermination," the idea that multiple institutions and structural relationships construct, or "overdetermine," the human subject, minimizing or even erasing unique, individual traits, personalities, preferences, talents and weaknesses (101). The plurality of structural relationships that construct identities such as "woman" or "black" are driven and enforced by the full range of powerful social institutions—familial, medical, psychotherapeutic, economic, political, religious, and legal—that frame and shape every aspect of social worlds. What this means, for example, is that a woman is never simply "human" but always a gendered being whose identity, status, and roles are constrained by social understandings of female gendering (Doddy 1900, Sered and Norton Hawk 2014).

In the grand scheme of *OITNB*, gender is so fully overdetermined that it's taken for granted. Set in a women's prison, the show, like the rest of American society, rarely questions the binary gendering that is foundational to the correctional system. While prisons are de facto racially segregated with far higher rates of blacks and Hispanics than whites drawn into the correctional system, they are officially and de jure segregated by gender. The hypermasculinizing gender "work" in male prisons has received more attention (Sabo, Kupers and London 2001,15; cf. Courtenay 2011, esp. 218; Sabo 2001, esp. 64), but women's prisons similarly carry out the cultural work of gendering in ways both obvious and subtle: calling prisoners "girls," telling them to "act like ladies," breaking up close friendships because of "female" tendencies to become overemotional, prohibiting sexual relationships between women, and a range of "gender sensitive" programs that tell women that they are overly reliant on relationships (Sered and Norton-Hawk 2015). Boundary-crossing gender expressions—as in the case of transgender Sophia—present unique challenges to the correctional system.

The replacement of individual characteristics with group stereotypes is an immensely more extensive and powerful social process for those in subordinate social positions than for those in dominant groups. In *Black Skin, White Masks* (1967) Frantz Fanon explains the mutually informing social processes of overdetermination from without and overdetermination from within. Racial and colonial stereotypes make it difficult for a black individual to be seen or heard for who he or she is, or even experience him or herself in an authentic way. A black person is never not-black: he or she is a black teacher or a black rapper or a "black crack whore" whose thoughts, actions and emotions are interpreted as a consequence of race. A white person is typically identified non-racially: as a teacher, a musician, an alcoholic, as a man or a woman, as rich or poor, or as a hillbilly, like Pennsatucky. In measurable ways, race reduces the effects of class for African Americans in ways that it does not for white Americans. For example, while economic and educational status are correlated with health status generally in the United States, that correlation is more true for whites than for blacks. In other words, being black neutralizes the health enhancing potential of wealth and education in a way that being white does not (Cutler 2007).

Unlike gender and race, class has a sort of underground existence in a society in which its unacceptable to ask about anyone else's income, in which people who work at jobs ranging from receptionist to executive consider themselves to be "middle class," in which politicians throw around the word "middle class values" as if it is some sort of code for "true American," and in which knock-off clothing is not noticeably different from its pricy model. Making matters murkier, we Americans claim that class (as opposed to caste) is by definition changeable and permeable, that an individual is not fated to remain in the class into which she or he was born (notwithstanding compelling evidence that the greatest predictors of adult economic status are one's parents' economic status (Fass, Dinan and Aratani 2009).

Both in *OITNB* and in the real world, gender and class intersect in complicated ways. As Erik Olin Wright (1996) explains, gender and class reciprocally affect one another both conceptually and in determining outcomes for individuals. Low-wage jobs filled mostly by women demand greater conformity with middle class appearances and dress codes, making it hard for poor women to be hired or requiring them to spend too much of their paycheck on job-appropriate clothing. While this is slowly changing, it is still the case that a working class identity for men—"blue collar"—is lauded; a man who lifts heavy things, sweats, does dangerous jobs is a "real" man who is respected for literally building America. Think, for instance, of the pride with which Pittsburghers wear the insignia of their football team—the Steelers (steel mill work is hard, noisy, dirty and dangerous). In contrast, women who work in low-wage female ghettos such as telemarketing and nail salons are ridiculed and demeaned (Sered and Fernandopulle 2007).

Unlike male low-wage workers who are expected to be gruff, rude and vulgar (think of construction workers' whistles), women as low-wage workers are expected to be pleasant, to show caring while changing diapers at nursing homes; to listen with interest to clients' complaints about leaf blowers, all while bent over a basin cleaning their clients' toenails at the mani-pedi salon; to exude sincere sympathy for guests' complaints about lost luggage and rude airlines while scrubbing hotel room toilets. This uncompensated emotional work takes a physical and emotional toll (Kang 1996). That kind of work is dramatized in *OITNB* in the relationship between Red and Healy. He, a free man with power over the women prisoners, demands from incarcerated Red a mixture of sympathy, language interpretation and marriage counseling.

In our gender-unequal society, women, more than men, are defined, evaluated, and constrained by their physical appearance. They are expected to take care of themselves "properly"; that is, appear well groomed, nice-smelling, clear skinned, and clothed in at least a reasonable proximity of whatever is the fashion of the moment, all enterprises that cost a great deal of money. Failure to meet those standards is not only socially stigmatizing but occupationally costly; women who do not "look nice" or who are overweight are more discriminated against in hiring than are comparable men (Shinall 2014). And finally, poor women (and especially black women) are often assumed to be more sexually available than their more affluent sisters, and many poor women find that they are compelled to engage in undesired sexual relations in order to keep a roof over their and their kids' heads (Krieger et al. 2006).

"Pennsatucky and the thousands of other young women growing up in rural communities in Appalachia, and across the American South and West, are not simply 'unlucky'—they are at high structural risk for rape and sexual assault" (Eisenberg 2015). In one of the states for which "Pennsatucky" is named, data from the Pennsylvania Coalition Against Rape and the Pennsylvania Office of Children, Youth and Families, show that rates of rape and child sexual assault were significantly higher in rural counties than in urban ones. According to Susan Lewis (2013), "To varying degrees, rural populations are often marginalized from the mainstream power structure, which holds the opportunities for assistance and services through resource and policy initiatives." Indeed, in Season 3, when more of Pennsatucky's back-story is presented, we learn that she was raped as a young teenager and she clearly had nowhere to turn for assistance afterwards.

Rapidly rising rates of opiate-related death and imprisonment among poor white women force us to think harder about how race and gender intersect with that great American unmentionable—class. Poor white women are medicated (and self-medicate) for the same socially construed gender weaknesses and pain as affluent white women, yet unlike their wealthier sisters they have to make do without the protections of good lawyers and platinum health insurance. Research published by the *Boston Globe* found that the number of babies born with opiates in their systems in Massachusetts is more than triple the national rate, and that the numbers in Maine and Vermont are even worse (Jan 2014). This research did not track race, but we do know that Maine and Vermont are two of the whitest states in the county (Vermont is 95 percent white and Massachusetts is 84 percent white) and that many of the opiate hot spots in these states are poor, white rural and semi-rural communities. In Fall River, for instance, approximately 72 percent of residents have received a prescription for opiates, a rate well above the state average of 40 percent (Fraga 2014).

Black men have been the face of incarceration in America for decades, and black men continue to be locked up at rates far exceeding those of other gender and racial demographic groups. But, over the past few years, just as the pace of incarceration finally began to decline for men and for black women, incarceration rates have risen by 47.1 percent for white women—almost all of whom are poor (Mauer 2013). In part, this may simply be a matter of white women catching up with everyone else in terms of arrests and incarceration; it may be a market phenomenon in the sense that the illicit drug and the prison markets for men and for African Americans are saturated and white women represent one of the few arenas into which drug dealers and the highly profitable prison industry still have room to expand.

But I believe that the evidence makes it clear that at this particular moment in American history social forces are coming together in ways that are increasingly and visibly deleterious for poor white women. Women like Pennsatucky—white women in America with less than a high school education—can expect to live five years fewer than similarly educated white women of the previous generation (healthaffairs.org). "For the first time in modern history, the life expectancy of a particular segment of the American population—non–Hispanic white women with low levels of education and income living in certain rural counties, is declining" (Cockerham 2014).

Overdetermination of "White Trash"

While overdetermined racial identities subsume, cover up, or neutralize class for the black and Hispanic women of *OITNB*, class is nuanced for the white women. And, as Fanon would have predicted, class becomes overdetermined for those white women associated with subordinate statuses. Thus Pennsatucky's prison name erases her individual identity, subsuming it to a class-linked geographic region—rural Appalachia, the home of hillbillies, trailer trash, rednecks, crackers, white trash, meth heads, gun lovers, Jesus freaks, and ignorant racists. In one of my favorite moments in Season 3 the writers offer an ironic twist on classic racist claims that "all blacks [or Asians] look alike" when Angie, a poor white woman with bad teeth, is mistakenly released in place of Sarah, another poor white woman. It seems the guards couldn't tell the two apart.

Pennsatucky's overdetermined class status is inherited from her mother, a woman who embodies "white trash" in every sense of the word. Her class is cut into her body—into her bad skin, rotten teeth, and tattoos. Pennsatucky can get all dressed up (as she does for the Christmas pageant in Season 1), but the costume cannot ever be transformative. She is stuck with being who she is. Ironically, the stickiness of class is most clearly articulated in a scene in which Pennsatucky does not star: College educated Soso unsuccessfully (and pathetically) tries to make friends with the poor white girls by showing her working class chops. "So Wal-Mart? How about Wal-Mart? I went there once; they have a lot of … CHEAP SHIT in there!" Not surprisingly, the other women don't buy it. You can't fake class in the fishbowl that is a women's prison unit.

"Many people who would bite their tongues and stifle such hostile language about other social groups seem to feel free to spew vitriol and even violent intentions towards 'rednecks,' 'hillbillies,' members of evangelical Christian churches and poor white people in general" (Leondar-Wright 2013). Thus, Pennsatucky is portrayed as a sort of timeless caricature of dishonorable traits. We learn that she and the house she grew up in are dirty. We learn that they eat unhealthy food and drink gallons of Mountain Dew. We learn that they are too ignorant to know that they need to clean their dentures. And above all else, we learn that they are too stupid to even know what actions would be in their own best interests.

Throughout the first three seasons of *OITNB*, Pennsatucky is shown as openly racist (asking for an all-white bathroom, for instance), a portrayal that reinforces common pejorative stereotypes but elides the historical and economic reality of how upper class white society in the south play poor whites and poor blacks against one another in efforts to maintain the economic and social hegemony of the plantation class (Dollard 1998). Following centuries in which poor whites were taught that "you may be poor but at least you're not black" and "we white folks need to stick together to stop 'them' from raping our daughters," we see today that legacy in the ubiquitous notion among poor whites that blacks get more than their fair share of government assistance and even, as I've been told by more than one low income white person in Mississippi—that black people automatically get welfare and then drive around in big cars while "we whites" have to work for our money. Animosity poor whites feel towards blacks is not a consequence of stupidity or moral failure, but rather of centuries of economic policies that ensured that poor whites would blame blacks and not wealthy whites for their circumstances.

Not only is Pennsatucky racist, she is also homophobic and instigates homophobic harassment in a setting in which everyone else (black women and non-poor white women) seem to accept fairly fluid sexual orientations. Her condemnation of homosexuality is framed around both her ignorance and her religious zeal. Repeatedly, especially in Season 1, she spouts blind faith in a Bible that she does not know nearly as well as does the clearly middle class white nun. And while the black and Hispanic women are portrayed as helping one another emotionally and materially, the poor white women do not stick up for one another and seem not to trust other women (even their own cohort). Stupidly, however, they repeatedly trust men. When Angie is released from prison she makes it as far as the bus station but is too clueless to figure out what to do next, and puts her trust in Caputo when he comes to pick her up there. Pennsatucky trusts in Healy (someone Piper immediately tags as a "tool") and trusts the van driver even when he has her pick up food from the ground with her teeth and crawl around like a dog. In short, she has neither the knowledge of the wider world possessed by the middle class white women nor the street smarts of the black women (especially the poor black women).

Around matters of sexuality the intersection of female gender, low class and white race takes a very particular form that is one part promiscuity and two parts ignorance. Pennsatucky is portrayed as both promiscuous and ignorant. In Season 1 we learn that she'd had multiple unwanted pregnancies—assumedly never figuring out how to avoid becoming pregnant. We learn in Season 3 that her mother taught her when she was ten that sex is something that men expect. Her notion of sex is shown as animal-like with her turning around and bending over so that the man can do what he wants. She'd already been sexually active for a substantial period of time before she even heard of the idea that women are supposed to enjoy sexual interactions. When she is raped as a young woman she doesn't know that what happened is rape; she needs middle class Boo to teach her the difference between sex and rape. For the first time, the show seems to encourage viewer sympathy for Pennsatucky, but in reality what is elicited is pity. The difference, I suggest, is that sympathy implies some level of respect and identification with the sufferer; pity, in contrast, is what one feels for a clearly inferior being.

The relationship between Pennsatucky and Big Boo that develops towards the end of the third season initially seems to be forced; nothing in previous episodes hints at this development. What could homophobic Pennsatucky see in Boo, and what could self-confident and self-accepting Boo see in Pennsatucky? Most obviously, the relationship is a mentoring one in which middle class Boo teaches white trash Pennsatucky basic information about hygiene (Pennsatucky doesn't know that she needs to clean her dentures), and self-respect. But at the risk of reading too much into the relationship, I wonder if the writers need Boo to fill in a key trait of female "trailer trash" that the meth heads are not able to embody. Because meth causes weight loss, Pennsatucky and her toothless cohort are not portrayed in that most negative of all physical states: fat.

Weight has become a marker of socioeconomic status in the United States. Studies show that poorer women are far more likely to be obese than wealthy women (in one study, poor women were six times more likely to be obese), that opportunities to consume a healthy diet and to exercise are more abundant for the well-to-do, and that different groups in American society assign different social and moral meanings to body size. The stigma associated with obesity as signifying a lack of impulse control echoes the well-entrenched belief among the affluent that poor people are less capable of controlling their impulses. "Dieting and fitness rituals are primarily a middle- and upper-class phenomenon.... [I]n middle-class American culture fat symbolizes loss of self-control ... [and] obesity is strongly stigmatized" (Freund and McGuire 1999). I suggest that Boo can be seen as class transgressive (in the way that Sophia is gender transgressive). Boo is clearly middle class in terms of education, speech patterns and family background. But unlike middle class white women she does not "take care of herself." She is not pretty, neat, refined—and above all—she is not slim.

Teeth: The Final Frontier of Class

The producers of *OINTB* offer viewers an especially clear visual cue to the racialized class divide: the first time Pennsatucky opens her mouth we see a hideous display of broken and missing teeth. More than any other marker, teeth indicate class status. Rotten teeth are hard to hide and tooth decay signifies that supremely unforgivable character trait: not taking care of oneself, a particularly serious flaw in women, who are expected to look attractive. Perfectly white and straight teeth—the kind we see on celebrities—belong to the super rich who can afford costly cosmetic dentistry. Nicely aligned and healthy teeth are the sign of professional and upper middle class individuals who can afford regular dental care and basic orthodontia. Crooked teeth with delayed root canal work and a few crowns means the mouth belongs to a middle-or working class individual who has access to basic dental care but nothing fancy. And rotted teeth, like those Tiffany and her friends sport, mark the women as poor—a status with both economic and moral meaning. As I've been told countless times by Americans who do not earn enough to scrape by, being too poor to have respectable teeth is like wearing an "L" for loser on your face (Ehrenreich 2010; Wildavsky 2002). Sarah Smarsh, a journalist who grew up in a community similar to Pennsatucky's, notes dramatically rotted teeth slide into being a marker for the most brutal and monstrous villains in popular fiction; for example, "a derelict serial killer in a movie actually called *Monster*" (Smarsh 2014).

Many of us assume that rotten teeth are volitional—that if someone had just brushed and flossed then they'd have nice teeth. That sense of choice was made clear in an antagonistic conversation between middle class Soso and poor white Leann. When Leann rages about Soso's perfect teeth and Poca-hontas hair, Soso simply tells her: "You choose meth over teeth." But it's not that simple. Dental health is not covered by standard health insurance and Medicare has no dental benefits, so about half of Americans don't have dental insurance. In recent years, the cost of dental care has been increasing faster than the cost of other medical care. And there is a significant urban/rural divide regarding access to dentists: 50 million Americans live in communities where there are no dentists at all (Sullivan 2012).

Tooth decay signifies poverty in pernicious ways. "Low class" drugs—crack cocaine (Joy's drug of choice) and crystal meth (Tiffany's drug)—are particularly portrayed as destroying teeth, and users of the drugs are por-trayed as toothless. As the national panic shifted in the 1990s and 2000s from crack to crank (meth), the "faces of meth" became poor white faces with rotted teeth, often attached to stories of women who neglected or endangered their children in their lust for the drug. (See, for example, the website *Faces of Meth* and especially the section "From Drugs to Mugs.") For women, missing teeth also signifies engaging in sex work to fund a drug habit and it signifies being a victim of domestic abuse. While we Americans pity victims, we also blame them for not being brave or strong or smart enough to get away from their abusers. More broadly, on one side of the class divide are those with normatively attractive bodies, respectable educational achievements and decent jobs. On the other side are those whose poor teeth and other "defects" are read as signs that they are incapable of managing their own lives.

I don't know Tiffany, but as a sociologist I have worked with many other poor, young, white women. Gina, a rural Idahoan, wears her blonde hair in a tightly bound ponytail. Of average height and weight with heavy glasses and sad, plain features, she has a peculiar mannerism of keeping her mouth closed even when speaking. Towards the end of our conversation, Gina explained why. She has always taken good care of her teeth and when she had insurance would go to the dentist regularly. Now she has not been able to afford to go for three years, and her front tooth has a cavity and is rotting away. She shows me. "You see there is a hole there, or a gap, and I've never had a gap there before" (Sered and Fernandopulle 2007).

In Massachusetts I have come to know Joy (Sered and Norton-Hawk 2014). Raised in a middle class family, she began to struggle with substance abuse in the wake of ongoing sexual abuse at the hands of a family "friend." By her early 30s, she had spent over a decade in and out of substance abuse treatment, psychiatric hospitals, the streets, shelters, and jails. I first met her in a rehab program where she looked well groomed and nicely dressed. When I asked her how she's managed to survive all that she'd been through she told me, "I take care of myself. Even when I don't have a place to live I go into the restroom at Burger King and brush my teeth." A few years later, Joy and I chatted about what she is most proud of having accomplished recently: "Going to the [drug treatment] program, attempting to get better, taking care of myself—brushing my teeth even though I don't have running water in my apartment." A few months later she called me in tears. She had gone to the dentist and was told that she has seven cavities but that she couldn't get them filled for another six months because she had maxed out her dental coverage under Medicaid. "By then I'll have to have my teeth pulled. I used to say bad things about people with no teeth and now I'm going to be one of them." In short, Joy realized that by losing her teeth she would be losing her class status.

And finally Carol, a vivacious rural Illinois woman in her early 70s, is still haunted by having had to declare bankruptcy because of medical debt over a decade ago. Carol is furious that Medicare does not cover the dental work that she needs as a result of not being able to treat her diabetes during the years she was uninsured. Over those years she watched her diet and kept her blood glucose levels under 200. "But … I lost teeth because of bad circulation and gum infections…. I'd eat salad and find a tooth in my hand…. That's another reason I don't go out much…. It affects your self-image, self-respect. I feel I should have a corn cob pipe and a jug and a hound dog." At this point her diabetes is under control; she has no other health problems, and would like to go back to work using her computer skills. "But there are not many jobs for a 67-year-old woman, especially since I lost my teeth."

Like her or hate her, Tiffany scores a victory over the system during the second season when the prison has to pay for a full, beautiful, functioning set of dentures to replace her few remaining rotting teeth. (Sadly, that's probably not what would really happen: I've never heard of anyone getting good dental care in prison; quite the opposite—women often lose teeth in prison.) When she gets her new teeth, she's visibly changed. Her lower-class white friends in prison start to think of her as annoying as she shows off her new pearly whites. Two her old friends accuse her of acting as if she is too good for them now. But in an era in which class divisions are increasingly permanent, shiny dentures are not enough to allow her access into the middle class white group that includes Piper and Nicky, women whose straight, even teeth are their own. For Pennsatucky, class remains overdetermined.

REFERENCES

Althusser, Louis. 1969. *For Marx*. New York: Pantheon Books.

Boddy, Janice. 1988. "Spirits and Selves in Northern Sudan: The Cultural Therapeutics of Possession and Trance." *American Ethnologist* 15(1):4–27.

Cawley, John. 2004. "The Impact of Obesity on Wages." *Journal of Human Resources* 39(2):51–74.

Courtenay, Will. 2011. *Dying To Be Men: Psychosocial, Environmental and Biobehavioral Directions in Promoting the Health of Men and Boys*. New York: Routledge.

Cutler, David M., and Adriana Lleras-Muney. 2007. "Education and Health." National Poverty Center Policy Brief #9.

Cockerham, William C. 2014. "The Emerging Crisis in American Female Longevity." *Social Currents* 1(3):220–227.

Dollard, John. 1998. *Caste and Class in a Southern Town*. New York: Taylor and Francis.

Ehrenreich, Barbara. 2010. *Nickel and Dimed: On Not Getting By in America*. New York: Henry Holt.

Eisenberg, Emma. 2015. "We Still Don't Know How to Talk About Pennsatucky: The reality of Rural Sexual Assault and How Class Plays Out in 'Orange Is the New Black.'" *Salon*, July 5.

Fanon, Frantz. 1967. *Black Skin, White Masks*. New York: Grove Press.

Fass, Sarah, Kinsey Alden Dinan, and Yumiko Aratani. 2009. *Child Poverty and Intergenerational Mobility*. Columbia University, National Center for Children in Poverty.

Freund, Peter, and Meredith McGuire. 1999. *Health, Illness, and the Social Body: A Critical Sociology*, 3rd edition. Upper Saddle River, NJ: Prentice-Hall.

Jan, Tracy. 2014. "Drug-Addicted Babies in Massachusetts are Triple the National Rate." *Boston Globe*, June 19.

Kang, Milliann. 1996. "Manicuring Race, Gender and Class: Service Interactions in New York City Korean-Owned Nail Salons." *Race, Gender & Class* 4(3):143–164.

Krieger, Nancy, Pamela D. Waterman, Cathy Hartman, Lisa M. Bates, Anne M. Stoddard, and Margaret M. Quinn. 2006. "Social Hazards on the Job: Workplace Abuse, Sexual Harassment, and Racial Discrimination: A Study of Black, Latino, and White Low-Income Women and Men Workers in the United States." *International Journal of Health Services* 36(1):51–85.

Leondar-Wright, Betsy. 2013. "Orange Is the Newest Redneck Bashing." *Classism*. http://www.classism.org/orange-newest-redneck-bashing/.

Lewis, Susan. 2013. "Unspoken Crimes: Sexual Assault in Rural America." Enola, PA: National Sexual Violence Resource Center.

Sabo, Don. 2001. "Doing Time, Doing Masculinity: Sports and Prison." In *Prison Masculinities*, ed. Don Sabo, Terry A. Kupers and Willie London, 61–66. Philadelphia: Temple University Press.

Sabo, Don, Terry A. Kupers, and Willie London. 2001. "Gender and the Politics of Punishment." *Prison Masculinities*, edited by Don Sabo, Terry A. Kupers and Willie London, 3–18. Philadelphia: Temple University Press.

Sered, Susan, and Maureen Norton-Hawk. 2011. "Gender Overdetermination and Resistance: The Case of Criminalized Women." *Feminist Theory* 12(3):317–333.

Sered, Susan, and Maureen Norton-Hawk. 2014. *Can't Catch a Break: Gender, Jail, Drugs, and the Limits of Personal Responsibility*. Berkeley: University of California Press.

Smarsh, Sarah. 2014. "Poor Teeth." *Aeon*, October 23. http://aeon.co/magazine/health/the-shame-of-poor-teeth-in-a-rich-world/.

Sullivan, Louis W. 2012. "Dental Insurance, but No Dentists." *New York Times*, April 8, A21.

Wildavsky, Aaron. 2002. *The Revolt Against the Masses: And Other Essays on Politics and Public Policy.* New Brunswick, NJ: Transaction Publishers.

Wray, Matt. 2006. *Not Quite White: White Trash and the Boundaries of Whiteness.* Durham: Duke University Press.

Wright, Erik Olin. 1996. *Class Counts: Comparative Studies in Class Analysis.* Cambridge: Cambridge University Press.

Pleasure and Power Behind Bars
Resisting Necropower with Sexuality

ZOEY K. JONES

The prison in *Orange Is the New Black* (*OITNB*), as it is in real life, is a *necropolitical* death world, a place that effectively operates to kill the inmates, socially, civilly, politically and even physically sometimes, despite official policy rhetoric that rehabilitation is its central purpose. This essay will argue that the prisoners in *OITNB* resist the killing power of the institution, in part, through a complex deployment of sexual power. This power is not easily accessed or expressed, and yet the inmates find ways to draw on sexual pleasure as a resource for nourishment, knowledge, rebellion and connection to oneself and others. The reality of the prison (and its actors) in *OITNB* is of a state institution constantly fighting to suppress, remove, undermine, and corrupt any power that the prisoners attempt to assert over their lives—or that they assert to prove that they *are* alive. As such, *Orange Is the New Black* provides a fictitious representation of prison and prisoners' experiences that provides fertile ground from which to examine necropolitics in depth, and explore how necropower and various iterations of 'death' might manifest at a micro level.

In order to describe these complex negotiations of sexual power and minute resistances to necropower, this chapter will draw on three subplots that occur throughout Seasons 1–3 of the show. These examples illustrate the killing power of the institution and showcase how expressions of sexuality can be (or become) transformative acts of living. Next, by discussing the love story of Daya and Bennett, this analysis will consider how Daya's sexuality is framed and utilized during her time at Litchfield. Finally, Suzanne's erotic writing, *The Time Hump Chronicles* offers a window into sexual power through self-expression, sexual creativity, and sexual exploration.

These three examples demonstrate that the prisoners in *OITNB* are not "dead" bodies within the death world of the prison. The institution may be represented as a death world, where the prisoners' ability to wield power over their life circumstances is profoundly and intentionally limited, often beyond the scope of their respective sentences. However, the prisoners grasp any shreds of power that they can with both hands and carve out living spaces and sexual experiences within the institution from which to resist the killing might of Litchfield Penitentiary and its actors.

Sensitizing Concept: Necropolitics

As of yet, there is no scholarly research examining how the necropolitical prison is represented in entertainment media. In order to begin that work, this section will briefly describe necropolitics and how it applies to the prison. Discussions of the prison within this chapter are grounded in an understanding of the prison as a political institution of power and social control, an approach informed by pivotal works on prison, power, and/or sexuality such as Michel Foucault's *Discipline and Punish* (1995) and *The History of Sexuality* (1990), Angela Davis' *Are Prisons Obsolete?* (2003), Gresham M. Sykes' *The Society of Captives* (2007), and David Garland's *The Culture of Control* (2001).

The prison has been theorized as a site of necropolitics by Sarah Lamble (2013) and Jessi Lee Jackson (2013) who frame the prison as a death world where inmates are subjected to civil, social, and political deaths (or half-deaths, where prisoners suffer from some loss of power/life, but not all). As Sarah Lamble (2013) writes,

> the prison is a site that produces the conditions of living death; it is a place where bodies are subject to regimes of slow death and dying. Not only are deprivation, abuse and neglect regular features of incarceration but the monotonous regime of caged life—the experience of "doing time"—involves the slow wearing away of human vitality and the reduction of human experience to a bleak existence [244].

Necropolitics as a concept includes analyses of mass physiological death, but also allows us to analyze situations where a demographic is targeted for 'deaths' of a kind beyond the biological, because the human experience consists of more than bare physiological life. If life is defined as "the deployment and manifestation of power" (Mbebe 2003, 12), a world—such as the prison—that functions on the basis of rendering people powerless is worth considering through a necropolitical lens.

Necropolitics literature speaks commonly of bodies, and that those traditionally subject to necropower are "marked for death," while others are "marked for life." This marking occurs at the level of a general descriptor—such as racial identity, nationality, gender presentation, sexuality—and constructs some people as worthy of life, while others are worthy of death. Judith Butler (2004) provides some insight into how bodies are marked for life or for death, even if she does not use quite those words. (Butler's work is commonly cited as biopolitical in nature, but her close engagements with life and death also contribute a great deal to understanding how biopolitics and necropolitics are inextricably linked and, as Lamble (2013) later describes, work in tandem.) In *Precarious Lives*, Butler writes that bodies are politicized and have a public dimension, not only a personal one. "Constituted as a social phenomenon in the public sphere," she writes, "my body is and is not mine" (26). As bodies are constituted in the public sphere, so does their treatment and inclusion (or exclusion) in this sphere impact *how* they are constituted. For example, Butler writes of violence inflicted upon sexual and racial minorities in the name of "a normative notion of the human, a normative notion of what the body of a human must be" (33). The result of this violence, of marking bodies outside of the human, is significant:

> I am referring not only to humans not regarded as humans, and thus to a restrictive conception of the human that is based upon their exclusion. It is not a matter of a simple entry of the excluded into an established ontology, but an insurrection at the level of ontology, a critical opening up of the questions, What is real? Whose lives are real? How might reality be remade? Those who are unreal have, in a sense, already suffered the violence of derealization [33].

By suffering this violence and this exclusion, particular people—in Butler's examples, people of sexual and racial minorities—are marked as "not real"; they are more likely to experience violence, and are more likely to *not* be grieved when that violence results in death. In this way, Butler helps us understand what it means to be marked for death.

Prisoners can be understood as a population that is marked for death. Their bodies are and are not theirs; their exclusion from the social sphere defines the worlds both inside and outside of prison, and prisoners regularly suffer the violence of being made less-than-human. Further, prisoners are more likely to belong to marginalized groups who are marked for death, as Butler describes. Others have made similar claims, such as Angela Davis' (2005, 41) assertion in *Abolition Democracy* that the prison functions to remove "dispensible" people from society, such as the homeless and the illiterate. And these people—women of color, women with mental health issues, women with sexualities and gender identities that are not hetero- or cisnormative, women from poverty-stricken backgrounds—are represented in *OITNB*. These representations are not without issue, as some have claimed that the show relies too heavily on racialized stereotypes (Rivera 2013; Gay 2013), but they are there. (Although it is also worthy of note that others, such as Ph.D. student blogger Anthony Oliveira [2013] and this essay, see transgressive mobilizations of racial stereotypes in their readings of the show.) The prison population in *OITNB* not only visually represents women that belong to demographics classically marked for death, but actively shows us the consequences of marginalization through flashbacks and story arcs. This concept can be further nuanced if we consider Angela Davis' (2005, 17) understanding of the American prison as an institution that historically absorbed the logic of slavery, resulting in a system that inherently marginalizes the people within it. As she says in *Abolition Democracy*, "punishment has been deployed against the human body as though it were a black body." Prisoners as a whole, then, cannot escape being marked for death, although for many of them, it is not the first time.

In some ways, necropower in *OITNB* manifests through the carceral system as a whole—from the arrest to sentencing, incarceration, and attempts to live on parole. The nature of incarceration is unapologetically geared toward removing liberty for prisoners, and this is the simplest explanation for the necropolitical prison; one could reasonably argue that even the most socially accepted and legally sound incarceration is still necropolitical in some way. But in *OITNB*, we only rarely come into conflict with the official policies that are meant to accurately and transparently manage prisoners as they serve their sentences. Instead, we are more often faced with policies that go above and beyond stated sentencing to interfere with the prisoners' lives inside and out, and are more often provided with representations of petty grievances and power plays of prison staff.

The prison as an institution and the individual people wielding the power of the prison within it seek the social, civil, and political death of the prisoners inside it and, occasionally, real physiological death. However, necropolitics alone does not provide us a sufficient framework to understand these representations, because this "death" is only in rare cases successfully and completely visited upon the prisoners. Instead, a constant theme running through this show is the resistance of death by the prisoners. Accordingly, instead of death, we will speak of *killing*—an action that is constantly taking place, and constantly being resisted. This conceptualization of killing (a verb) instead of death (a noun) allows us to recognize and analyze the myriad ways that the women prisoners in *OITNB* fight to live.

In this world, prisoners grasp power wherever and however they can, and use their scraps of power to defy the homicidal institution, by living. They fight to have social, civil, political, sexual lives, to wield some kind of economic power, and to feel joy within an institution that denies them that right. This analysis of Seasons 1 through 3 of *Orange Is the New Black* shows that one of the prisoners' most powerful avenues of living is sexuality.

The Power of Pleasure

Prisoners in *OITNB* resist necropower through the pursuit and enjoyment of sexual pleasure. This is in itself a transgressive act, as they take and give pleasure within an oppressive environment that works to reduce them to the state of functioning, but miserable, bodies. In the face of an institution that attempts to squash each prisoner's sexuality, women make love, they fuck, they masturbate, and they enjoy it immensely. In so many ways the prisoners fight to wring enjoyment out of the lives they live within their walls; they fight to be functioning, living human beings, and in this way constantly resist being killed—most of the time. Piper Chapman's experiences with sexuality in the prison perfectly exemplify both the institutional attitude towards sexual pleasure and enjoyment, and the transgressive nature of pursuing fulfilling sexual relationships in prison.

When Piper is admitted to the prison during that first episode of *Orange Is the New Black*, her newly contested sexuality remains a secret to prison officials. Healy, her assigned counselor, tells her that people like them need to stick together. During their first conversation, Healy informs Piper that there are lesbians in prison, but she does not need to participate in that behavior for safety or friendship—if she's worried about something, she should come to him because, as he states emphatically in Season 1, Episode 1, "you do *not* have to have lesbian sex." In that first interaction, it seems that Healy has made several assumptions about Piper: first, that because she is unlike other prisoners in class, she is not as "Other" as her fellow inmates; and second, that she would find sexual advances from another woman to be both unappealing and threatening.

Unbeknownst to her homophobic counselor, Piper's ex-lover and ex-partner in crime, Alex Vause, is imprisoned in the same institution. As the season progresses, Piper and Alex's relationship evolves from hostility to friendliness and flirting. The subtle attraction growing between the two women becomes more overt in "Fucksgiving," Season 1, Episode 9. The scene opens with a prison guard, nicknamed Pornstache, taping a poster to the wall—the poster reads "Suicidal?" in both English and Spanish, and features a crying woman prisoner.

> Pornstache: Listen up, turdbags! We're going to let you have your little going away party, but do not make our lives more difficult by hanging yourself, with a sheet, or a tampon string, or whatever the fuck you like to get all arts and craftsy with. *No Thanksgiving suicides*. Chapman. What are we not do to on this day of thanks?
> Piper: Commit suicide?
> Pornstache: Exactly. We are the pilgrims, you bitches are the Indians. This is the holiday where we cooperate.
> Other inmate (Boo): Yes. We bring you maize, and you give us smallpox blankets.
> Pornstache: Exactly. Everybody wins.

This exchange between Pornstache, Piper, and the other inmate shows a contradictory approach to the lives of prisoners. The poster offering help for suicidal thoughts seems, at face value, to be an attempt to protect the prisoners from harm. However, Pornstache's tone, word choices, and comments to the inmates—that smallpox blankets given to prisoners would be a "win" for everybody—demonstrate otherwise. Here, the bio-necropolitical spectrum is fully realized and overlapping, where the overt actions of the state (somewhat biopolitical, in the interest of protecting life) are subverted by the informal actions of an actor of the state. Further, this overlap actually undermines the biopolitical motive present, as the authority figure intended to convey the anti-suicide message is directly perpetuating the subjugation of these prisoners. This attitude could directly contribute to suicide through communicating disrespect, condescension, distaste, and a disregard for their lives, while making a casual and horrific comparison between the prisoners' relationships to the prison guards and the genocide of Native American peoples in the United States. This treatment of suicide and self-harm in *Orange Is the New Black* draws attention to the conflicting purposes and mandates of the prison, official and unofficial, and the complexity of bio-necropolitics as it is realized in this fictional death-world.

As the scene develops, we find that today is Thanksgiving, and the prisoners are holding a going away party for Taystee, a fellow prisoner who has reached her release date. Piper and Alex start to dance together—first platonically, but quickly shifting to intimate and flirtatious dance moves and interactions. As Piper coyly dances up and down the height of Alex's body, Pennsatucky, a fervently religious inmate, complains to Pornstache about the "lesbian activity." Enjoying the view, he shrugs her off, and Pennsatucky runs to find Healy to report Piper and Vause for "lesbian sexing." Pornstache's visual consumption of the prisoners' bodies and sexualities at this moment and many others reflects a common theme in mainstream media by heterosexualizing lesbianism, a process through which lesbian sexuality is framed as "hot" for heterosexual viewers (Jenkins 2005). However, in this case, by placing that heterosexualization on Pornstache's voyeuristic shoulders, the show seems to critique that very process.

Against Pornstache's protests, Healy imprisons Piper in the Solitary Housing Unit (SHU) for the "attempted rape" of a fellow inmate, his explanation for the dancing that he witnessed (an explanation that mirrors real-world American prisons' tendency to conflate consensual and non-consensual sexual activity in prison [Jackson 2013]). As the episode progresses through other subplots, we are treated to occasional glimpses of Piper in her cell. Usually shot from above, these short scenes emphasize the barrenness of the cell (and her time there), the literal chill, and the psychological impact of her confinement as Piper's composure visibly breaks down. We also witness her fiancé experiencing classic administrative barriers of the prison—he cannot gain full information on her confinement or the reasons for it, cannot reach any powerful prison officials due to the holiday, and her human rights take a back seat to the working hours of the institution. At one point, he yells on the phone that Piper is being "held there illegally—my father is a lawyer, I know her rights!" "It's a holiday," the person on the phone answers in a dry, bored tone. "You can call back on Monday."

One final scene from this episode begins with Piper lying on the cold, concrete floor of her cell in solitary, eyes blank and glazed, face almost absent of expression. Her head rolls to one side, and the screen fills with the red paint of the metal door, where a previous inmate has scratched "KILL ME NOW." Piper raises one eyebrow briefly, possibly in sympathy and understanding, when the door clangs and the plate over the window is drawn open. Piper jumps up. A few inches of Mr. Healy's face are visible.

> Healy: You needed a little time-out to think about your behavior.
> Piper: My *what*? I was dancing.
> Healy: Provocatively. Sexually. *Gay* sexually.
> Piper: This is illegal. You can't keep me in here.
> Healy: See, that's where you're wrong. Chapman, I tried to be nice to you because I understand where you come from. … You should be *thanking* me. Alex Vause is *sick*. I *get* you! You're not like her.
> Piper: The only sicko here… is *you*. And under different circumstances, what, I'd be your girlfriend? Is that it? Did I make you jealous? You *put* me in this *hellhole* for *no* reason. Wake up, Healy! Girls like me, *we don't fuck pretentious, ignorant old men with weird lesbian obsessions.* We go for tall, *hot* girls, and we *fucking love it.* So that leaves *you*. On the outside. Living your sad, *sad* little life. You don't *get me! Ever!* So go fuck yourself!"
> Healy: [After a pause, smiles.] Happy Thanksgiving, Chapman. [Slides the window closed]
> [Piper backs up from the window, clearly still infuriated, until she seems to realize what she has done. Her jaw drops, she spins back around to stare at her cell door, and the scene ends.]

The development and treatment of Piper's sexuality exemplifies the notion of the carceral state as an agent of sexual death. Piper is experiencing the brunt of necropower because finally, after nine episodes, she has failed to provide the heterosexual performance required of her by her counselor. Where her compliance with Healy's expectations had previously granted her privileges and positive feedback, rejecting those expectations—and the heterosexual performance (and avoidance of "lesbians") required of her—has resulted in her detainment in solitary.

However, Piper responds to the attempted killing of her sexuality (and self) with resistance instead of capitulation. In the face of Healy's homophobia, she throws her pleasure up like armor: "We go for tall, *hot* girls," she states defiantly, "and we *fucking love it.*" During her time in the SHU, she experiences severe mental health distress and at times appears to be broken, speaking to a (possibly hallucinated) voice as her mind breaks down. But

Piper emerges from confinement furious and determined. As we watch her re-enter the general population, she strides to Alex, takes her hand, and leads her to the chapel. Piper kisses Alex passionately, and the scene ends—presumably leaving them to consummate their newly rekindled relationship.

Healy may have tried to kill Piper's erotic spirit—by using every tool at his disposal to remove her ability to engage in sexuality he abhors—but he did not succeed, in the end. While Piper, Alex, and other women in *OITNB* continue to face trials in their pursuit of intimate physical relationships with one another, they cannot be stopped, and in their assertions of these relationships declare to us that they are very much alive.

Piper's dramatic reunion with Alex represents a major theme in *OITNB*—the mobilization of sexuality as a form of resistance to necropower, a way to wield power of a kind through sexuality and resist being killed. At times, this power comes from pleasure, for experiencing pleasure in this punitive and retributive environment is in itself transgressive. The show forces us to witness and examine sexual pleasure in a way that only rarely graces our mainstream television screens, from the practical "you do me, I'll do you" exchange between Nicky and Morello to a long shot of Boo, a big butch lesbian prisoner, in the throes of an orgasm she gives herself. In fact, sexual pleasure felt by the women prisoners in *OITNB* is represented in stark dissonance to the ways that the sexual pleasure of male prison guards is represented. In the first instance, we frequently see women's faces while they orgasm with each other or alone, and their joy is apparent on their faces. In contrast, while male characters are involved in sexual relationships (with prisoners and, occasionally in flashbacks/flashes out of prison, with free women), we rarely see men orgasm. Sex with men or male masturbation either occurs off screen (as in the case of the majority of Daya and Bennett's sexual activity) or is framed as boring, creepy, practical, or disgusting. Joyful, positive sexual pleasure is only directly seen on our screens when it is being felt by the prisoners. And through this, *OITNB* represents sex and pleasure as power—the power to live and feel joy in an institution geared toward preventing either.

Within this framework, the majority of visible representations of sexual pleasure are felt or caused by white prisoners. While those prisoners span gender presentation, class, and sexual orientation, they are mostly white women. Some women of color in *OITNB* do mobilize their sexualities to fight the necropower of the institution, but in markedly different ways than the white women. Significantly, with the black women prisoners, we see only unfulfilled sexual attraction. For example, the classic trope of a lesbian falling in love with a straight woman is portrayed in the case of Poussey and Taystee, while Suzanne's ("Crazy Eyes") attraction to Piper is framed as unrequited and unappealing to Piper. Suzanne's love interest at the end of Season 3 with a white woman, Maureen, is positive in framing, but never results in on-screen sexual pleasure, while Poussey's flashback of a sexual interlude with her (white) ex-girlfriend ends badly when her ex-girlfriend's father bursts into the room. The actual sex scenes in *OITNB* are not entirely whitewashed—Nicky's graphic sex with Soso (a prisoner with Japanese and Scottish heritage) being one outlier—and yet, the majority of on-screen, pleasurable sexual relationships occur between white women.

This pointedly excludes Piper's relationship with Larry. While Piper has an inferred sexual relationship with her fiancé, all on-screen attempts at sexual activity result in tears or non-performance, while his solo masturbation is framed as similarly pathetic and dissatisfying. Similarly, the majority of the sexual relationships portrayed that involve the prison staff are negatively framed (with one notable exception). For example, Joe Caputo's on-screen sexuality is limited to masturbation at work, unrequited attraction to a female guard, hate sex with Figueroa, and flashbacks that show a history of bad experiences in romance. Healy's wife despises him and refuses to try to learn to speak English to speak to him, while Pornstache sends unreturned love letters to Daya. This framing emphasizes the situation of sexual pleasure as a currency of the prisoners alone.

The Power of/for Family

Dayanara Diaz (Daya) is a young Latina woman and one of the main characters in *OITNB*. During Season 1, Daya develops a flirtation and then a relationship with one of the male guards, John Bennett. The representation of their relationship provides us with an incredibly nuanced platform from which to analyze various complex themes surrounding sexuality, power, and sexual agency.

Daya and Bennett's relationship is born both in the disparity of power and a disruption of that power. Walking down a set of stairs in Season 1, Episode 2, Daya asks Bennett (who is chewing gum) if she can have some gum. Bennett stiffly declines, then drops the official persona for a moment to add "It'd look funny. Like I liked you." Later, she finds a stick of gum in her bunk. This is Bennett's first overt flirtation and his first break with the rules of the institution for Daya.

During the next episode (Season 1, Episode 3), Pornstache is sharing his attitudes regarding the prisoners with Bennett (a new employee). Pornstache's mentorship of Bennett includes derogatory comments about the prisoners with a decidedly sexual overtone. Near the end of this scene, Pornstache draws close to share some advice: "I tell you what, grasshopper," he says. "Some of these bitches would suck it for half a cigarette." As we hear the word "bitches," the shot cuts to Daya walking past the open doorway to the guard's control room, glancing inside. At "for half a cigarette" the shot switches to Bennett looking back at her.

In this way, the romance between Daya and Bennett starts out in the full context of the institution, official and not: on one hand we have the official rules of the prison which condemn fraternization between the inmates and guards, while on the other we have the sexually oppressive and disrespectful oversight of Pornstache—along with some awareness of how Daya can be objectified, dehumanized, and theoretically coerced by staff. From the first few episodes their relationship is complicated by background policies and comments, even if their one-on-one flirtations closely mimic conventional relationships, aside from the not-insubstantial measures they take to avoid being caught by prison staff and other prisoners.

In this context, Daya becomes/is represented as a sexual being with a sex life of her own. However, unlike Piper and Alex, Nicky and Morello, and various other (white) prisoners in on-screen relationships, we rarely see Daya actually feeling sexual pleasure with Bennett (the one exception being on Valentine's Day in Season 2). Instead, her sexuality manifests visibly to us in two ways: first by becoming pregnant, and second by using her body to protect her future family. Daya's sexual activity, ensuing pregnancy, and decision to keep said pregnancy to term is transgressive by pursuing an aspect of life strictly forbidden to prisoners in an institution without conjugal visits or real access to furlough. As she is behind bars with her mother and half-sister and has regular access to her love interest and father of her child, she maintains a complex family life—one that she is largely not supposed to have. This family's main concern throughout the first three seasons of the show is Daya's pregnancy and the related drama.

One of the chief sources of conflict for Daya's biological and prison family is the need to protect Bennett from termination and arrest if he were found to be the father of Daya's child. In Season 1, Episode 11, Red (a prisoner and head cook) tells Daya and her mother, Aleida, that Daya has to have sex with Pornstache. He is lecherous enough to be easily seduced, and when Daya reports the activity as rape, he will be fired from his job and held accountable for her pregnancy. Further, Pornstache is a danger to the inmates and on Red's bad side after using her smuggling route to bring drugs into the prison (which results in the death of one of the characters). After some disagreement, Daya decides that this is the only route to take to fully protect her family.

Daya seduces Pornstache to protect her love interest, her unborn child, and the future she pictures their family having together. These sexual interactions are shown on-screen and framed as both practical and distasteful for Daya. During the first scene, we see the beginning of their sexual interlude in a broom closet; Pornstache's insistence on wearing a condom foils the original plan to use semen as evidence of rape. Daya seduces him a second time, and her friends and family make sure that they are caught in the act by Joe Caputo, an administrative official in the prison. Before being interrupted, we see Daya's face—looking bored and uncomfortable—and Pornstache's twisted in an orgasm. The scene itself does not seem meant to be pleasurable or exciting for the audience; as one blogger wrote, "if it was possible to be anti-turned on, this is it" (Allen 2015).

In this subplot, we see one woman using her sexuality to grasp the power she needs to exercise control over her situation. The show's representation(s) of Daya's true power in the prison is ambiguous and ever-changing—at times, the show gives us scenes of intimacy and joy between Daya and Bennett that are represented in a positive light, while at other times Daya is responsibilized for "framing" Pornstache for rape. As Bennett angrily tells her later, "He didn't rape you, you framed him." "Yeah, but as far as they know," she replies. The show does not dwell on the fact that Pornstache is not actually being "framed" for rape in prison—despite Daya's intentions, completely consensual sex between an inmate and a guard within prison walls is still legally rape— potentially because it would draw too direct attention to Daya's relationship with Bennett.

Daya not only disrupts the normal power disparity of the institution for herself, but also for her prison family as they develop a more casual attitude towards him (complete with teasing disrespect and blackmail in Season 2). Through Daya's sexual and romantic relationship with Bennett, along with the temporary removal of a corrupt and abusive prison guard, she and her kin gain a level of power normally denied to prisoners. This is never uncomplicated—as Daya confronts Bennett with in Season 2, he could give her a "shot" at any time, if he so desired—and yet the show regularly represents the vibrant life that Daya and her family have as a consequence of her refusal to be sexually dead during her incarceration.

This does not mean that Daya's pregnancy is completely positive in nature, or naturally engenders power. At times, Daya expresses frustration at feeling trapped in her pregnant body, and her storyline allows us to see various ways that the prison constrains the choices available to the prisoners. Still, Daya's sexuality (and her related pregnancy) provide her an avenue to grasp *some* power with which to fight the killing effects of the prison. Even at the end of Season 3, the circumstances of her newborn child highlight both the power she has to make decisions as a mother and the powerlessness of a mother in prison.

Daya's presence as a pregnant woman on the show is not unproblematic; throughout three seasons of the show, the two prisoners who we see pregnant in prison are Latina (the other is Maria Ruiz), compared to one well-off white woman's achingly normal pregnancy outside of prison (Polly, Piper's friend and business partner). With such a low number of pregnant characters, it is difficult to announce this simply as a stereotype, a fine line upon which *OITNB* walks regularly. One blogger, Rivera (2013), a self-identified Latin@ woman, struggles with this herself:

> I wanted to be mad about Daya getting pregnant, like damn of course the Latin@ folks are the only characters with pregnancy as part of their storylines because all we do is pop out babies, y'all. Opp! I just popped out another one while writing this. But then it's like—why does that upset me so much? It's not like it isn't part of real life. … Am I playing into some unchecked shame shit?… Or am I justified in wishing that the pregnancy storylines weren't just for the Latin@ folks? I don't know. What are we supposed to do when we see stereotypes that aren't completely ridiculous and speak to elements of our everyday lives?

Daya and Maria hearken to a classic stereotype of Latina women as always pregnant (López and Chesney-Lind 2014), while Daya's framing of Pornstache holds echoes of the "Vamp" stereotype—the Latina character who "uses her intellectual and devious sexual wiles to get what she wants" (Merskin 2007, 137). And yet, Daya's pregnancy is a regular plot point involved in her assertion and mobilization of sexual power and agency, while her controversial entrapment of Pornstache challenges the Vamp stereotype through the decidedly unsexy framing of the sexual acts and the predatory tone to his character. Daya is far from the stereotypical "Hot Tamale" or "firebrand" Latina woman that smolders and seduces (Cofer 2005, 247), as her sexual relationships are typified by a mixture of blunt honesty, kindness, and shared interests.

This juxtaposition of classic stereotypes and complicating nuances are seen throughout the rest of the Latina characters on the show. For example, when the Latina women gain control of the kitchen, the show positions the group of Latina women in a stereotypically domestic role for little narrative purpose, and prisoners comment that the eggs have gotten too spicy (reflecting the often-seen trope on television that Latina women and spicy food belong together [Merskin 2007]). However, the representations of Latina characters also challenge typical television stereotypes. For example, Daya is critiqued for not being able to speak Spanish, a skill that some of the other Latina women think that she should have; Marisol "Flaca" Gonzales leaves the Latina women in the kitchen to pursue more lucrative employment; and the Latina women form a heterogeneous group with a wide range of body types, sexual histories, intelligence, and personal styles. In these ways, *OITNB* seems to engage in a complex dance that both borrows from stereotypes and complicates them, a process which is also present in one final example of sexual power at Litchfield.

The Power of Sexual Creativity: The Case of The Time Hump Chronicles

During Season 3 Suzanne pens *The Time Hump Chronicles*, a series of erotica chapters involving aliens and very creative interpretations of what sexual activity can look like. Suzanne's experience putting her thoughts to paper provide an interesting look into the treatment of black women's sexuality in *OITNB*, along with giving us another example of how splinters of power can be gained through sexuality (in this circumstance, the creative expression of sexuality).

Season 3 introduces us to Berdie Rogers, a new black woman prison counselor who wants to make changes to Litchfield. (She faces extreme resistance from Healy, who we have found has serious issues with women; as she says to him in a later episode, "I can't pin down whether you're a misogynist, or a racist, or a winning combination of the two.") Rogers runs a drama class for the prisoners, and asks them to write a script. In Season 3, Episode 7, Rogers gently confronts Suzanne about the content of her writing:

> Suzanne: You asked us to use our imagination.
> Rogers: I asked you to re-imagine a primary life experience, not write a kinky sex fantasy set in space.
> Suzanne: It's not just sex, it's love. It's two people connecting, with four other people, and aliens.

Following the rejection of her story, Suzanne storms out of the office, smacking herself in the head with the rolled up papers and muttering about how "stupid" she is. When Taystee interrupts to ask what is wrong, Suzanne responds with "She said it's dirty and it's wrong, and she hated it!" As the supportive friend, Taystee assures her that she should keep writing, and scans the pages quickly with evident shock, curiosity, and disgust. Still, Taystee encourages Suzanne to keep writing, even if Rogers' class is more accepting of Chang's violent script than Suzanne' sexual one. As Taystee states, "This is America. Violence is all good and fine, but sex? [gasps] Lord, no!"

The introduction of this subplot seems to borrow on a long history of the mainstream media's tendency to pathologize black women's sexuality, historically constructing it as inherently immoral, uncontrollable, and hypersexual (Hammonds 1999; Davis and Tucker-Brown 2013; Young 2002; Stephens and Phillips 2003). Suzanne's sexuality in *OITNB* up until this point fits this trope perfectly: her advances to a white woman (Piper) are unwanted and perceived by Piper as downright dangerous, while the show frames Suzanne's expressions from a lens colored by markers of mental illness. When *The Time Hump Chronicles* arrive in Season 3, this just seems par for the course as far as Suzanne's inappropriate expressions of sexuality are concerned.

However, this subplot holds transgressive nuances as Suzanne continues to explore her erotic voice outside of the bounds of prison programming. Taystee passes the first pages to Poussey in horror, after explaining that she cannot read any more—"She's got a sentence that goes on a whole paragraph about some lady's clit that turns into a caterpillar!" "Well, you can't blame her for wanting to escape, alright?" Poussey responds. "It's lonely as fuck in here."

Poussey, a character who is dealing with severe loneliness and an escalating alcohol dependency, finds solace in Suzanne's writing and becomes her first fan. From there, Suzanne discovers that she is becoming popular through her writing—previously unknown prisoners come visit her in her bunk to ask about the next plot developments, debate their favorite characters and scenes, and ask for more chapters. As the episodes go by and Suzanne's erotica spreads, her character also undergoes a change; while the attention is annoying at times, Suzanne becomes more assertive in dealing with her fans, she walks with more confidence, and she seems to be suffering less from grief, loneliness, and her mental health difficulties.

One such scene occurs at the beginning of Season 3, Episode 9. Suzanne strolls down the hallway of Litchfield with her head up and a smirk on her face. One of the old-timers greets her jovially, and Suzanne responds with a casual one-fingered salute as she continues walking down the hall. Another admirer calls out a compliment on Suzanne's latest chapter. Then a new character, Maureen (a young white woman), stops Suzanne to rave about a particular reference she felt was made in one of Suzanne's chapters. Suzanne confidently walks on into the cafeteria. Her three admirers gather in the hallway. "She has a *beautiful* mind," Maureen tells the other two, awestruck. "Yeah, sick as fuck, but beautiful," another responds.

Later in this episode, Suzanne is having lunch in the cafeteria with some of the other black women when her fans start to sit down at the table, quizzing her about her process, inspiration, and what she's going to do next. Suzanne evidently is enjoying the positive attention, and shares a secret with her fans: the inspiration for one of the main characters in *The Time Hump Chronicles*, Admiral Rodcocker, was none other than W. Donaldson, one of the guards supervising the cafeteria. "I never thought I'd have a thing for bald dudes, but *damn*," Babs drawls as she looks him up and down, impressed and intrigued. Donaldson's fictional doppelganger is the subject of lust throughout the prison; in Babs' favorite scene in *The Time Hump Chronicles*, Rodcocker's clothes are vaporized to expose that he has two penises and "he gives [Edwina] a shocker made of penis instead of fingers." In the end, when Suzanne's erotica is found, she has to meet with both Healy and Donaldson to discuss the issue, to Donaldson's obvious discomfort.

This subplot is complex, and does not easily fit into one analytical box. On one hand, it borrows on mainstream (white) culture's understandings of black women's sexuality as immoral, extreme, perverse; Suzanne's sexual creativity cannot be controlled by the institution, and at first glance appears framed as disgusting for the viewers as well. But *The Time Hump Chronicles* quickly catapults Suzanne into her five minutes of fame and brings excitement to prisoners of all racial groups, a fact Suzanne is proud of. Her erotica is represented as both disgusting and intriguing, inappropriate and empowering, comedic and arousing. While Suzanne herself firmly occupies the position of 'deviant' as far as the prison officials are concerned, her creativity earns her respect and admiration from many of her fellow prisoners; aside from Taystee's first expressions of alarm at the content, we see no other negative feedback from the prisoners.

Further, Suzanne's taboo expression of sexuality undermines and objectifies a member of the prison staff. Donaldson is a tall white man, and largely unremarkable in the plot of *OITNB*. He neither seems overtly abusive (like Pornstache) or overly sympathetic (like Susan Fischer). Instead, he generally serves as a placeholder for the more official aspects of prison authority. But after the dissemination of *The Time Hump Chronicles*, prisoners in the third season subtly refer to him as Admiral Rodcocker with giggles and lustful glances, pulling him down from his position as a face of institutional power. With her erotica, Suzanne and the other prisoners, just a moment, make Donaldson serve *them*—even if it is only for a quick moment of sexual fantasy. Donaldson becomes subject to the "female gaze" (Perfetti-Oates 2015) of both the characters and, potentially, the audience, resulting in his immense discomfort and a manifestation of the prisoners' resistance.

The remainder of this subplot continues to be rich in meaning. Suzanne's erotica draws the attention of Maureen, who develops feelings for Suzanne and attempts to seduce her with a poem. Suzanne is intrigued and flattered, but afraid; as she tells Morello in Season 3, Episode 10, Suzanne does not actually understand sex, and has no experience with it. Through the remaining episodes, Suzanne and Maureen find a place of innocence from which to begin to explore their interest in each other.

In the end, Suzanne both represents and resists classic stereotypes about black women's sexuality. As Hammonds (1999) writes, "Black women's sexuality is often described in metaphors of speechlessness, space, or vision; as a 'void' or empty space that is simultaneously ever-visible (exposed) and invisible, where black women's bodies are always already colonized. In addition, this always already colonized black female body has so much sexual potential it has none at all" (94). Suzanne is both hyper-sexual and non-sexual, perverse and innocent; her space-set erotica draws direct comparisons to the void or empty space that black women's sexualities are sometimes seen to occupy, while disrupting the voiceless nature of such (Lewis 2005). In this season, Suzanne exercises her voice. She shares her thoughts, "kinky" though they might be, and finds power through that process. *The Time Hump Chronicles* serve Suzanne as an avenue to social power, as people finally begin to notice her for positive reasons, and sexual power, as she starts the beginning of a relationship within which she can be herself. In other words, in this season Suzanne finds a way to *live*, and the chief means through which she does so is the expression of her sexuality in writing.

Conclusion

Orange Is the New Black showcases powerful sexuality in the necropolitical world of the prison. Sexuality and womanhood form the core of the show, from up-close-and-personal shots of orgasmic bliss to used tampon applicators being repurposed to deal black market cigarettes. These representations of sexuality are by no means always positive (as Pennsatucky's past and present force us to confront), but they consistently form a base from which the prisoners can gather power.

This essay has outlined three different avenues through which the power of sexuality is mobilized to fight the killing power of the prison. First, Piper's outright, transgressive enjoyment of taboo sexuality is framed as a tool of resistance to the necropower of prison. Second, Daya's expression and practical utilization of her sexuality allows her to both create life and protect her new family. And third, Suzanne's discovery and assertion of her sexual creativity and voice provides a subplot that subtly challenges the authority of the prison and brings new vibrancy to her incarcerated life.

Litchfield Penitentiary is a death world, a place where the prisoners have been marked as worthy of civil, social, political, and sometimes biological death. But in this death world, these prisoners see power in the cracks and grasp it with both hands. They refuse to submit to the institution and allow themselves to be killed. Through these three subplots and many others, *Orange Is the New Black* gives us transgressive representations of women prisoners engaging with and mobilizing their own sexualities to fight the killing power of the prison.

REFERENCES

Allen, Rebekah. 2015. "All 17 Sex Scenes on *Orange Is the New Black* Ranked!" *Shewired.* March 15. http://www.shewired.com/television/2015/03/15/all-17-sex-scenes-orange-new-black-ranked?page=full.
Butler, Judith. 2004. *Precarious Life: The Powers of Mourning and Violence.* New York: Verso.
Cofer, Judith Ortiz. 2005. "The Myth of the Latin Woman: I Just Met a Girl Named Maria." *Experiencing Race, Class, and Gender in the United States* (4th ed.), edited by R. Riske-Rusciano and V. Cyrus, 246–248. Boston: McGraw Hill.

Davis, Angela Y. 2003. *Are Prisons Obsolete?* New York: Seven Stories Press.
Davis, Angela Y. 2005. *Abolition Democracy: Beyond Empire, Prisons, and Torture.* New York: Seven Stories Press.
Davis, Sarita, and Aisha Tucker-Brown. 2013. "Effects of Black Sexual Stereotypes on Sexual Decision Making among African American Women." *Journal of Pan African Studies* 5(9):11.
Foucault, Michel. 1990. *The History of Sexuality.* New York: Vintage.
Foucault, Michel. 1995. *Discipline and Punish.* New York: Random House.
Garland, David. 2001. *The Culture of Control: Crime and Social Order in Contemporary Society.* Chicago: University of Chicago Press.
Gay, Roxanne. 2013. "The Bar for TV Diversity Is Way Too Low." *Salon.* August 22. http://www.salon.com/2013/08/22/the_bar_for_tv_diversity_is_way_too_low/.
Hammonds, Evelynn M. 1999. "Toward a Genealogy of Black Female Sexuality: The Problematic of Silence." *Feminist Theory and the Body: A Reader*, edited by Margrit Shildrick and Janet Price, 93–104. New York: Routledge.
Jackson, Jessi Lee. 2013. "Sexual Necropolitics and Prison Rape Elimination." *Signs* 39(11):197–220.
Jenkins, Tricia. 2005. "'Potential Lesbians at Two O'Clock': The Heterosexualization of Lesbianism in the Recent Teen Film." *Journal of Popular Culture* 38(3):491–504.
Lamble, Sarah. 2013. "Queer Necropolitics and the Expanding Carceral State: Interrogating Sexual Investments in Punishment." *Law Critique* 24:229–253.
Lewis, Desiree. 2005. "Against the Grain: Black Women and Sexuality." *Agenda* 19(63):11–24.
López, Vera, and Meda Chesney-Lind. 2014. "Latina Girls Speak out: Stereotypes, Gender and Relationship Dynamics." *Latino Studies* 12(4):27–49.
Mbebe, Achille. 2003. "Necropolitics." Translated by Libby Meintjes. *Public Culture* 15(1):11–40.
Merskin, Debra. 2007. "Three Faces of Eva: Perpetuation of The Hot-Latina Stereotype in *Desperate Housewives*." *The Howard Journal of Communications* 18:133–151.
Oliveira, Anthony. 2013. "A Question of Taystee: On Racist Stereotypes in Orange Is the New Black." *Notes from Maxwell's Demon.* August 22. https://maxwellsdemoniac.wordpress.com/2013/08/22/a-hymn-to-taystee-on-racist-stereotypes-in-orange-is-the-new-black/.
Perfetti-Oates, Natalie. 2015. "Chick Flicks and the Straight Female Gaze: Sexual Objectification and Sex Negativity in New Moon, Forgetting Sarah Marshall, Magic Mike, and Fool's Gold." *Gender Forum* 51.
Rivera, Gabrielle. 2013. "Orange Is the New Black: Things We Should Talk About." *Autostraddle.* July 21. http://www.autostraddle.com/orange-is-the-new-black-7-things-we-should-talk-about-186228/.
Stephens, Dionne P., and Layli D. Phillips. 2003. "Freaks, Gold Diggers, Divas, and Dykes: The Sociohistorical Development of Adolescent African American Women's Sexual Scripts." *Sexuality and Culture* 7(1):3–49.
Sykes, Gresham M. 2007. *The Society of Captives: A Study of a Maximum Security Prison.* Princeton: Princeton University Press.
Young, Lola. 2002. *Fear of the Dark: Gender, Racism, Ethnicity.* London: Routledge. http://www.myilibrary.com?ID=46291.

Anatomy of a Binge
Abject Intimacy and the Televisual Form

ANNE MOORE

Television has always had a bit of a chip on its shoulder. From "golden age" shows that performed canonical theatrical works to HBO's erstwhile slogan "It's not TV," television has continually pretended to be something it's not. Whether it's series creator David Chase comparing *The Sopranos* to short films (Mittell 2015, 29) or the *New York Times Book Review* debating the "quality" of Quality TV by asking the question "Are the New Golden Age Television Shows the New Novels?" (Kirsch and Hamid 2015), it's clear that escaping the déclassé taint of TV is a key to middlebrow respectability.

This dismissal of television is linked to its status as a gendered media. Unlike film, which is historically associated with the public sphere, television is a more intimate—and thus understood to be a more feminine—medium. Daytime programming, especially soap operas, is linked to women, and to the abject position of women's work. In their book *Legitimating Television: Media Convergence and Cultural Status*, Michael Newman and Elana Levine argue that "much of what gets praised about prime time seriality is framed in masculinist terms that work to distance such programming from its feminized other"—the soap opera (Newman and Levine 2012, 82).

And it seems to have worked: from college courses on *The Wire* to Emily Nussbaum's regular television column in *The New Yorker*, television's cultural moment seems be finally arriving. Furthermore, there's no greater sign of cultural legitimacy than acquiring copycats, and television has recently found these, courtesy of the Internet. The streaming services Netflix, Hulu Plus, and Amazon Prime all feature original programming, which they call "television shows," and are carefully presented as such through a series of cultural markers: for instance, Netflix and Amazon Prime have submitted their shows for (and won) Emmys, and both list their original programming alongside traditional network shows on their streaming platforms. However, if we define media forms at least in part by their mode of distribution, then these narratives shouldn't be called television at all. If, as Raymond Williams claims, television is identified by the uninterrupted "flow" from programming to commercial break that discourages viewers from changing the channel, then series from streaming services disrupt the nature of the form (Williams 2003, 91). Netflix series are released all at once, and the shows themselves utilize so many of the narrative and stylistic strategies of television serials that they border on formal parody. In this way, Netflix forms a kind of fun-house mirror for HBO's self-aggrandizing claim that it's "not TV." Despite the fact that Netflix has changed the mode of distribution so much that it's technically inaccurate to describe its original programming as television at all, the company's slogan seems to be "more TV than TV."

Orange Is the New Black stands out among shows which have garnered the middlebrow accolade "Quality Television" in that it has upended the gendered hierarchy which Newman and Levine critique. In setting the so recently abject form of television as its aspirational goal, it has embraced effeminate elements of the medium that were previously discarded in other shows' anxiety to be taken seriously. For instance, AMC marketing campaigns around the network's breakout hits *Breaking Bad* and *Mad Men* which lionized antiheroes Don Draper and Walter White often undermined the shows' feminist content. Instead of distancing itself from the taint of the soap opera as so many "Quality Television" shows have done, *Orange Is the New Black* centrally and unapologetically features many of the generic markers of the soap opera—cliffhangers, a sprawling cast of characters, multiple overlapping serial plots, and melodrama.

At the same time as it embraces this abject form, the show emphasizes the feminine concerns of intimacy, both on the level of plot and in its adoption of the serial tropes that elicit readerly devotion and binge viewing. This intimacy is compounded by the series' insistent focus on the abject details of daily life, especially in its attention to the characters' bodily needs—the sense of lived closeness with the characters comes from the show's focus on food and toilets. In this way, the intimacy elicited by the form is directed toward political ends, shifting the reader's identification further and further toward those elements that are absent from or debased within mainstream media, and simultaneously decentering the perspective away from the Trojan Horse of white wealthy protagonist Piper toward the other inmates: mostly poor and/or people of color. Historically, this process of identification has been used to value the Other based on her similarity to the presumably white viewer or reader. However, *Orange* turns this machinery of empathy back on the viewer by steadily degrading Piper's position as a lens through which the narrative can be interpreted. As Piper's perspective is troubled, she is implicated in the larger social problems of white supremacy and capitalism which structure the narrative and the prison-industrial complex in which it is set. And so is the viewer.

It's Not the Internet, It's Netflix

The first way that *Orange Is the New Black* signals its alignment with abjection is through its refusal to distance itself from the effeminacy associated with the television form. The show's clearest declaration of its "TV-ness" is so structurally fundamental that it almost goes without saying: the division of the narrative into hour-long episodes. The length of the narrative (roughly 13 hours per season) does necessitate splitting it into manageable pieces, but the possibilities of the streaming platform make it possible for episodes to be longer or shorter than a typical television show, or even for episodes within a single series to vary widely in length. The hour-long format aligns *Orange Is the New Black* with prime time television dramas and soap operas: from *Hill Street Blues* to *Days of Our Lives*, this hour-long format has, with a few rare exceptions, been the standard for serialized drama. At the same time, this format opens up the possibility that episodes will be syndicated on a traditional network. While the finales of the second and third seasons are 90 minutes long, this still lines up with the "very special episode" status that a season finale often receives, and follows the model offered by traditional narrative television shows such as *Lost* and *Battlestar Galactica*.

The formal break between episodes is central to establishing the sense of intimacy with a fiction world. In his essay "Broken on Purpose," Sean O'Sullivan (2009) argues for the importance of the serial gap: the art of the serial, he claims, "calls attention to itself as an array of parts; it is the art of fracture, of separation, and it is the art of the energy required to stitch together those pieces" (59). Netflix's user interface discourages viewers from lingering too long in those gaps, but the cliffhanger ending of nearly every episode and the signature smash-cut to an orange screen that precedes the end credits highlight the segmented nature of the show and encourages viewers to invest interpretive energy into the serial breaks, even if they only have to wait fifteen seconds before the next episode begins to autoplay. The break elicits the kind of devotion that leads to "water cooler" buzz, even though the actual reader doesn't have time to walk to the sink for a glass of water before the next episode begins. In this way, viewers get all the anticipatory pleasure with none of the pain of waiting. For this viewer, at least, the recurrence of the floating "Netflix Original Series" title card kicks off the same pleasure center associated with the "next one" in any binge (a cigarette, a piece of candy, a game of computer solitaire): the sneaky voice in my head that tells me "just one more."

The show acknowledges its compulsion-inducing nature, particularly through references to media fandom, and it does so in a way that emphasizes the intimacy of the televisual form. For instance, although we learn during Larry's ill-starred NPR interview that he and Piper never had any official conversation about cheating before she was incarcerated, she does make him promise on his first visit that he won't watch *Mad Men* without her. Not only that, but she makes him promise to watch it in the most intimate way possible:

> Piper: Promise me that when I get out of here we're going to binge-watch it in bed with take out from…
> Larry: Gertie's?

The communal experience of watching a show together is aligned with sex and food, and is (of course) a direct reference to the viewer's own current experience of watching the show itself. From the bedroom setting to the moment of Larry finishing her sentence for her, binge-watching a show is the *ne plus ultra* of relational intimacy.

In a 2014 interview with the Writer's Guild of America, series creator Jenji Kohan claimed that the binge format has not affected the way she writes the show, but she did acknowledge how much it has affected the way people consume it: "They bathe in it," she mused. "They become so involved in a way, because they've been so immersed in a way that is different—that a more spread out episodic show didn't allow for before." Piper's promise from Larry (broken almost immediately) that he will refrain from their intimate scene of televisual domestic bliss repurposes *Mad Men*'s TV-ness as a strength of the form, not an effeminate taint that needs to be outrun or erased. Television's link to intimacy is explicitly tied here to its domestic setting.

Suzanne's foray into serial erotica in Season 3 similarly plays on the link between serial narratives and intense affective investment, and does so through references to the debased genre of science fiction. While the element of communal participation has been part of the way serial narratives have been consumed since the Victorian era (Hayward 1995), a more contemporaneous object of the joke of Suzanne's rabid fan base would be television fan communities, particular as they manifest in spaces like online message boards. In this way, the show draws a parallel between the binge format and early time-shifted television viewing, especially among science fiction fandom—the sci-fi content of Suzanne's stories only serves to strengthen that link, and the parallels between the viewer and Suzanne's super-fans both riff on the depth of attachment associated with the serial form and how embarrassing that attachment can feel.

While the cliffhanger plots and flashback structure acknowledge the influence of pulp television such as the groundbreaking addictive science fiction series *Lost*, *Orange*'s reliance on melodrama and coincidence to move the plot forward gestures further back to the even more denigrated genre of the daytime soap. This can be seen most clearly in the central relationship between Piper and Alex Vause, her former lover and the woman who named her to the FBI—who just happens to be housed in the same facility. In Kerman's memoir, Piper does end up rooming with the Alex character, but only after they have both been transported to the facility where they are awaiting trial, thus grounding the encounter in the realism that characterizes the memoir genre. Further undoing the "reality effect" of the memoir, the televised versions of Piper and Alex are both traditionally attractive: thin, white, and magazine-pretty. In the book, Kerman describes Alex as "a fireplug" with "a French bulldog face"—a far cry from the glamorous Laura Prepon. In the show, Alex's presence at Litchfield is played for full dramatic effect, and her final confrontation with Piper is the shocking final image of the first episode, enticing the viewer to come back for more.

The appearance of Vee in Season 2 further cements the role of coincidence in the show's plotting. While the arrival of Taystee's former foster mother in Litchfield does not push the limits of realism too heavily (after all, she and Taystee lived in the same region and both were presumably arrested for their work in the drug trade), Taystee's psychological turmoil at the return of this mother figure, the turmoil it causes in her romantic friendship with Poussey, and Vee's own villainous machinations within the prison are all played for full melodramatic effect. The final revelation of Vee's seduction of and subsequent setup for murder of her foster son RJ dials the emotional tenor of the show up to a fever pitch.

Orange's reliance on melodrama is most apparent, however, in the story of Daya, an inmate who arrives the same day as Piper. Upon arrival, she discovers that her mother is also a prisoner at Litchfield, and their initial meeting is highly dramatized, with Daya's mother, Aleida, slapping her across the face and stomping away wordlessly. We soon discover that Aleida's anger is at least in part based in sexual jealousy over Daya's angry dalliance with her mother's boyfriend. Daya's romance with the prison guard Bennett is soapiest of all: the sentimental piano theme that accompanies their scenes together through the first two seasons encourages the viewer to see their connection as a star-crossed romance instead of a rape, a blurring that has an ignominious track record in soaps.

Intimate Matters, or, So Much Peeing

The show also demonstrates its debt to soaps through its combination of multiple overlapping plots, all of which prioritize connection and relationality; even when the show features violence, that violence is almost always in service of a plot based around relationships. For instance, for the first two seasons, Alex and Piper are only interested in each other, not in influence over the other inmates. It's Piper's investment in power over her fellow inmates which marks her descent into villainy in Season 3, in much the same way that Vee's obsession with power and influence marked her as the central villain of Season 2. For the most part, the machinations of the plot are more focused on traditionally feminine concerns: motherhood, romance (familial, romantic, or platonic), sexual violence, and the detritus of daily life.

The show's commitment to exploring the relational consequences of violence is particularly clear when it is compared to other self-consciously "quality" television. Brian Ott argues in his essay "Cocksucker, Motherfucker, Tits" (2008) that HBO uses explicit content, particularly profanity, nudity, and violence "as a way to position itself outside of televisual normativity" (125). Violence, especially shocking moments of violence, has become one of the key signifiers of cinematic "quality" on cable dramas: whether it's Tony Soprano garroting an FBI stoolie, a bathtub and decomposing body crashing through the ceiling in *Breaking Bad*, or a ritually posed murder victim in *True Detective*, intensely violent scenes demonstrate the lengths to which cable dramas are willing to go in order to distinguish themselves as edgy and thus distance themselves from standard televised fare.

Orange Is the New Black is also invested in a discourse of exceptionalism, but the gendered and racial politics of its methods of distinguishing itself from its predecessors are notably different. If there's a move that most parallels the "distinguishing" scenes of violence so popular among its Quality predecessors, it's *Orange Is the New Black*'s interest in toilets. I've watched a lot of television in my life, and never have I seen so many women peeing on screen. The series begins in a bathroom, as Piper rushes through her first prison shower, and the first flashback scene in the pilot features her sitting on the toilet and weeping the night before she leaves for Litchfield. The bathroom is a central plot location as well: not only is it one place where Piper and Alex and Morello and Nichols escape for sex, but it's also the setting for a racial turf war in Season 2. Furthermore, Piper's quest to find a time to use the toilet alone is a running gag throughout the first season. The opening episode of the second season shows how impossible that wish for privacy is in a prison setting, when Piper is housed in a temporary holding cell in Chicago with a single shared toilet in the cell, so she has to watch her cellmates defecating.

While the show does contain violent moments (Poussey, Red, Pennsatucky, and Sophia are all badly beaten at different points), it tends to present violence in more day-to-day, relational terms, often centering on bathrooms and food—bodily functions. The best example of this (and the most shocking) is Red's initial ploy to starve Piper out after Piper insults the prison food, serving her a bloody tampon in an English muffin for breakfast. When Piper rejects Suzanne's romantic advances, Suzanne responds by peeing on the floor outside Piper's bunk. Susanne's aggression is based on blurring the boundaries of privacy, not on the threat of physical harm. Vee uses the bathrooms as the site by which she attempts to gain control of the prison economy; not only does she bar the "Spanish" crew from using the clean(er) toilets in the black section after their bathrooms are flooded with sewage, but the conduit for her cigarette business is empty tampon dispensers.

By continually emphasizing the unavoidable and unavoidably intimate daily needs of the body, the show highlights the multifaceted nature of institutionalized violence. Piper's first-season fear of getting "shivved" by her roommate, for instance, is an example of her racist reliance on stereotypes, not reality. The real violence comes through the "smaller" concerns of the body which are historically coded as female—Sophia cannot get access to her medication, Ruiz's baby is taken away from her immediately after childbirth, all the women are denied decent food after the prison is privatized. By narrativizing the most private details of the characters' daily lives, the show uses the feminist strategy of elevating "women's concerns" to show the connection between these seemingly small-scale concerns and larger patterns of oppression.

"It ain't just about the food"

If the focus on toilets and urination revels in the connection between women and the abject needs of the body, then the show's emphasis on food demonstrates the way it structurally highlights traditionally feminine concerns: not just eating food (which has been a central concern for many "Quality" shows, including the Sopranos), but the raced and gendered work of food preparation. For instance, part of Vee's appeal to her foster children is the promise of maternal love demonstrated by her homemade butternut squash soup, and it is the contrast between the menacing way she first attempts to lure Taystee into the drug trade when she is a kid and her later domestic fortitude which is an early signal to the viewer of the complicated hold she has over the other women at the prison. Along the same lines, Red's position as the "mother" among the white inmate clique is solidified by her position in the kitchen; her removal from that position coincides with her loss of power and status among her fellow inmates. Even after MCC empties the kitchen position out of any real meaning (and any opportunity to build job skills for the other inmates who work there) with its switch to boil-in-the-bag meals, Red's lottery for private meals renews her position of power in the internal prison economy.

Over the course of three seasons, the show steadily drifts away from the perspective of its initial white protagonist. It does so in part through its focus on the daily work of food preparation. When Gloria takes over management of the kitchen, she brings in her fellow Latina inmates to work as her prep crew, and the food is noticeably different than when Red was in charge. She also takes advantage of the position as a source of social power, but Gloria's power is linked to her practice of Santeria. The basics of what the position offers are similar, but the difference between the details adds up. If the show is making the argument that small details form the basis of larger, more explicitly political trends, then this difference among cuisines demonstrates how not all experiences are reducible to the same core feelings, and backs away from easy humanism. Flavors which are comforting to some groups alienate others. The show takes the variety of experiences seriously, not because "we're all the same," but because all those experiences deserve respect in and of themselves.

One of the most striking instances of the show's steady shift in focus away from a white perspective comes in the episode "Ching Chong Chang," which follows the inmate Chang throughout a typical day, giving insight into her background through an extended flashback. Chang is one of the characters who is least developed in the first season, and who most resembles the racist trope of the inscrutable Chinese: she speaks only rarely, and in a thick accent; when Healey chooses representatives for his ill-fated women's caucus, Chang represents "Other." Even after the show drifts away from Piper in the second season to more deeply explore characters and dynamics within the black and Spanish cliques, Chang remains a relatively one-note character, especially since she is not aligned with any of the main prison cliques. The episode that centers on her takes her experience and her isolation seriously, and on its own terms. Moments which presented her as a stereotype in previous episodes are given depth, defusing their effectiveness as racist shorthand. For instance, when she only orders peas and two milks at lunch, building on the stereotype of the "strange" eating habits of Asian people, we see how she is actually hoarding ingredients to make a veggie cake for herself, which she enjoys alone while watching Chinese soaps in the prison yard on an illegal cell phone. Even though her backstory demonstrates connections to organized crime and the kinds of violence that I mentioned earlier which often serve to distinguish masculine "Quality" television (at one point, she orders a fellow gang member to cut out someone's gall bladder), the show devotes considerably more narrative time to her food preparation. These small details—the detritus of daily life—are given narrative priority over what would more frequently be considered the "big-picture" issue of violence.

Along the same lines, Cindy's conversion to Judaism shows the connection between the intimate details of lived experience and identity. At the beginning of the third season, Cindy is one of the many inmates who requests the superior kosher meals. Unlike the other inmates, Cindy maintains her commitment to Judaism even after a rabbi from MCC arrives to investigate the sudden spike in inmates who keep kosher. Her self-identified Judaism is played for laughs throughout the season, but this takes a sudden turn in the season finale when she has an emotional conversion experience. Food is central to the experience beyond just her initial motivation to convert, and she acknowledges this directly to the Rabbi as she tries to convince him of her sincerity, telling him: "It ain't just about the food—although, the more I been learning, the food a big part of it, am I right?" She has even used food to enable her study of Jewish culture, paying one of the two Jewish inmates who had been serving as her tutors in granola bars to teach her the Hebrew alphabet.

Her monologue demonstrating her faith is played completely straight (rare for this character who is so often a source of comic relief): the conversation is a standard shot/reverse-shot, with no music to guide audience response. With this lack of visual or extradiegetic cues, the viewer is left to fully focus on Cindy's tearstained face and searching monologue. For this viewer, at least, the result is deeply affecting, not least because the commitment to seriousness is so rare for the character. When she is told that the conversion will not be official until they can perform a *mikvah*, her disappointment is palpable, and the ensuing flashback further explores the place of food in Cindy's spiritual life, showing a scene around a dinner table where her terrifying father quotes Deuteronomy at her, threatening hell for her sin of tasting dinner before grace has been said. Just as the kosher meals offered her an unexpected door to a new faith and new identity, the oppressive mealtime environment of her childhood alienated her from the faith she was born into. With this emphasis on the connection between lived experience and identity, the show makes an argument against essentialism, demonstrating how identity is always rooted in the intimate, embodied details of daily life.

Faces, Voices

Just before Cindy's flashback, there's a shift from the scene's naturalistic camera work: immediately before the scene cuts, the camera zooms in on Cindy's face until it almost fills the frame, and we hear the first few lines of her flashback before the visual cuts over. This visual focus on the character featured in the flashback occurs throughout the episode. Unlike most episodes, the premiere and finale of season three both contain flashbacks for a number of different characters, all organized around a single theme. During these themed episodes, we get one of these shots just before each flashback, in which the face of the character upon whom the following scene will focus takes up nearly the entire frame. Throughout the show, the flashbacks deepen our understanding of the characters, and these establishing shots demonstrate the intimacy they aim to create.

What is particularly interesting to me about *Orange*'s use of the flashback structure to create a sense of intimacy with characters is that the flashbacks give viewers a deeper understanding of the characters but don't flatten out these experiences into an easy sameness. The Season 3 premiere's focus on motherhood is perhaps the most notable in this way, since rhetoric around motherhood is so frequently used as a way to create an idealized sameness among women that can in practice be stifling or exclusionary. Each of the flashbacks presents a very different experience of motherhood, from Poussey and Aleida's idealized moments of connection between mother and child to Pennsatucky's mother pushing her to drink Mountain Dew so her hyperactive reaction might allow their family to get more money from Social Services to Healey's nightmarish mother caught in the midst of a schizophrenic rant. It is the inclusion of Sophia's experience, pre-transition, awaiting the birth of her son that most fully complicates the picture, and opens the episode up to a reading based on multiplicity, discouraging the viewer from seeing it just as a catalog of Good Mothers vs. Bad Mothers.

These group flashback episodes work as a microcosm of what seems to be the show's mission: to look more closely at a range of women, and to see them on their own terms, rather than in some transition from Other to sameness. The opening credits follow the same pattern, and can be read as a thesis statement for the show overall. It is a series of women's eyes and mouths, shot in extreme close-up and intercut with shots of small details of prison life: hands being cuffed or fingerprinted, a row of payphones, a shot from below of a barbed-wire fence. This is played over a jangly Regina Spektor song written for the show, "You've Got Time." The faces are of real prisoners, recruited from a nonprofit organization that helps women transition out of gang life, and they were asked to think of a peaceful time, a person who made them laugh, and a time they wished to forget (Dunne 2013). With a few exceptions, however (two smiling mouths and one woman throwing her head back to laugh), the expressions on their faces are not nearly so legible as the cues would suggest.

What instead strikes the viewer is the almost overwhelming variety and closeness of the faces, especially in relation to the song. The faces often change with the drumbeat of the song, but not consistently, so the expected rhythm is thrown off with these pauses. Then, with the first drum roll that leads to the chorus, the faces change with each beat of the roll, so fast that they can no longer be distinguished from each other. This happens again with the second chorus, but this time it is pictures of mouths that roll by, too quick to read. The effect of all this is a sense of the overwhelming variety of human experience, and the basic opacity of other people's experience. The best example of this last quality is one of the last faces we see: eyes framed by rectangular black glasses, reminiscent of those worn by the Alex character—however, the face in the credits is older than Laura Prepon, and significantly more weathered. At first, it appears that the character is crying, but upon looking more closely what appears to be a tear is just a skin tag in the corner of her eye. We're tricked, for a moment, into thinking we know her experience, and the misreading serves as a reminder that every assumption of sameness comes with the danger of projecting a presumed experience onto the other person. At the same time, the "realness" of these women, and their distance from the glamorized doubles in the show, works as a reminder of their embodiment, and thus their difference from you, the viewer. Even as we identify with these characters, the credits work as a reminder every episode that we aren't getting the full story of what prison experience is like.

Initially, the studio that designed the credits (also responsible for the jazzy paranoia of the *Homeland* credits and the eerie repeating suburbanites of *Weeds*) wanted to "create a semi-surreal main title sequence of images from Piper's point of view that would starkly contrast the hard, cold reality of her new imprisoned life against the imagined luxuries of her previous life" (Dunne 2013). Kohan objected, saying that she wanted the credits sequence to demonstrate the show's commitment to showing the stories of a wide variety of formerly incarcerated women, not just Piper's. In an NPR interview when the show premiered, Kohan was frank that Piper was meant to work as a "Trojan Horse": "you're not going to go into a network and sell a show on really fascinating tales of black women and Latina women and old women and criminals. But you take this white girl, this fish out of water, and you follow her in, you can then expand your world and tell all those other stories" (*Fresh Air* 2013).

Unpacking the Trojan Horse

The series may use Piper's privilege as a way to draw viewers in, but by the end of the first season, identifying with Piper is profoundly uncomfortable for the viewer, and by the end of the third season, she has transformed into a full-fledged villain. The show follows this decentering of Piper's perspective and steady problematization of her point of view. In the pilot, many of the social differences between Piper and the other inmates are played for laughs at the inmates' expense: Aleida slapping Daya in greeting marks them as "hotheaded Latinas," and Big Boo is the prison trope of the butch daddy. One early clue that Piper's perspective will be steadily troubled comes when her fiancé Larry gets a coveted interview on the show's *This American Life* stand-in. He talks at length about his paternalistic concern for Piper's safety and relays stories about the "wacky inmates" she has met. When we see the "real" characters behind these tropes who are devastated by Piper's descriptions of them, the implications of relying on stereotypes to understand these characters is turned back on the viewer who, like Larry, is a voyeur in the world of Litchfield. Even though Piper is herself devastated when her initial impressions are aired to the prison community, she doesn't do anything to repair the damage she has done, and has no answer when her roommate confronts her with the question "Is that what you think of me?" If the show uses its emphasis on intimacy to push its readers toward an empathetic response, it's clear from Piper's lack of progress even though she is, in her own words, "So, so, so sorry," that merely feeling bad is insufficient to address one's own position of privilege.

As the seasons go on, Piper's narcissism continues unabated, and this inability or unwillingness to consider her own culpability in the larger structures of power marks her transformation into full-on villainy by the end of Season 3. The best example of this comes in the recurrence of one item: the screwdriver Piper accidentally steals from the electrical shop early in the first season. Because she is not used to being monitored (a result not only of her new arrival in prison, but because of her social position as a wealthy white woman), she unthinkingly pockets the screwdriver during her work shift and only realizes she has it after Janae, the black inmate who runs the desk, has been sent to solitary confinement for her mistake. Unlike Janae, Piper is able to use the corruption of the system to her advantage, and she just waits for the guard responsible for the electrical shop to replace the item. Boo steals the screwdriver, and while at first it's teased that she will use it as a weapon, the bawdy joke that ends the episode is that she has in fact stolen it as a masturbatory tool. Following the rule of Chekhov's gun, the screwdriver returns in the season finale, when Piper begins to carry it as protection against Pennsatucky, who has attacked her in the showers with a razor and presents a genuine threat to her safety. However, the final scene's use of the visual language of horror movies tells a different story, one that foreshadows Piper's descent into villainy.

The scene opens with Pennsatucky following Piper into a dark alleyway. Piper is in the foreground of the scene, and takes up much more screen space than Pennsatucky. Pennsatucky's angel costume is on one level meant to be read ironically, since her faith is what makes her so dangerous, but the combination of her costume and her homemade weapon—a wooden cross sharpened into a stake—makes it impossible not to read Piper as a vampire. And in the context of her recent arguments with Larry and Alex when she calls herself "a selfish, manipulative, narcissist," this characterization is not far off base. At first, Pennsatucky is the more frightening character by far—her previous attack on Piper is genuinely terrifying, and ends with Piper smeared in Pennsatucky's blood, only saved by the timely arrival of a guard. The opposite dynamic seems to be at work in this scene: a guard arrives, but it's Healey, who leaves Piper to her fate. Pennsatucky easily disarms Piper, and draws first blood, which splashes dramatically on the snow. Her diatribe at Piper is similarly menacing, both in its vitriol and its demonstration of her religious fervor: "God loves me; he don't love you because you ain't worthy of God's love—you ain't worthy of anybody's love."

It is here when Piper snaps, and the scene changes dramatically. Of course, as a poor, mentally ill, drug-addicted woman, Pennsatucky is repeating the message which has been aimed at her for her entire life, both directly and through the systems which have surrounded her. She has remained frightening partly because the viewer has been encouraged to follow Piper's belief in her own helplessness, or that, as she says to Taystee after her shower attack, that she is "not equipped to deal with this." When she begins to beat Pennsatucky, however, and actually uses the power that she has possessed all along, the viewer finally gets an external view of her character. Again, Piper is framed like a horror movie monster, shot from a low angle, her face an unrecognizable mask of rage that finally fades to an orange screen (a departure from the smash cut usually used to end episodes). From a position that prioritizes Piper's perspective as a white, wealthy woman, it would be possible to read this final scene as a victory: Piper finally recognizes her own power and stands up for herself to patriarchal religious intimidation. Through an intersectional lens, however, one that takes Pennsatucky's perspective seriously, Piper looks very different. Viewed from below, she's monstrously powerful.

The screwdriver does not return until Season 3, in a way that shows another side of Piper's power, one that builds on the allusion to vampirism in the previous scene. Over the course of the season, she builds an underground business selling used panties she makes from extra cloth at her job in the prison sweatshop. The enterprise is originally played for laughs, especially the scene where Piper recruits her fellow inmates to wear the panties: she adopts a smooth persona, which stands in contrast to her description of the operation as "selling stinky panties to perverts." She offers to pay them in ramen flavor packets—the only thing that makes the new MCC food palatable. Piper has used her external wealth to buy out the commissary, knowing that this will work as a form of currency. Revealingly, Piper uses leftist and feminist logic to convince the others to work for her. When Boo points out that she will be the one taking home the profit from the arrangement, she offers up that Boo will be "supporting local business." When Yoga Jones complains that it's "gross," Piper counters with the argument that it is only shame "bred into them by the patriarchy" which prevents them from participating. She even refers to them as "sisters," with patriotic music swelling behind her.

Her later behavior, however, reveals the lie of this sisterly rhetoric. As the business picks up, Piper becomes an ever more ruthless boss, firing Flaca for her attempts to unionize the workers, and setting up money transfers to pay them: the same system, Alex reminds her, that drug kingpins use to pay dealers. It is her behavior after she is crossed by her new partner (and love interest) Stella that most clearly shows how selfishness has become her defining characteristic. When she discovers that Stella—another character who, like Pennsatucky, lacks Piper's financial security—has stolen all her profits from their business so she will be able to have money when she is released, Piper loads her bunk with contraband, including the fateful screwdriver, and reports her to the guards. Instead of being sent home, Stella is sent to maximum security, and Piper's position as a criminal power is solidified.

As Piper's position as the conduit for the viewer becomes steadily troubled, it becomes clearer and clearer how her "window into Litchfield" role in the first season is rooted in the same passive racism that structures the underrepresentation of people of color throughout mainstream media. When we see Litchfield (and the world) through Piper's eyes, it seems naturalized because it mirrors so many other representations on TV and in movies directed toward "mainstream" (read: white) audiences. As Piper is steadily decentered, however, we cannot avoid the ways in which her perspective was always sorely limited. The show's insistence on intimacy with all its characters opens up this possibility, since it contextualizes Piper's experience. *Orange*'s structural commitment to elevating previously abject techniques and subject matter (AKA soap operas and tampons) is mirrored through its focus on poor women and women of color. Not only have we been looking in the wrong places for Quality, *Orange* tells us, we've been looking at television— and class and race—in the wrong way.

Conclusion

In the recent explosion of public discourse around intersectionality and its relationship to white privilege, empathy hasn't come out very well. Activist Hari Ziyad, for instance, writes on the popular blog *Black Girl Dangerous* (2005) that "the belief that empathy can solve the world's ills relies on the idea that we are all similar enough that someone else's pain can be understood through the understanding of our own." With its dual focus on the breadth of experience among Litchfield inmates and its indictment of Piper's toxic narcissism, *Orange Is the New Black* demonstrates one way that empathy can be used as a jumping-off point for greater action. It is not enough, the show argues, for viewers like Piper—the wealthy white people who are the presumed "mainstream" audience toward which most media is pitched—to feel bad for the women at Litchfield. Piper feels bad, too—her emotional connections with Miss Claudette and even Suzanne are real. But her apology to Suzanne for Larry's NPR interview is revealing. She says, "I'm not mean. I didn't mean to be mean to you." And this, of course, is the limit of the use-value of empathy: good intentions are great, but they are a far cry from political action, as Piper's steady vilification makes clear.

The show uses melodrama like another feminist Trojan Horse: through the use of flashbacks and the immersive affective power of the serial form (especially in its binge format), viewers are encouraged to "feel for" a wide variety of characters who are rarely afforded attention in most narrative media, much less subjectivity. But the show takes this intimacy to more radical ends, refusing to stop in the realm of intimate feeling. Instead, it pushes intimacy past the limit of comfort and good taste with its insistence on the embodied nature of experience. While the Daya/Bennett plot features the tinkly piano cues of High Sentiment, it also features episode-long plotlines addressing Daya's pregnancy constipation. With this insistent emphasis on the abject realities of daily life, it's unsurprising when their romantic plot unravels. Daya and Bennet want to enter into a romantic story that is bigger than they are: star-crossed lovers, torn apart by an unjust system. But even melodrama on *Orange* is grounded in the specific and discomfiting details that make easy universality impossible, and they ultimately cannot escape the reality of their surroundings.

While the show utilizes empathy as a way to get readers to connect with these characters—the kinds of characters who are rarely so fully drawn in mainstream media, that empathy becomes a less and less comfortable position for the viewer as the structural details of these women's lives are more clearly drawn. One common complaint about empathy as a political tool is that it does not go far enough. Our hearts break for Jo the street sweeper in *Bleak House*, and the assumption is that this heartbreak will then motivate some kind of (always vaguely defined) action to fix his situation, and that of the countless boys like him. And this fix usually takes the form of some way incorporating abject figures like Jo into normative structures. In *The Female Complaint* (2008), Lauren Berlant puts it this way: "melodramatic conventions that locate the human in a universal capacity to suffer and romantic conventions of individual historical acts of compassion and transcendence are adapted to imagine a nonhierarchical social world that is post-racist and 'at heart' democratic because good intentions and love flourish in it" (6). Melodrama encourages women in positions of power to generously invite the Other into their hearts (if not their homes) because "deep down, we're all the same."

Orange begins in this vein: Piper embarks on what we assume will be her ongoing realization that she's not so different from these other women after all. However, as the show goes on, it becomes clear that she cannot follow through on the potential of that fellow-feeling (how she is "so so so sorry") without examining or relinquishing her own position of power. In this way, the show examines the implications of the phrase "Black Lives Matter." The first step is empathy: an acknowledgement of the basic humanity of all people. The problem, however, is that this emphasis on sameness opens up a quick logical slide into "All Lives Matter." Even Healey has a tragic backstory, after all. *Orange*'s ongoing emphasis on underrepresented and systematically oppressed people, *taken on their own terms*, makes it clearer and clearer how systems of inequality cohere to ensure that some lives—White, wealthy lives—matter much, much more. Piper's ongoing decentralization in the narrative can be read as a model for a political strategy: there is an initial stage in which parallels are drawn between the experience of the dominant group and the abased one. However, the facts of daily life complicate those easy equivalencies and, more importantly, the narrative features the voices of underrepresented people more and more clearly and more centrally, finally displacing the dominant voice altogether. Piper does not get a single flashback in the third season, as her position is rendered strange in its easy access to power. Piper embodies the problem of white feminism, especially in her appeals to universality combined with her interest in acquiring power and her unwillingness to listen, but the show itself does the opposite, using the intimacy of the television form to prioritize the intimate reality of oppression. If Piper were to listen, the way that the show forces its audience to through the flashback structure and the intimacy of the immersive binge format, she would see that it's impossible to follow through on her initial fellow-feeling while maintaining her position of dominance. Whether readers do the same is an open question, but the show encourages them to do so.

References

Berlant, Lauren. 2008. *The Female Complaint: The Unfinished Business of Sentimentality in American Culture*. Durham: Duke University Press.

Dunne, Carey. 2013. "Move Over, Dove: 'Orange Is the New Black' Celebrates Real Women." *Fast Company Design*. 20 August. http://www.fastcodesign.com/16731 32/move-over-dove-orange-is-the-new-black-celebrates-real-women#1..

Hayward, Jennifer. 1995. *Consuming Pleasures: Active Audiences and Serial Fiction from Dickens to Soap Opera*. Lexington: University of Kentucky Press.

Kerman, Piper. 2011. *Orange Is the New Black*. New York: Spiegel & Grau.

Kirsch, Adam, and Mohsin Hamid. 2015. "Are the New 'Golden Age' TV Shows the New Novels?" *New York Times Book Review*. 25 February.

Kohan, Jenji. 2013. *Fresh Air*. Interviewed by Terry Gross, National Public Radio. 13 August.

___. 2014. "An Orange by Any Other Name." *Writer's Guild of America, West*. Interviewed by Dylan Callaghan. 17 January. http://www.wga.org/content/default. aspx?id=5388.

Mittell, Jason. 2015. *Complex TV: The Poetics of Contemporary Storytelling*. New York: New York University Press.

Newman, Michael Z., and Elana Levine. 2012. *Legitimating Television: Media Convergence and Cultural Status.* New York: Routledge.

O'Sullivan, Sean. 2010. "Broken on Purpose: Poetry, Serial Television, and the Season." *Storyworlds: A Journal of Narrative Studies* 2(1):59–77.

Ott, David. 2008. "Cocksucker, Motherfucker, Tits." *It's Not TV: Watching HBO in the Post-Television Era.* New York: Routledge. 123–151.

Williams, Raymond. 2003. *Television: Technology and Cultural Form.* New York: Routledge.

Ziyad, Hari. 2015. "Empathy Won't Save Us in the Fight Against Oppression. Here's Why." *Black Girl Dangerous.* 11 August. http://www.blackgirldangerous.org/2015/08/empathy-wont-save-us-in-the-fight-against-oppression-heres-why/.

"You don't feel like such a freak anymore"

Representing Disability, Madness and Trauma in Litchfield Penitentiary

LYDIA BROWN

"You're a freak." I heard it from the other kids at school and I began to tell myself the same thing. At first, I struggled to reject the "freak" label, and then I attempted to reclaim my freak-ness in a rebellious, defiant act. I didn't have the words growing up to express that I figured out that what it really meant was that I didn't belong, and that there was something about the way I spoke or moved or *felt* that marked me as a constant outsider—as a freak. As an adoptee of color with white parents, or as a questioning asexual in the campus pride group, or as a political leftist at my parents' evangelical church, or as an autistic in a world of neurotypicals, I have almost never felt that I belonged. Even now, the word "freak" weighs heavy for me, as it does for Aurora Levins Morales and Eli Clare (2015, xiv).

Disabled people, alongside others at the margins, have long grappled with the image of the freak, from "monsters and goblins and beasts; from the freak shows of the 1800's where physically disabled folks, trans and gender non-conforming folks, indigenous folks and people of color were displayed side-by-side" as spectacle for the normate gaze (Mingus 2011). Deviance— real in the most essentialist sense, imagined in the most constructivist sense, or some combination of both—can exist only in opposition to an imagined normal. Against a constructed normative body, any deviation in human existence becomes pathology (Walker 2013). I operate from an understanding of disability as *disablement*—both the process (and product of that process) of constantly renegotiated, complex interactions between biological/neurological embodied realities and sociocultural values about bodies. Disablement as process/product necessarily depends on the culturally hegemonic pathology paradigm. The core contention of the pathology paradigm, as articulated by Nick Walker in his seminal 2013 essay, is that there is one normal, default template for human existence and that any deviation from that default is pathology. While culturally, temporally, and geospatially contextual, the imagined normal central to the pathology paradigm in our present context is not only white, cisgender, masculine, heterosexual, etc., but also ambulatory, sighted, hearing, and neurotypical. The pathology paradigm depends on ableism to shape "attitudes, policies and systems that ultimately dehumanize, pathologize and criminalize people whose bodies do not fit into socially constructed notions of what constitutes a 'normal' human being" (Ndopu and Moore 2012).

In this essay, I seek to identify, describe, and analyze various representations and invocations of disability in Netflix's award-winning show *Orange Is the New Black* (*OITNB*), which first aired in 2013, within a broadly anti-ableist paradigm. By drawing connections between disability, madness, and trauma, I also aim to suggest possible reimaginings of pathologizing disability narratives in the show that reject compulsory ablenormativity and instead welcome vulnerability and realness. Finally, I argue that while *OITNB* makes visible those who inhabit atypical bodies and minds like mine, we must interrogate those representations and demand visibility that subverts and dismantles ableism.

OITNB has received critical acclaim for its portrayal of women of color, queer women, and transgender people. Much less attention has focused on the show's representation of disabled people in comparison, although *OITNB*'s three seasons offers incredibly rich possibilities for critically examining representations of disability, madness, and trauma in the popular imagination. No discussion of the show's representation of racialized, gendered, classed, incarcerated, or maternal bodies can be complete without an analysis of disabled, mad, and traumatized bodies. Ableism, like all systems of oppression, is both dependent on and necessary for every other system of oppression to (re)produce itself. As a result, disability carries implications for every marker of identity and experience—"gender reaches into disability; disability wraps around class; class strains against abuse, abuse snarls into sexuality; sexuality folds on top of race" (Clare 1999, 123). In the context of prisons, "incarceration and institutional subordination are central to much of the sexual violence directed at disabled people, both because disabled people are so likely to be targeted for incarceration and because unchecked sexual violence is so prevalent in institutions specifically designed to incarcerate disabled people, such as nursing homes and psychiatric hospitals" (Arkles 2015, 78).

OITNB is replete both with explicitly disabled characters and with characters whose portrayal implicates disability. The show consistently invokes the specter of disability—whether in the three instances of a punch line, "He's not an eggplant; he's retarded," or in the presence of a service dog in training (for an unidentified disability-related service). Grappling directly with disability invites us to complicate discussions of the show's portrayals of racial, sexual, gender, and socioeconomic diversity. It also challenges compulsory ablenormativity and neuronormativity as necessary pre-conditions for empowerment, visibility, and desirability.

Commodifying Madness for the Neurotypical Gaze

What is telling about Suzanne's portrayal is that her specific form of neurodivergence—mental disability or neurological atypicality—is never named. *OITNB* makes widespread use of the problematic "ambiguous mental disorder" trope, from white inmates Lorna Morello, Tiffany Doggett, Mazall, and Lolly Whitehill to white counselor Sam Healy's mother. This is as much for shock value and entertainment as to suggest a social consciousness of "mental health issues" dependent on the pathology paradigm's assignation of moral value to psychiatric treatment for its credibility.

The *OITNB* fandom is singularly fascinated with, sympathetic for, and entertained by Suzanne Warren, the black inmate known mostly as Crazy Eyes both to her fellow prisoners and to the show's audience, largely because of her apparent disability. We first meet Suzanne when she develops a crush on the rich white protagonist Piper Chapman that soon leads to a spurned Suzanne urinating on the floor outside Piper's cube. The show depicts Suzanne as generically mentally disabled (the specific nature of her disability remains ambiguous). Reviewers and fans alike frequently describe her as "mentally ill" while the autistic community often reads her as one of our own. A promotional poster for *OITNB* shows Suzanne holding a pie, with pie on her face, sucking on her thumb, with caption, "slice of crazy." The well-liked black counselor Berdie Rogers says that Suzanne "functions as a six-year-old," invoking the ableist notion that adults with mental disabilities are actually cognitive/emotional children trapped inside adults' bodies (thus rendering paternalism and infantilization acceptable) rather than adults with atypical emotional and cognitive experiences.

In Season 2, we are treated to one of *OITNB*'s characteristic flashback scenes showing a ten-year-old Suzanne sitting in a circle with five- and six-year-old girls at a slumber party as they tell a story together line by line. The other girls establish that there is a princess in a castle, but Suzanne adds a dragon burning down the castle and killing the princess; the younger girls tell Suzanne that she and her idea are stupid. It seems we are meant to feel some pity for Suzanne's marked difference from the other children (and the implication that she is not invited to socialize with her age peers). Mostly, the scene seems to push for its audience to be taken aback with the violence in Suzanne's addition and to consider the incident an early symptom of her later behavioral problem or emotional disturbance. In keeping with Berdie's assessment, Suzanne is portrayed as gullible, naïve, or impressionable due to her apparent disability. In particular, Suzanne is the only one who still believes that fellow black inmate Yvonne Parker (Vee) is a good person after Vee disrupted multiple inmates' lives and interpersonal relationships by physically attacking several others, encouraging Suzanne to attack others, and attempting to frame Suzanne for one of Vee's own violent attacks. Vee was the only one who treated Suzanne like a person, and the only one who never called her Crazy Eyes (a name that Suzanne clearly dislikes), telling Suzanne that she was not crazy but unique.

Discussions about mental illness on *OITNB* frequently reference Suzanne as a talking point, and typically conclude with an exhortation to reform mental health services. While purporting to be supportive and humanizing, assertions that inmates with psychiatric disabilities need treatment (often in specialized mental health facilities) rather than incarceration fail to acknowledge the painfully ironic reality that institutions (from psych wards to mental hospitals to large-scale public residential institutions) are another form of incarceration (Chapman et al. 2014, 17). Institutionalization operates parallel to the penal system, and the lines are constantly blurred by detainment pending competency hearings, indefinite confinement in an institution once adjudicated not guilty by reason of insanity, or civil commitment to a psychiatric unit.

The first episode of Season 3 includes a short flashback to Healy's childhood. We see a chubby boy holding a plate of food and staring in terror at his mother in a bedroom with 1950s-era décor. She stands on the bed, drawing on the wall with lipstick, then suddenly hurls an ashtray toward young Healy's head followed quickly by asking him to dance with her on the bed. Perhaps as if to bookend the season, the final episode of Season 3 also flashes back to Healy's childhood, where he is sitting outside a church praying for God to heal his mother. The show's portrayal of Healy's mother, encapsulated in these two brief vignettes (where she is bodily present in the one and hovering over the other despite her physical absence), is rife with the ambiguity of generic "mental illness."

Later underscoring the imposition of ambiguous mental illness, Healy comments to an inmate that his mother underwent electroconvulsive therapy, which he describes as "very effective"—a stark contrast to the experiences of activists from disabled, mad, and psychiatric survivor communities, which have been coercive, involuntary, paternalistic, and ineffective far more often than not. Healy's mother never receives her own name. Her brief appearance and subsequent references to her simply allude to her apparent violence, irrationality, and instability—the baseline for depictions of madness as unreason that must be mediated through psychiatric intervention.

Similarly, we never quite learn what psychiatric disability Morello is supposed to have. For all of Season 1, we believe she is planning for her eventual wedding with her fiancé Christopher. Early in Season 2, we learn that Morello had only gone on one coffee date with Christopher. Morello stalked him incessantly and rigged a bomb under his girlfriend's car. Later, Morello takes advantage of her job as prison van driver to visit and break into Christopher's home. Morello's depiction suggests delusions, obsessions, unpredictably violent behavior, and irrationality—again with sufficient ambiguity to invoke the specter of madness without explicit reference to any particular experience. Likewise, Tiffany's portrayal as violent, religiously zealous, ignorant, and socially oblivious suggests potential cognitive, learning, or psychiatric disabilities—none of which are specified or confirmed.

In the same vein, the first episode of Season 2 introduces Mazall (first name never provided), an inmate who becomes rapidly obsessed with Piper's astrology based on the exact day and time of her birth. Mazall describes herself as manic, suggesting that she may have bipolar. In keeping with the disorienting milieu of Season 2's first episode (where Piper is suddenly whisked to Chicago after a prolonged period in solitary confinement), Mazall seems to be intentionally played as creepy. Finally, the show introduces Lolly at first as a potential threat to another inmate—Lolly meticulously records Alex Vause's daily activities and is frequently caught staring at her. When confronted, Alex learns that Lolly is terrified that Alex works for the NSA, and Alex calms Lolly only by claiming to be a double agent working for the CIA instead. The apparent paranoia around government conspiracies is consistent with popular representations of mental instability or disconnect from reality, and calls to mind the possibility of schizophrenia.

The *OITNB* writers go to great lengths to suggest humanity and personhood for various characters in the ensemble cast. Yet for as long as madness exists primarily as spectacle for neurotypical entertainment while reifying dangerously ableist ideas of what psychiatric disability or madness *ought* to look like, the show cannot possibly do justice to people with any kind of mental disability.

On the basis of fundamentally ableist assumptions about our (lack of) capacity, competence, and presence, we "are presumed not to be competent, nor understandable, nor valuable, nor whole.... The failure to make sense, as measured against and by those with 'normal' minds, means a loss of personhood" (Price 2011, 26). The show is easily co-opted by narratives of institutionalization as an acceptable if not desirable alternative to penal incarceration for those with mental disabilities and of violence being intrinsic to madness. An intersectional feminism that incorporates disability justice must reject such narratives and demand representation without catering to neurotypical desires to mock, confine, or medicalize caricatures of our lived realities.

Deviant Bodies and the Outer Limits of Desirability

OITNB presents its viewers with a multitude of bodies—fat bodies, elderly bodies, physically disabled bodies, neurodivergent bodies, and otherwise atypically shaped and formed bodies—many of which are simultaneously marked by queer, trans, and racialized existence. The show presents itself as a model for media representation of people whose bodies exist outside the bounds of normative beauty and desirability in multifarious ways. Disability theory allows more nuanced exploration of these categorizations, and demands an interrogation of beauty and desirability.

Within the pathology paradigm, bodies that more closely resemble the imagined normal have much more claim to value, worth, and desirability than those markedly deviant from the imagined normal. With respect to sexuality, Gayle Rubin (1984) offers a framework to guide our thinking about desirability and acceptable expressions and experiences of sexuality ranging from an inner charmed circle ("good, normal, natural, blessed") to its surrounding outer limits ("bad, abnormal, unnatural, damned"). Drawing from Rubin's work, Bethany Stevens (2011) suggests a similar framing for disability/ability—naming as abnormal and unnatural (and thus "undesirable and worthless") various categories of impairment, from visual, hearing, and mobility to cognitive, psychosocial, and learning. While Stevens (2011) notes that her examples are not a complete list of possible impairments, her chart does not make space for the bodies that are simply *ugly*—not (necessarily) impaired or conventionally considered disabled, even within disabled people's movements, but that embody a deviant *aesthetic*. Fat bodies, elderly bodies, and atypically shaped and formed bodies are not necessarily also *disabled* bodies, though the inherent physicality of their deviance from the imagined normal invites a disability analysis. Non-normative bodies invite us to return to the image of the freak, or "that piece of disability and ableism where bodies that are deformed, disfigured, scarred and non-normatively physically disabled live" (Mingus 2011), and challenge us to radically reconceptualize the pathology paradigm's insistence on borders between desirable/undesirable and whole/broken.

Midway through Season 3, we learn that a suitor rejected Chinese inmate Mei Chang immediately upon seeing her face as ugly, unattractive, and thus undesirable. While Chang's facial appearance does not evince any particular disability, she may have had dermatitis or she may have simply had atypical coloration for no identifiable reason. When Chang confronted the suitor later, he told her that she was an ugly girl that no one will ever want and nothing would ever change that. The show has also considered the ugly body in Tiffany's meth mouth—severe tooth decay and tooth loss caused by her drug use—which was ultimately "fixed" when she received dentures. *OITNB* presents uncritically both Tiffany's insistence on and pride in her new dentures (designed to be normatively beautiful) and Chang's rejection for her conventionally unattractive face. While Tiffany's attempts to receive complimentary attention for her new teeth are ignored and Chang later exacts revenge on the suitor, the show ultimately fails to critique the underlying ideas that Tiffany's dentures fixed her appearance (that is, brought it in closer alignment with the imagined normal) and that Chang's suitor was justified in rejecting a body he saw as ugly.

Earlier, by the time Season 2 had concluded, the show had gradually developed more nuanced characterization of Cuban inmate Rosa Cisneros—originally introduced as the older woman with cancer, bald from chemotherapy when Piper first arrived. Much later, we learn that Rosa was a repeat bank robber before going to prison. Rosa's portrayal as at once thrill-seeking, practical-minded, and curmudgeonly contrasts with how most fictional characters with cancer lack dimension or individual subjectivity, and are portrayed "as either tragic victims or heroic overcomers without much characterization [whose] only goals are to emotionally manipulate the audience and make the lead characters feel equal parts shitty and inspired" (Miller 2014). Yet despite seeming here to criticize the tragedy/inspiration porn dichotomy that entraps so many portrayals of disabled people, the very same article again depends on ableist narrative when the author writes that "there's a lot of complexity and texture added in Season 2 that fills Miss Rosa into a more fully-developed, humanized character not limited to or defined by her body" (Miller 2014). Miller clearly associates the sick and disabled body as an impediment or accessory to full humanization, invoking the familiar rhetoric of humanity *despite* disability. Toward the end of Season 2, Rosa's learns that the prison system will not pay for the cost of the only surgery that might save her life from a now-terminal prognosis. Upon return to prison from her last appointment, the prison has gone into lockdown over a separate crisis. In a moment of spontaneity, Morello leaves the keys in the ignition and hops out of the van, imploring, "Don't die in here, Miss Rosa. Go do it your own way." Rosa speeds away to a soundtrack of "(Don't Fear) the Reaper." We learn in Season 3 that Rosa died by driving into a quarry.

Without the clear nod to ableist and ageist invocations of a sick or disabled body as fearsome or not worth inhabiting, this scene could be read as exemplifying themes of bodily autonomy and self-determination against the backdrop of the prison-industrial complex's inhumanity and indifference to human suffering. Instead, the director had Rosa's flashback actor (a younger woman with hair) switch positions with Rosa's primary present-day actor (an older woman who appears bald) as though her present-day self were reimagining her body as though she were young and unimpaired—in other words, as though she inhabited a different (and implicitly, more desirable or genuine) body and is thus dying triumphantly and in control of her own destiny. Most importantly, the more desirable or genuine body of Rosa's fantasy is depicted as abled, young, and healthy. In response to the overwhelmingly dominant narrative that it is better to be dead than disabled, writers like Rachel Cohen-Rottenberg (2014) argue for an acknowledgement and embrace of bodily vulnerability, debility, and dependence in the elderly and disabled bodies that challenge "the youthful, strong, and independent ideal" of the imagined normal (213–214). In her critique of an image intended to be inspirational that depicts an elderly woman in a wheelchair imagining her shadow as an able-bodied young woman dancing—quite like *OITNB*'s depiction of Rosa imagining herself as younger and without impairment—Cohen-Rottenberg (2012) writes that "the onus is on the elderly woman to imagine herself to be someone else, rather than on other people to see her—and to treat her—as someone who is beautiful, valuable, and respected [as she is]." We must question why Rosa cannot be admired and loved in the sick, vulnerable, and aging body she presently inhabits and why her triumphant exit must be mediated through ableism and ageism.

Inspoporn/Overcomer Tropes, Disability Pity and Subversive Possibilities

Media representations of disabled people—fictional and nonfictional—are so often dependent on the discourse of inspiration. In the disabled community, we call it inspiration porn, or inspoporn for short—capitalizing on the exploitation inherent to romanticized or fantasized images of disabled people for the edification and voyeurism of abled people. "This boy's kindness to classmate with autism will bring you to tears. Click to watch this heartwarming video." "Girl with Down Syndrome wins statewide art competition. What's your excuse?" We so often find that the only acceptable narratives for disability are that the disabled person's activities (whether mundane or truly extraordinary) serve to inspire the abled people around them or that the disabled person achieves success and deserves praise for overcoming their disability by more closely approximating the impossible standards of compulsory ablenormativity and neuronormativity. In both of these narratives, the disabled people are not permitted subjectivity or agency and instead exist only for the edification of the nondisabled people around them. *OITNB* offers material that can be read simultaneously as within the inspoporn/overcomers narrative and as subverting it.

Beyond the insporporn/overcomers narrative, *OITNB* falls into other disability tropes. The audience is meant to pity Suzanne at least somewhat. John Bennett, a white guard, has his prosthetic leg become a convenient plot device. Norma Romano, the white inmate who chooses not to speak because she stutters becomes something of a cult figure referred to as a "magical mute." Jimmy Cavanaugh, an elderly white inmate convinced she is 23, is dropped off at a bus station with no support system in a fictionalized version of compassionate release; other inmates respond with outrage but insist that she needs to be in a full-time care facility—again, ironically ignoring that institutions simply constitute other forms of incarceration. The internal discourse surrounding Jimmy's narrative presents an opportunity to turn to disabled people's movements in demanding peer-led community care systems as alternatives to institutions of any kind.

Ableism-conscious viewers can find ample material to resist the pressure of pathologizing and condescending disability tropes. Toward the end of Season 1, a group of justice-involved youth arrives at Litchfield as part of a Scared Straight program. One of the youth is Dina, a young woman of color in a wheelchair who ran her own gang and robbed a liquor store, portrayed as the toughest of the group and least impressed by the intimidation tactics. Black inmate Poussey's attempts to intimidate Dina fade into the awkwardness that so often characterizes abled people's interactions with disabled people. Dina responds, "I don't need nobody to hold doors for me. I can do anything anybody else can do. They told me I couldn't rob a liquor store, 'cause I'm a roller. But I showed them. They told me I couldn't gang bang. And now I got my own gang." Later, Tiffany throws Dina from her wheelchair to the ground attempting to "heal" her before being hauled to the psych ward.

To understand Dina, who only appears in one episode, we must peel through multiple layers of analysis. Dina is a disabled woman of color, in contrast to the primarily white characters in whom disability is implicated, whose physically disabled body leads to Tiffany's confinement for supposed psychiatric disability. Does Dina (a disabled woman of color) exist solely as a plot device for Tiffany's narrative? Does Dina's self-narration invoke the inspoporn/overcomer trope, or does she resist and subvert it? Dina's narrative calls into question the images of both the abled white savior and the angry black woman, as well as the inspoporn/overcomer trope's presumptively good, compliant, and docile disabled person.

In Season 3, we encounter Joe Caputo (a white Litchfield administrator) as a high school star wrestler. During a tournament, Caputo agrees to an exhibition match with another high school's student who has Down syndrome.

Kendall Barnes, who is actually played by an actor with Down syndrome (unlike most characters in whom disability is implicated), is clearly not a regular competitor, as the announcer describes him as a "very special wrestler" and Caputo's coach implies that he is not a regular team member. Caputo promises to let Kendall "feel like he's really doing it." Such condescending exhibitionist matches and showcases featuring people with disabilities are meant as feel-good experiences to reassure nondisabled participants/organizers of their moral upstandingness. As it happens, Kendall is so strong he injures Caputo severely enough to end Caputo's career. Caputo's episode is entitled "We Can Be Heroes," suggesting that Caputo himself believed he was a hero for volunteering to wrestle with the student with intellectual disabilities. We might applaud *OITNB* for subverting the usual narrative here by presenting Kendall as someone most certainly not to be pitied or presumed subpar.

For all that *OITNB* does to weave disability into its narrative strands, suggesting an ordinariness of disabled experience, we must be careful not to become so enamored with casual presence that we then demand disability be made invisible and left unacknowledged.

Transgressing Shame

Disabled people so often live with the shame of internalized ableism—building outposts in our minds to reinforce the hegemonic ablesupremacy of the pathology paradigm. We learn to hide and hate our bodies, to glorify and strive for passing as abled, to participate in disability hierarchy by insisting that if *we* escape the self-contained segregated classroom, the sheltered workshop, the institution, the group home, that someone *else* inevitably belongs there instead. We learn that we are undesirable and that our own desires are dangerous—that the only outcomes of our desires are rejection, reluctant coupling with other deviants, or the perverse reproduction of disabled existence. In *OITNB*, disabled shame etches itself most clearly in the bodies of Norma Romano and John Bennett, stretching its tendrils slowly around their narrative portraits in momentary expressions caught all too painfully for the camera.

For Norma, who stutters, shame brought her, tentative and uncertain, to the healing circle of a culturally appropriative white "guru" who, upon realizing she was ashamed to have her voice heard, assured her that she never need speak in his presence. For decades, Norma lived with the cult leader, ceremonially marrying him alongside dozens of other young women enamored with his charisma, until she was the only one of his wives left. His life in shambles, he curses at Norma, bemoaning how of all his wives, she is the only one still with him. He tells her that she is only a follower, that he knows the reason she does not speak is because she does not think. In anger, Norma shoves him from a cliff to his death, screaming—and stuttering—"Son of a bitch!" Norma never overcomes her shame—she never speaks aloud again.

For Bennett, an amputee with a prosthetic leg, shame writes itself into the careful shadows of his face as he looks, pained, when Dayanara begins to undress him during their first sexual liaison, knowing she is about to discover his prosthesis. Mirroring the shame, fear, and internalized ableism of so many disabled people who learn over and over that we are either automatically undesirable or exotic bodies to be fetishized, Bennett seems afraid of how Daya might react. Instead, she touches him with tenderness, and the shame slowly evaporates. He is capable of both desire and desirability, mutuality and coercion, presence and absence; his character demands attention to multiple layers—the inescapable power relations between a guard and an inmate, the sexual possibilities for disabled bodies, the particular shame inscribed in the bodies of those who become late disabled by accident.

Disability Invocations and the Pathologized Body

Analyzing disability invocations allows us to consider the various ways in which *OITNB*'s characters deliberately use disability (or some specter of disability) as a means of survival or of enacting violence. In childhood, Tiffany's mother had her chug Mountain Dew to fake a learning disability to receive more monetary benefits—this portrayal veers into the territory of disability fakery accusations levied upon disabled people who rely on state support to survive. In prison, Tiffany removes herself from van driving duty with the guard who raped her by faking an epileptic seizure—this portrayal, in contrast, is viscerally painful, invoking the collective trauma of having to perform disability to survive.

Vee's emotional manipulation of Suzanne began slowly, first by telling Suzanne, "Everybody else around here underestimates you, but not me." We are expected to understand that Vee's ability to manipulate Suzanne derives from Suzanne's presumptive incapacity. After Vee uses Suzanne to take the fall for her nearly murdering Galina Reznikov (Red), gaslighting Suzanne into doubting her own memory and believing she very well might have attacked Red. Vee instructs other inmates to blame Suzanne, who is easily scapegoated for the crime as someone with atypical behavior and a history of institutional violence. For neurodivergent people, this sequence is painful and devastating in an incredibly *personal* way—the one person who Suzanne has begun to trust, the one person who had spoken to Suzanne respectfully, that person so callously uses and abuses Suzanne.

While distinct from the depictions of Tiffany and Vee that clearly invoke disability, the show's acclaimed portrayal of Sophia Burset, a black inmate and the only transwoman among the cast, may call to mind the fraught connections between disabled and trans identities/experiences. Like disabled bodies, trans bodies are treated as both spectacle and pathology requiring medical/psychiatric surveillance and control. And as a result, the trans community has long engaged in the practice of disavowal—seeking to "resist alliances with people with disabilities in no small part because of long struggles against stigmatization and pathologization that may be reinvoked through such an affiliation" (Puar 2015, 46)—by asserting trans identity/experience as valid and natural (but "actual" psychiatric disability as disorder in need of psychiatric surveillance and intervention). Foucault's notion of the disciplined body requires that we understand both how the pathology paradigm forces compliance (here, with ablenormativity and cisnormativity) on deviant bodies and how those of us who inhabit deviant bodies learn to discipline and punish our own bodies for their deviance. Ablenormativity requires performing abledness and neurotypicality—apparent disability cannot be tolerated. Cisnormativity requires performing hyperfemininity or hypermasculinity—intersexuality cannot be tolerated. In imposing the power of the pathology paradigm's compulsory ablenormativity and cisnormativity, deviant bodies must be rendered sites for psychiatric or medical intervention. Here, the tensions and possible alliances between trans and disabled experiences are unavoidably present—if latent—in the medical bureaucracies and psychiatric surveillance that Sophia must navigate as a post-transition transwoman.

(Re)Producing Trauma and Disability in the Prison-Industrial Complex

Prisons produce and reproduce disability, particularly by enacting new traumas borne of carceral violence. Ableism is inherent to the prison-industrial complex. We can find ableism in older configurations of criminality as evidence of mental deviance (madness) or imbecility (cognitive disability) as much as in the ways in which present-day mass incarceration systematically targets disabled, low-income, black and brown people and inflicts repeated trauma on its targets. Gabriel Arkles (2015) writes that "imprisonment demands major infringements on the bodily autonomy and self-determination of prisoners" in the form of "strip searches, body cavity searches, and nonconsensual medical interventions on prisoners: acts that have much in common with other forms of sexual violence" (71). Disability justice demands that "we must examine the devastating effects that prison has on people's psyches [as] both detrimental for people with disabilities and responsible for creating new experiences of disabilities" (Ware et al. 2014, 164). In this section, I turn to trauma as a means of complicating disability by discussing representations of various traumas within *OITNB*.

It is possible to draw a clear connection between trauma and debility (borne of disability), as trauma implicates both precarity and instability (Carter 2013), thereby invoking Nancy Hirschmann's (2013) configurations of disability as "helplessness, weakness, and incapacity" (650). Trauma, crip, disability, and queer theories similarly point to the impossibility of the coherent, stable, or normative body (Carter 2013, 3). While trauma and disability are not interchangeable, the traumatized body and disabled body are frequently co-constitutive and share "undeniable overlaps in both subjective embodiments" (Carter 2013, 1).

Hirschmann (2013) writes that "disability is configured as helplessness, weakness, and incapacity, all conceptually related to the ways women have been seen throughout history" (650). Nevertheless, relatively few disability theorists have connected criticism of gender and sexuality to criticism of disability constructions (Samuels 2002, 59). Hirschmann (2013) has criticized feminist theorists of reinforcing other normative embodiments, particularly neuronormativity and ablenormativity, writing that feminists "tacitly operate from a particular specialized body [and] assume certain reproductive capacities, certain body parts, certain capabilities" (650–651). My discussion of trauma here thus seeks to explore the show's representations of disability and madness as they relate both to narrative impact and to the material conditions experienced by real-life, off-screen prisoners faced with institutional apathy and a national conversation dictated primarily by the pathology paradigm.

Institutions of any kind—including penal and psychiatric—thrive within the pathology paradigm. They strip their subjects of autonomy, deny access to meaningful choice, and disrupt healing and intimacy. When Brook Soso, a biracial Chinese/Scottish inmate, shares that she is dealing with depression, Healy tells her that people don't like sad people and she should go on psychotropic medication. When Brook finally goes to the pharmacy, she swipes a bag of pills and quietly overdoses, nearly killing herself. This sequence represents one of the few times where *OITNB* did not uncritically depict the psychiatric establishment—Brook had had a positive relationship with the other counselor, Berdie, who provided non-medication support for Brook's struggles, whereas Healy is portrayed as disconnected from Brook's experiences and thoroughly uninvested in her personhood, leaving his recommendation for psychotropic medications hollow.

Suzanne has been in both solitary and the psych ward before, and describes psych as far worse than solitary. We glimpse the reality of the psych ward once Tiffany is sent there after her faith healing crusade has gone awry. Locked standing inside a cage, wearing a paper uniform, Tiffany tells the doctor that she can prove she's not crazy if he would only talk to the other inmates she had healed—revealing the vicious, long-term nature of the prank the other inmates played on Tiffany when pretending she had healed them of everything from an injured knee to being gay. The doctor sedates her with psychotropic medication instead. Later, Tiffany is lying in four-point leather restraints when a nurse enters, telling her that if she weren't crazy, she wouldn't have to work so hard to prove she's sane. Because of Suzanne's insistence on the inhumanity of psych, Piper (who was responsible for the last incident with Dina that sent Tiffany there) decides to confess the truth so Tiffany will be released. By the time Brook arrives and has nearly fatally overdosed, Suzanne convinces her fellow black inmates that they should take care of her—that they should do whatever possible to prevent the administration from discovering Brook's suicide attempt and sending her to psych.

The institution ignores, exacerbates, and sometimes directly causes disability and trauma in other contexts. Red lives with chronic back pain, possibly induced by an earlier attack by Vee. Maria Ruiz and Dayanara Diaz, whose pregnancies may theoretically afforded certain protections under the Americans with Disabilities Act, endure pregnancy in prison, where their many real-life counterparts are denied necessary reproductive care and shackled leading up to and sometimes through delivery. Gina Murphy is burned all over her face and body. Sister Jane Ingalls is subjected to humiliating and painful forced feeding while restrained, after going on a hunger strike. Incarceration demands compliance, which itself is so often framed in the language of "emotional disturbance" or "behavioral problems."

In turning toward a discussion of *OITNB*'s depiction of trauma, the recurring theme of sexual violence and survivorship dominates as much as the theme of familial trauma and displacement, and sometimes overlap. We witness Sophia Burset repeatedly subjected to dehumanizing sexual comments steeped in transmisogyny and later attacked by fellow inmates demanding that she display her genitalia—another iteration of the freak show. We witness Tricia Miller's past as street homeless, catching a passing reference to a rapist stepfather. We witness Piper Chapman standing to be searched during lockdown only to have her breasts groped and squeezed by a guard. We witness the routine violence of the strip search.

In particular, we witness Tiffany Doggett, who has been repeatedly traumatized through rape from her youth where she was raped for refusing to have sex in exchange for soda to her adulthood where an increasingly controlling guard rapes her. Tiffany's character in particular epitomizes the classist caricature of low-income, rural working-class white people as boorish and brutes (Kadi 1996, 43; Clare 1999, 45–46)—as uneducated, drug users, likely to have frequent sex with multiple partners, religiously conservative and zealous. Against this caricature, disability and trauma become legible, thus demanding complexity in unpacking the ableism and classism in Tiffany's depiction as "stupid" and "unstable."

Themes of familial, generational, and the traumas of displacement, abandonment, and isolation mark *OITNB* as much as themes of sexual violence. Sophia Burset struggled with coming out to her wife and son as she transitioned. Gloria Mendoza could not bring herself to leave her abusive boyfriend until he hit her son. Aleida Diaz was absent for much of Dayanara's childhood, leaving Daya to care for the children while Aleida was involved with her boyfriend's drug operations; Daya initiated a relationship with the same boyfriend when Aleida went to prison, and Bennett watched as that boyfriend held a gun to one of the children's heads to make him eat his food. Carrie Black struggled with parents who refused to accept her gender presentation and constantly demanded that she wear clothing that she was uncomfortable donning for the sake of their comfort and convenience. Tiffany Doggett's mother told her that men demanding sex was inevitable and that if she was lucky, a man would be quick like a bee sting. Nicky Nicholson struggled with her rich, absentee mother. Leanne Taylor chose to leave her family and community after her parents were shunned over her actions. Tasha Jefferson (Taystee), never selected as an adoption candidate, lived in what was likely a series of group homes for children in state custody, ultimately landing with Vee as a maternal figure, only for Vee to disrupt her chosen family by arranging for a corrupt police officer to murder her other functionally adopted child—Taystee's friend who was like a brother.

Unlike Taystee, Suzanne was adopted (at an unspecified age) by a white, educated, and upper class adoptive family that was possibly obsessed with "normalizing" her for the sake of compliance with the arbitrarily defined standards of the imagined normal. In remembering her mother's past pressure to perform publicly, Suzanne dissociates following a meltdown at the prison's Christmas pageant, where while hitting Piper she said, "I don't want to! You're always pushing me to do these things! Pushing me! No more, Mommy!"— evoking Suzanne's earlier flashback where she fled from her high school graduation's stage after her mother implored her to "show them how great you are." Cate Young (2014) argues that we should read Suzanne's white adoptive mother's responses to her daughter as fundamentally steeped in racism borne of colonization, the white gaze, and white supremacist conflation of blackness with mental instability. Rather than accept Suzanne's mother's suggestion that another mother's reluctance to include Suzanne at a birthday party with younger children might have been marked by racism, Young posits that Suzanne's mother assumed that Suzanne "had a propensity for misbehavior or violence because of her blackness." For Young, a sensible assumption would have been that Suzanne's weirdness led to the other mother's reluctance. In Suzanne's mother's attempt to address and confront racism, she instead fixated on the possibility of racism even where ableism was likely more salient to the immediate interaction. Yet Young's (2014) rhetorical framing depends on a pathologizing, behaviorizing paradigm—she writes, "As a child who clearly wasn't getting the help she needed, Suzanne likely would have been difficult to manage even for someone with the best of intentions, let alone an unwilling parent. It is the most obvious reason for why she experienced so much alienation growing up."

Instead of attempting to ignore Suzanne's blackness in their attempt to be "color blind," Young (2014) argues that her parents should have seen Suzanne's "difficult behaviour not as an indication of a disease that she could have received help for" and "made the effort to get her the mental health care that she so desperately needed." This framing clearly places the onus on Suzanne's mother to seek treatment in the conventional medical model of mental health, and suggests that any disconnection from peers or difficulty with parents arises from failure to obtain mental health treatment. Young strongly implies a connection between Suzanne's mother failing to seek "mental health care" for her daughter and Suzanne's later incarceration, suggesting that presumptively responsible/proper psychiatric intervention would have kept Suzanne out of prison. Young further uncritically accepts the validity, effectiveness, and safety of mental health care in her assertion that "the only indication that Suzanne receives treatment of any kind is [when she describes] how difficult it is to be held is the prison's psych ward."

A disability justice analysis demands further critique and exploration—how can we reject the automatic pathologization of madness as defect and disorder and the presumptive authority and credibility lent psychiatric professionals, while making space for coping, survival, and healing? How can we recognize the white saviorism so often endemic to adoption of children of color into white families and the racism that adoptees of color experience within their own families—and complicate the trauma of adoption with the racism and ableism embedded in response to a white family's response to a disabled adopted child of color?

Some Concluding Thoughts

Visibility and Power

For disabled people, it's a step in the right direction to feature John Bennett as openly sexual—both him expressing sexual desire/attraction and receiving it in return, and entering into a long-term sexual/romantic relationship. But of course, we must contend not only with his whiteness, masculinity, and (likely) heterosexuality, but also the insurmountable and disturbing power dynamic between him as a white male guard and Dayanara as a brown woman and a prisoner. There is little truly revolutionary about *OITNB*'s portrayal of a white man's heterosexual intimacy, except that we are expected to develop some amount of emotional investment in the unequal relationship only for John to disappear without explanation. Nevertheless, even whiteness, heterosexuality, and masculinity may be impacted by the ableist presumption that disabled people must always lie outside the outer limits of acceptable or even conceivable sexuality. There is both vulnerability and power in visibility.

For those of us in the autistic community, we can explore multiple possibilities for reading Suzanne specifically as autistic. We can envision ourselves quite easily in Suzanne's place when her sister begs her to please not be weird, and again when Suzanne becomes too anxious to perform a song in front of her graduating high school class amid titters of laughter from her classmates and her abled white mother's intense stare pressuring her to perform both talent (potentially to "compensate" for disability) and abledness (by not having or overcoming a moment of panic and anxiety). As Suzanne flees from the stage, hitting herself, her classmates laugh. It is often nearly impossible to encounter fictional representations that allow autistic to be ordinary, let alone feminine, racialized, queer, or (realistically and relatably) marked by multiple traumas. Instead, the networks bombard us with the magical autistic as in Fox's *Touch* (featuring a non-speaking autistic boy with superpowers) or shallow caricatures of stereotypically autistic traits as in CBS's *The Big Bang Theory* (featuring a physicist widely perceived as autistic). Unlike flat caricatures of predominantly cisgender, heterosexual white autistic men, I can see myself in Suzanne's expressiveness, in how she hits herself when frustrated and hopeless, in how she pulls and holds her sleeves partially over her hands, in her tentative gestures toward intimacy with Maureen Kukudio (who could be read as autistic herself), in her choice to leap to the dragon's destructiveness in her childhood storytelling, in her franticly intense echolalic lines during her interrogation. Visibility transgresses shame, erasure, and involuntary isolation, by allowing those of us branded freaks to recognize ourselves and build community together. As Suzanne says, "You don't feel like such a freak anymore."

The Liberatory Power of a Disability Justice Analysis

While *OITNB* frequently resorts to pathologizing and limiting tropes in representations of disability, the show simultaneously suggests both disabled ordinariness and exceptionalism. The diversity of disabled visibility allows further exploration of disability's role in mediating transgender identity, disabled sexuality and intimacy, inspoporn/overcomer narratives, and the production and reproduction of trauma. In making disabled existence visible,

OITNB allows its viewers to consider possibilities for embracing vulnerability and precarity as part of human wholeness and complexity, while resisting the demand of compulsory ablenormativity that empowered femininity must erase any specter of disability.

What potential does *OITNB* have for informing, educating, raising consciousness, and providing additional impetus for disability justice work in transforming the criminal (in)justice system? Can we strengthen feminist theory *and* praxis by making space for vulnerability, instability, and debility? More importantly, can we strive for present and future communities that adamantly demand space and ongoing affirmation for disabled people, in all our wobbly, lopsided, flappy, drooling, stuttering, twitching, mad, and sick magnificence? This is not a conclusion but an invitation.

ACKNOWLEDGMENTS

I am grateful for support and comments from Jennifer Scuro and Shain M. Neumeier in preparing this chapter, as well as the incredibly helpful comments from my editors, April Kalogeropoulos Householder and Adrienne Trier-Bieniek.

REFERENCES

Arkles, Gabriel. 2015. "Regulating Prison Sexual Violence." *Northeastern University Law Journal* 7:1, 69–124.

Bartmess, Elizabeth. 2015. "Writing Autistic Characters: Behaviorizing vs. Humanizing Approaches." *Disability in Kidlit*. Original publication April 14. http://disabilityinkidlit.com/2015/04/14/writing-autistic-characters-behaviorizing-vs-humanizing-approaches/ (accessed November 12, 2015).

Carter, Angela M. 2013. *Cripping Trauma: Reconceptualizing the Discourse of Debilitation*. Paper presented at Debilitating Queerness, the annual DC Queer Studies Symposium, College Park, Maryland, April 5.

Chapman, Chris, Allison C. Carey, and Liat Ben-Moshe. 2014. "Reconsidering Confinement: Interlocking Locations and Logics of Incarceration." *Disability Incarcerated: Imprisonment and Disability in the United States and Canada*, edited by Liat Ben-Moshe, Chris Chapman, and Allison C. Carey, 3–24. New York: Palgrave Macmillan.

Clare, Eli. 1999. *Exile and Pride: Disability, Queerness, and Liberation*. Cambridge: South End Press.

Cohen-Rottenberg, Rachel. 2012. "Ableism and Ageism in One Tidy Little Package." *The Body Is Not an Apology*. Original publication June 22. http://thebodyisnotanapology.tumblr.com/post/76528664013/ableism-and-ageism-in-one-tidy-little-package (accessed September 23, 2015).

Cohen-Rottenberg, Rachel. "What Bodies Do: Meditations on Crip Hatred, Elder Hatred, and the Vulnerable Body." *Criptiques*, edited by Caitlin Wood, 211–218. May Day, 2014.

Foucault, Michel. 1977. *Discipline and Punish: The Birth of the Prison*. Translated by Alan Sheridan. New York: Vintage.

Foucault, Michel. 1990. *The History of Sexuality: Volume 1: An Introduction*. Translated by Robert Hurley. New York: Vintage.

Foucault, Michel. 2006. *History of Madness*. Translated by Jonathan Murphy. London: Routledge.

Ghai, Anita. 2003. *(Dis)Embodied Form: Issues of Disabled Women*. New Delhi: Har-Anand Publications.

Hirschmann, Nancy J. 2013. "Disability, Feminism, and Intersectionality: A Critical Approach." *Radical Philosophy Review* 16:2, 649–662.

Hochberg, Gil Z. 2010. "Introduction: Israelis, Palestinians, Queers: Points of Departure." *GLQ: A Journal of Lesbian and Gay Studies* 16:4, 493–516.

Kadi, Joanna. "Stupidity 'Deconstructed.'" *Thinking Class: Sketches from a Cultural Worker*, 39–58. Cambridge: South End Press, 1996.

Kafer, Alison. 2013. *Feminist Queer Crip*. Bloomington: Indiana University Press.

Levins Morales, Aurora. 2015. Foreword to the 2015 Edition of *Exile and Pride: Disability, Queerness, and Liberation* by Eli Clare, xi-xx. Durham: Duke University Press.

Lockett, Dee. 2015. "*Orange Is the New Black*'s Laverne Cox on Why Playing Sophia's Shocking Punishment Was an Out-of-Body Experience." *Vulture*. Original publication June 24. http://www.vulture.com/2015/06/laverne-cox-orange-is-the-new-black-sophias-shocking-punishment.html (accessed October 15, 2015).

McRuer, Robert. "Compulsory Able-Bodiedness and Queer/Disabled Existence." *Disability Studies: Enabling the Humanities*, edited by Sharon L. Snyder, Brenda Jo Brueggemann, and Rosemarie Garland-Thomson, 88–99. New York: Modern Language Association, 2002.

Miller, Taylor Cole. 2014. "*OITNB*'s Miss Rosa on 'Tit Hairs,' the Prop in Her Freezer, and F**king with Cancer." *Huffington Post*. Original publication July 21. http://www.huffingtonpost.com/taylor-cole-miller/orange-is-the-new-black-miss-rosa_b_5602426.html (accessed October 15, 2015).

Mingus, Mia. 2011. "Moving Toward the Ugly: A Politic Beyond Desirability." *Leaving Evidence*. Original publication August 22. https://leavingevidence.wordpress.com/2011/08/22/moving-toward-the-ugly-a-politic-beyond-desirability/ (accessed October 1, 2015)

Mingus, Mia, Mariama Lockington, and So Yung Kim. 2010. "Transcript: Recognizing Each Other: Adoptees of Color Video." By Mia Mingus. *Leaving Evidence*. July 16. https://leavingevidence.wordpress.com/2010/07/16/video-recognizing-each-other-adoptees-of-color/ (accessed October 16, 2015).

Mollow, Anna. 2012. "Is Sex Disability? Queer Theory and the Disability Drive." *Sex and Disability*, edited by Robert McRuer and Anna Mollow, 285–312. Durham: Duke University Press.

Nakamura, Karen. 2012. *Trans/Disability: Disability, Queer Sexualities, and Transsexuality from a Comparative Ethnographic Perspective*. Paper presented at Shōgai, Kuia, Shitizunshippu (Disability, Queer, Citizenship), forum held at the Center for Barrier-Free Education at the University of Tokyo.

Ndopu, Edward, and Darnell L. Moore. 2012. "On Ableism within Queer Spaces, or, Queering the 'Normal.'" *PrettyQueer*. Original publication December 7. http://www.prettyqueer.com/2012/12/07/on-ableism-within-queer-spaces-or-queering-the-normal/ (accessed October 10, 2015).

Ndopu, Edward. 2013. "Our Lives Matter: Toward An Intersectional Politics Of Disability." *The Feminist Wire*. Original publication November 18. http://www.thefeministwire.com/2013/11/our-lives-matter-toward-an-intersectional-politics-of-disability/ (accessed September 25, 2015).

Price, Margaret. 2011. *Mad at School: Rhetorics of Mental Disability and Academic Life*. Ann Arbor: University of Michigan Press.

Puar, Jasbir K. 2015. "Bodies with New Organs: Becoming Trans, Becoming Disabled." *Social Text*, 33:34, 45–73.

Rubin, Gayle. "Thinking Sex: Notes for a Radical Theory of the Politics of Sexuality." *Pleasure and Danger: Exploring Female Sexuality*, edited by Carole S. Vance, 3–44. Boston: Routledge & Kegan Paul, 1984.

Samuels, Ellen J. 2002. "Critical Divides: Judith Butler's Body Theory and the Question of Disability." *NWSA Journal* 14:3, 58–76.

smith, s.e. 2011. "I'm Not a Feminist, and I Wish People Would Stop Trying to Convince Me Otherwise." *xoJane*. Original publication November 16. http://www.xojane.com/issues/im-not-feminist-and-i-wish-people-would-stop-trying-convince-me-otherwise (accessed September 25, 2015).

Stevens, Bethany. 2011. "Interrogating Transability: A Catalyst to View Disability as Body Art." *Disability Studies Quarterly* 31:4.

Walker, Nick. 2013. "Throw Away the Master's Tools: Liberating Ourselves from the Pathology Paradigm," *Neurocosmopolitanism*. Original publication August 16. http://neurocosmopolitanism.com/throw-away-the-masters-tools-liberating-ourselves-from-the-pathology-paradigm/ (accessed October 10, 2015)

Ware, Syrus, Joan Ruzsa, and Giselle Dias. "It Can't Be Fixed Because It's Not Broken: Racism and Disability in the Prison Industrial Complex" *Disability Incarcerated: Imprisonment and Disability in the United States and Canada*, edited by Liat Ben-Moshe, Chris Chapman, and Allison C. Carey, 163–184. New York: Palgrave Macmillan, 2014.

Young, Catherine "NinjaCate." 2014. "Race, Racism and Mental Health: A Look At *OITNB*'s Suzanne 'Crazy Eyes' Warren." *The Powder Room*. Original publication July 24. http://powderroom.kinja.com/race-racism-and-mental-health-a-look-at-*oitnb*-suzann-1610174118 (accessed October 5, 2015).

Piper Chapman's Flexible Accommodation of Difference

H. RAKES

In this essay, I read the character Piper Chapman as preoccupied with "being down" with difference, understanding this preoccupation as precluding possibilities for *being with*. "Being down" is a form of what I call flexible accommodation, an imperialistic, neoliberal practice of stretching just enough to manage calls for accountability. I track Piper's practices of flexible accommodation to demonstrate how white and abled audiences of the show are encouraged to critically distance ourselves from her.

I define neoliberalism as a global, ongoing practice of imperialism, in which the "freedom" of global markets is the deregulated entitlement of Global North entities and corporations to exploit labor, environments, and people in Global South spaces, as well as spaces within the Global North that have been ghettoized in order to contain people of color and their contributions. Neoliberalism economically, militarily, and politically produces conditions of precarity for Global South and ghettoized subjects or "surplus people" (see Lorde 1984) who do the dirtiest and most dangerous jobs. "Precarity" describes conditions that are socially and politically produced, making certain lives more vulnerable than others. We need to take these seriously in their centuries-long histories related to imperialism, which means questioning what we are laughing at when watching *Orange*. When we encounter Piper, we are confronted with a subject who has not experienced these conditions of precarity, and whose confinement at Litchfield is, if anything, a completely new precarity for her. So is her sense of entitlement funny, dangerous, or both?

This precarity produced by neoliberalism is deeply intertwined with demands for flexible labor, where the precarity and insecurity of jobs—and the precarious "life chances" (Spade 2011) of those who do them—means that workers have little choice but to accept "flexible" hours, part time employment without a consistent schedule, lack of benefits packages, and so forth (Harvey 1989; Hong 2006). I insist, along with transnational feminist scholars, on understanding these operations of neoliberalism as updates to imperialism (Alexander 2006; Erevelles 2011) and thus not particularly new. What *is* new about neoliberalism is the squeeze it is putting on predominantly white, abled, cisgender professional, managerial, and middle class labor. I argue that the newness of the labor flexibility required of U.S., middle class white subjects has produced majoritarian flexible subjects, whose intersections of identity are not all privileged, but who nevertheless try to maintain their centrality and privilege through what I'm calling flexible accommodation. Crip theorist Robert McRuer (2006) reads flexible subjectivity in the character Melvin Udall in the film *As Good as It Gets*. Whereas *As Good as It Gets* portrays flexibility positively, *Orange Is the New Black* parodies it in order to invite the accountability of being with rather than being down.

My reading of Piper's practices of being down operates on two levels. The first is understanding her as a character who is exemplary of flexible accommodation, and the second level is understanding the show as positioning her practices as entitled and undesirable—laughable, but in ways that warn white audiences to take care rather than "let it all go" as we crack up. While there is a danger of playing the "good white"—and good abled person—by laughing at Piper, there is also potential for a more critical engagement, especially if we appreciate the arc of Season 1. This arc exposes the unsustainability of these majoritarian practices of flexible accommodation. I hone in on scenes in which Piper's flexible accommodations are most prevalent: in her attempt at an apology to Suzanne, which I interpret in the larger context of *psychiatrization* and *sancism* in the moniker "Crazy Eyes" and attending discourse around her; in her "scary butch rapist" performance to Dina, a woman of color and wheelchair user brought to Litchfield to be "scared straight"; and finally her complete loss of even the flexibility to deal with others at all when she goes for the kill with Tiffany, the bigoted character that Piper—and audiences of the show—can feel good about hating. Related to these points, I have made some choices as to how I refer to the characters, so as to avoid the more problematic nicknames of certain characters while using nicknames when I think there are indications that they are self-given or otherwise playfully and joyfully inhabited. Thus I refer to Suzanne as "Suzanne," to Tiffany as "Tiffany," and to Taystee, Poussey, and Flaca, accordingly.

Flexibility Is the New White: Centrality, Sameness and Being Down

Piper's subjectivity must be contextualized within the broader projects of the prison-industrial complex (PIC), a specific set of arrangements in neoliberalism that also reach back through imperialism and, for my purposes, settler colonialism in the U.S. (see Miranda 2010; Mogul, Ritchie and Whitlock 2011). Angela Y. Davis has defined the PIC as "an array of relationships linking corporations, government, correctional communities, and media" (Davis 2003, 84), emphasizing the need to unlink the phrasing and ideology of "crime and punishment" to understand that rising violent crime has never been the rationale for building more and more, bigger and bigger prisons. Instead, various practices of containment and confinement based in racism, colonialism, homophobia, transphobia, and ableism have culminated in a prison-industrial complex. Given the pervasiveness of the PIC in the lives of women of color, I ask what it means to *meme* incarceration in the series and in its title, "*Orange Is the New Black*"—wherein a central character is not a target of the PIC but rather is an entitled, majoritarian subject who committed a crime out of boredom. Below I will further discuss what is new and what is not about the PIC, flexibility, and privilege. In order to argue convincingly for what can be gleaned from critical engagement with the series, it is necessary to attend to the newness of Piper's precarity/confinement as well as the question of genre. Is there rage behind this comedy-drama? Because, as José Esteban Muñoz (1999) insisted: "Comedy does not exist independently of rage" (xi).

But what happens to the violence of the prison-industrial complex when we are invited to laugh? And who is this "we"? Does comedy itself invite a kind of "being down" rather than being with? The ability to laugh—even and maybe especially *at ourselves*, for white audiences—and show that we are "down"? *Orange* has won or been nominated for a very long list of awards, in both categories of comedy and drama. I think we have to ask if popular culture is stuck in a binary circuit of tragedy vs. comedy, in which the only alternative to a paternalistic, tragic rendition of economically oppressed, imprisoned women/ of color is to comically render the situation. No doubt much of *Orange*'s playfulness is preferable to the objectifying frames and gazes of pity. And yet, the comfort of laughter by majoritarian audience members is discomforting. In a similar vein, Megan Comfort's (2014) contribution to the Public Books, "Virtual Roundtable on *Orange Is the New Black*," importantly insists: "Prison is no joke." According to these understandings of the neoliberalism and the PIC as well as the warnings about comedy, Piper's role in the series and the question of her centrality must be situated by interpreting white, abled, middle class labor insecurity and flexibility as a new form of old practices of imperialism and global capital which Global South, of color, and disabled subjects have long been exploited by (see Erevelles 2011), and finally, bringing together the queer, crip critique of neoliberalism with a disability justice orientation toward *flexible accommodation*.

What can we learn from Piper's flexible accommodation of difference, from her normatively privileged, uncritical mistakes? Her trajectory, especially throughout Season 1, moves from flexible to inflexible. McRuer's reading of Jack Nicholson's character, Melvin Udall, in the 1997 film *As Good as It Gets* interprets Melvin's character development along a trajectory of becoming flexible, moving from inflexible and intolerant to flexible and tolerant. Melvin's trajectory culminates in a flexibility that is probably already inhabited by the intended majoritarian audiences of the film. He must *become* what many audiences applaud themselves for already being, even as they laugh at his racist, sexist, homophobic and ableist jokes. By contrast, Piper's practices at the beginning of the show are already flexible, and she becomes increasingly inflexible during Season One especially. The upshot of my comparison between the two characters is the possibility for reading *Orange* as representing flexibility as undesirable, whereas *As Good as It Gets* makes it the telos of Melvin's positive development. My reading of Piper argues that her flexibility is not, overall, promoted by the show, and instead is exposed as unsustainable and irrelational. My intervention poses Piper's subjectivity as inhabiting *flexible accommodation*, in which the flexible subject accommodates difference rather than being accountable to difference and accountable for privilege. This new flexible accommodation entails multiple intersections of normativity, including abled privilege as well as Global North whiteness and abledness, and their ongoing practices of genocide, enslavement, and various forms of confinement such as incarceration, as well as the institutionalization of people with physical, emotional, intellectual or psychological disabilities.

One of the ways *Orange* may encourage critical engagement is by consistently questioning Piper's centrality. Whereas Melvin in *As Good as It Gets* is central as the main character, Piper's centrality is unsettled by send-ups throughout the series, highlighting the question of why she is central. The show's ensemble cast allows for the development and backstories of many other characters and their relationships to one another, many of which do not make Piper important. As María Lugones insists in "On the Logic of Pluralist Feminism" (2003), white women tend to block identification with the parts of themselves that are reflected back to them by women of color, and one reason for this is the refusal to recognize a multiplicity of selves: "we are also more than one and … not all the selves we are make you important." Mecca Jamilah Sullivan, in the Public Books "Virtual Roundtable on *Orange Is the New Black*" (2014) writes, "[I]t is the place of whiteness—not of blackness or brownness—that makes the show's race politics most problematic. By centering Piper's perspective on race and power, *Orange Is the New Black* constructs a fantasy of whiteness extremely useful in the candy land of the contemporary post-racial imaginary. It offers a fantastical landscape in which whiteness can interact more or less confidently with several racial others, can acknowledge and comment authoritatively on racial difference, and can observe, joke about, and benefit from racial, sexual, and gender power imbalances, all without relinquishing whiteness's privileges, and, perhaps most importantly, without ever being accused of racism." I agree with Sullivan's assessment, as I also read the series as exposing that fantasy of whiteness it is displaying by directly questioning Piper's centrality and importance, as well as exposing the unsustainability of her flexible accommodation. *Orange* does risk reproducing the fantasy without audiences engaging in any critique. I run a similar risk in this chapter by giving a sustained critique of Piper's privilege and flexibility, thus potentially recentering whiteness and her other privileges. I take this risk because I think there are even greater risks in ignoring how dangerous and violent her privilege is, and how dangerous and violent flexibility is as well. While Piper experiences many call outs on the part of her women of color interlocutors, these do not put her subjectivity in crisis because of her flexible management of the threat of crisis. In normative flexibility, only limited awareness can be brought to the normative subject's crisis, in order to resolve it; it would be *inflexible* to bring more than a little awareness (McRuer 2011, 17). Likewise, there is another danger to flexibility that lets normative subjectivity off the hook if we do not look at what these subjects are already getting away with. In other words, one of the features of the emerging normative flexible subject is the avoidance of an "inflexible" attention to difference, and to one's multiple forms of privilege. That would be too awkward for this new majoritarian subject.

If we read Piper's centrality as consistently in question, at the same time what we recognize her possessive investment in her own centrality, we can apprehend how much space she takes up even when she's hardly around. In the first few episodes of Season 2, Piper is completely absent from the story; all of our audience time is spent with the other characters and we are given a glimpse into what the show could be without her presence, however decentralized it may be. The relationship between Piper's sense of her own centrality and her flexible accommodation of difference is directly evident in an important scene from Season 1, wherein Piper schools her mom on visitation day. Her mother wants to confirm that Piper does not belong in prison, but, interestingly, Piper takes some responsibility for why she's there. In the very same gesture, however, she reduces the myriad reasons why the other women are there—reasons organized by the imperialist, racist, homophobic, transphobic, ableist carceral logics of the PIC—to *sameness*. In Piper's words, "I'm in here because I'm no different from anybody else in here and being in here is no one's fault but my own" (*Orange* 2013, Season One, Episode 6). What's most telling about this moment is that many different audiences might identify with her need to disagree with her mother's insistence on her difference from the other women, on the terms that she doesn't belong there and they do.

And yet the reduction to sameness is supremely disturbing when we consider how much her involvement in the drug trade, which landed her at Litchfield, can pretty much be summed up under the heading of "boredom"—unlike most of the other inmates, Piper hasn't been targeted by the PIC because of any of her identities. Claiming responsibility comes at the expense of justifying and further normalizing the role of the PIC in the other women's lives, and it reifies the "crime and punishment" ideology that Davis and many others have insisted on rejecting.

On Piper's part, no awareness is cultivated in terms of the role of homophobia in Poussey's life as it made her vulnerable to incarceration; no understanding of Taystee's experiences of school-to-foster care-to-prison pipeline; no thoughtful reflections on Sophia's credit card fraud to pay for her medical transition—astronomically expensive and not covered by insurance—to inhabit her gender. Thus Piper's reduction of difference to sameness is her way of flexibly accommodating difference in this scene; she can only flex or stretch enough to suggest that she is the same as the other women. She can only express accountability for her actions, and accommodate their difference from her, by asserting a false sameness. However, because of the ensemble structure of the show, the audience can understand what Piper will not. It is the complexity often given to other inmates' stories that breaks the monolithic, lazy, and uncritical way that Piper excuses the PIC. As we engage with the stories of the ensemble characters, white middle class audiences might be encouraged to inhabit whiteness differently, rather than rush to false solidarities or assume we are relating across difference when we are not. Mecca Jamilah Sullivan (2014) also refers to this scene, in order to argue that "the show uses Piper's encounters with women of color to invoke rhetorics of racial sameness as the allegorical undercurrent of its 'adventure' frame." In a similar vein, elsewhere in a collaborative piece with early Americanist Emily García, we suggest a reading of Piper's adventure story as a 21st century captivity narrative, in which it is not the "Other" in the form of American Indians who have captured her, nor the "Other" as women of color. It is the state that has put her in captivity, but her affective orientation throughout the series is marked by the sense that she is an outsider who does not belong in prison, even if she says otherwise. And when she does say otherwise, as we have seen, she does so by refusing to question the assumption that the women of color at Litchfield belong there. She reduces her differences from them to sameness, much like white women who wrote captivity narratives did when they had been "converted" to their captors' ways. Here, my reading of the flexible accommodation of difference—at times accommodating difference by reducing it to sameness—might open up possibilities for constructive distancing from Piper's behavior, whatever the intentions of the series' writers and creator. I am less concerned with creator Jenji Kohan's now-famous intent to use

Piper as a Trojan Horse than I am with effects. Sullivan's critique is similarly concerned with effects, and accurately so. If the series can be read as representing an *undesirable whiteness*, invested in its own centrality, giddy for the adventure of being down with women of color, much can be learned and hopefully avoided.

What Is New and What Is Not

As precarization of labor affects even those whose positionality would previously have been shielded from employment insecurities, and often from incarceration, what sorts of effects does this produce in terms of possibilities for solidarity or accountability? To whatever extent majoritarian subjects are being precarized in terms of their middle class labor, their own precarization does not automatically guarantee solidarity with subjects who experience multiple identity-based oppressions. As Lauren Berlant (2011) warns: "Competing precarities can morph in an instant to sound like grounds for solidarity" (203). Piper's precarity, and to some extent her flexible subjectivity, are recent products of her incarceration; she is white, wealthy, cisgender, abled, and Global North positioned prior to being imprisoned and she takes these modes and practices of identity with her into her confinement. Orange, as a color that indicates incarceration, is new to Piper. Orange, khaki, stripes, and various other-colored jumpsuits, as the carceral colors signifying the imprisonment of imperialism and settler colonialism's others, are not new. Criminalization and imprisonment of black, brown, Asian American, Amerindian, disabled, queer, trans, and gender nonconforming people spans centuries of North American settler colonialism (Ben-Moshe 2013; Davis 2003; Miranda 2010; Mogul, Ritchie and Whitlock 2011; Ogden 2006; Spade 2011; Stanley and Smith 2011; Sudbury 2004). Nor is it very new to call something "the new black," although this has a much more recent history; "fill-in-the-blank is the new black" is maybe a decades-old meme.

If orange is new to Piper, it is so as a riff of her new precarity; incarceration makes her a formerly upper middle class subject, or at least temporarily "on hold" upper middle class subject. At Litchfield Correctional Facility for Women, Piper's freedom of movement is precarized, as is her labor and her capital. In Season One, Piper tries to maintain the small business—making and selling aromatherapeutic soap—that she started with her best friend. Prior to Litchfield, she was already engaging in "employment at will" as a flexible form of labor, but this was a choice she could make because of her and her fiancé's financial support from their parents, and their class privilege. In Season 3, she works in the newly privatized prison's corporate mini-factory, sewing underwear for a company that is meant to invoke Victoria's Secret, an exploiter of prison labor. Piper concocts a scheme to make additional underwear from scrap materials and have a group of the other women wear them, then smuggle them out to sell on the Internet to fetishist connoisseurs of underwear with vaginal effluvia. She even union-busts the group, firing Flaca when she organizes them for better wages, later accusing Flaca of stealing money from her without any proof. This all takes place within the Season of the show that, so far, most explicitly attends to neoliberalism, with the privatization of Litchfield as perhaps the most important arc of Season 3. This privatization arc implicates prison labor as well as the corporatization of prisons in their privatization: the hierarchies in play; the CEO who will move on to another CEO position before the financial quarter is over so that it will not affect his portfolio; and the union prevention and union-busting of guards, an interesting representation in and of itself because prison guard unions are some of the few viable unions left in the U.S. In terms of flexibility, the requirements of flexible labor inside and outside of prisons and as effects of imperialism and globalization—along with the preference for flexible labor on the part of those who do not need to work but choose to do so—have produced features of subjectivity that McRuer associates with compulsory heterosexuality and able-bodiedness. He pairs David Harvey's critique of flexible accumulation through the use of flexible, contingent labor and Emily Martin's study of the shift toward framing the healthiest immune systems as the most flexible. He does so to argue that labor, employment and bodies have been required to be flexible in the extreme, insisting that a new mode of majoritarian subjectivity has emerged: flexible subjectivity. Thus it is not simply the self that labors which has been transformed by the mandates of flexibility; subjectivity itself has changed and the emerging majoritarian subjectivity must be attended to as a flexible subjectivity that can maintain privilege and centrality.

A newfound precarization of abled but also normatively classed, gendered, raced, regional and sexual subjects actually *deepens* the normative practice of flexibility, providing yet another "alibi" for privilege ("I'm not responsible because I am precarized too"; or "I was working really hard at a crappy, meaningless job too"). Piper's newfound precarity does not position her in solidarity with the other inmates. In fact, the assumption that they share experiences is one of the most common ways she is called to task in the show, as we saw above in Piper's self-righteous assertion that she is at Litchfield because she is the same as everyone else there. These moments in the series can offer majoritarian audiences a space to distance ourselves from her in critical ways. Laughing at Piper might encourage critical engagement, or it could problematically confirm that white audience members are "good whites" if we can laugh at her and ourselves. My reading of the show claims the space for distancing as a critical gesture that also refuses the "good white" paradigm, instead centering relationality and accountability. When audiences encounter Piper's differences from the other inmates, when they call her "College" or they engage with each other about their experiences with institutional oppression, there is a possibility for audience members to distance ourselves from her practices on the basis of her assumptions of shared experiences, and to reflect critically on our privilege if we have it. We cannot disavow privilege, but we can work to let go of the practices that protect it.

Flexible Accommodation as Managing the Crisis of Majoritarian Subjectivity

The disability justice inflections of my use of the term "accommodation" are intentional, and this relate specifically to Piper's flexible accommodation of difference as a kind of managing what would otherwise be a crisis of majoritarian, abled subjectivity. The disability rights movements of the U.K. and U.S., and the resulting (U.S.) Americans with Disabilities Act (ADA) have made crucial interventions in the mandate of "reasonable accommodation" for individual persons with disabilities, and these gains should not be diminished. At the same time, disability *justice* claims demand a more radical and thoroughgoing accessibility, which would require that the structures of the built world—and our relationships to each other—be changed (Mingus 2011). "Reasonable accommodation" is the bare minimum that should be required but is often treated by ableist individuals and institutions as if it were full accessibility, and this sense of what is reasonable is quite biased in favor of the ways the world is already built to privilege certain bodies, movements, cognitive processes, and emotional experiences. Just as the work of ADAPT and other disability justice organizations have emphasized a shift in expectation—*from* disabled people having to adapt to the ableist built world *to* their abled counterparts and institutions adapting to promote accessibility—accommodation should be understood as the bare minimum, or more accurately as a mode of flexibility that uses neoliberal tactics of inclusion/exclusion to alternately keep out and discipline. Flexible accommodation is not flexible *toward* disabled people, on the way to full accessibility, so much as it is flexible *for* the abled and ableist neoliberal institutions, as a mode of their being "down" with disability difference. Broadening the horizons of a critique of accommodation, not to conflate racial, gender, sexuality, and ability differences but to understand similar mechanisms of neoliberal institutions, we can better evaluate the practices of flexibility that protect multiple different forms of privilege.

As I have shown in my reading of Piper so far, the flexible subject avoids accountability to difference—and for its own privilege—in the performance of flexibility, of being "down" with difference. "Being down" is an irrelational orientation, a kind of insistent lack of accountability that avoids really being with others who are differently positioned. It may even use words like accountability and privilege to disclaim or avoid the work; it may even engage in acknowledging its own privilege in order to either not have to accept any call out, or even to *re-cement the burden on others to call me out*. Being down means being always already flexibly attuned, protected from one's own subjective sense of crisis, of being decentered.

McRuer (2011) articulates the "success" of the flexible subject as the ability to "perform *wholeness* through each recurring crisis" (17). This flexible accommodation, as practice of being down with difference, can discuss certain stereotypes without having to relate to relevant critical intellectual and activist histories, for example. Throughout the three seasons of *Orange* so far, Piper consistently performs being down with difference, knowing just enough to show (off) that she is not entirely ignorant. But Suzanne, Taystee, Sophia, Daya, Cindy and Poussey consistently put the burden back on her. In general, one of the ways Piper practices her flexible accommodation of difference is by apologizing to other characters, and in doing so she is managing the crisis that she would otherwise feel about her own subjectivity. She actually apologizes quite often, yet there are clues as to her lack of accountability, and many of them come in the form of how the apology is received, lending credibility to her interlocutors. One of the most poignant of these scenes is late in Season One. Piper's white, financially-supported-by-his-parents fiancé Larry has been struggling to become a writer, and he strikes gold by using Piper's incarceration to write a story. He is then invited for an interview on a radio show that is clearly meant to invoke *This American Life*, perhaps even nodding to the website "Stuff White People Like" (http://stuffwhitepeoplelike.com/), which has included *This American Life* and National Public Radio on its list. In the interview, which all the inmates listened to, Larry described Suzanne as "this insane girl—I mean like really insane, like belongs in a psychiatric hospital not a prison" (*Orange*, 2013, Season One, Episode Eleven, 47:50). As Liat Ben-Moshe has argued, well-meaning liberals make this gesture quite often, either calling prisons the biggest mental hospitals now that so many mental facilities have been defunded and closed, or otherwise appealing to the need for more mental hospitals to treat those who are "really" mentally ill and not "criminals." In fact, psychiatrization and institutionalization of those deemed mentally is another form of incarceration that needs to be questioned alongside our critiques of the PIC (Ben-Moshe 2013; see also Price 2011).

As the host is asking Larry if he worries about Piper's safety, the audio of the interview continues and the visual switches from Larry in the radio studio to Suzanne listening with headphones on, crying. Shortly after the radio program airs and Larry uses Piper's stories of the other inmates to further his own career interests, Piper has her first encounter with Suzanne while they are both cleaning the bathroom. Audiences are asked to confront Suzanne's vulnerability and the mean-spiritedness of the "outside" and all of the ways Piper represents it on the "inside," and we are likewise encouraged to shift our own identifications and critically reflect on our prior laughter at Suzanne's expense. Piper, as well as audiences of the show, are called to task for the moniker "Crazy Eyes," as Suzanne explains how cleaning is therapeutic for her when she feels overwhelmed by her emotions, reminding us of an earlier scene in which she asks why everyone calls her "Crazy Eyes." After this critical scene and throughout Seasons 2 and 3, Suzanne is more often referred to by her name rather than by the pathologizing nickname. It is even more significant in the broader context of Litchfield and the series, wherein almost everyone is referred to by a nickname and/or by their surname by the guards and other inmates alike. Suzanne becomes "Suzanne" to most of the other women, just as Sophia has always been "Sophia" throughout the Series, in an important if subtle trans-affirming move on the part of the show. Suzanne's own interventions, along with this shift in how she is named by others, can move us to be critical of the medicalization and psychiatrization of "crazy" and "insane," as well as their everyday use as modes of repathologizing. In terms of Piper's flexibly accommodating apologies, this one best exemplifies her being down rather than accountable, being just flexible enough to say "sorry," but still expecting Suzanne to make her feel better about herself, to alleviate her guilt. Still inhabiting a colonizing attitude toward Suzanne. She apologizes for her part in what Larry did, and tries to convince Suzanne that she's "great," just the way she is. But Suzanne needs no convincing on this point (arguably she has a stronger sense of herself and what she understands and does not understand). Refusing the mandate of flexibility, refusing to mediate with Piper's worst selves, she turns the question of goodness, validation, and recognition back on Piper. As she so eloquently puts it: "You're not a nice person" (*Orange* 2013, Season One, Episode Twelve).

Whether or not flexible accommodation is always or inherently unsustainable, it is certainly represented as unsustainable in *Orange*. Piper's practices of being down with difference cannot be maintained consistently. This is especially so in the arc of Season One, wherein Piper's earlier flexibility and tolerance shifts to an inflexibility, a hateful and murderous orientation toward Tiffany, the economically oppressed white character referred to as "Pennsatucky." A critical engagement with the series exposes Piper's movements from flexible to inflexible, drawing majoritarian audience attention to the crises and her preempting of feelings of fragmentation. This can encourage a desire for accountability in the very gesture of framing Piper's behavior as undesirable. Flexible accommodation is enabled through being "down" with difference, using flexibility to avoid relational practices of stretching and account-ability. Being always already "down" functions as a kind of fixed positionality that does not need to move or stretch too much, a position from which Piper can take what she wants. Flexibly accommodate.

McRuer (2011) insists that neoliberal flexibility allows for managing the subjective crisis; flexible subjects "adapt and perform *as if* the crisis had never happened" (17). This "as if" is where Piper lives, whether at home lacking the discipline to finish a cayenne pepper cleanse with her fiancé Larry, or in prison fucking her sometime girlfriend Alex (Laura Prepon) and/or flirting with Stella (Ruby Rose). Although there are painful initiations, punishments for "lesbian behavior," and disillusionment with Larry's willingness to exploit the other women's stories, there's no shift in her relational politics, no account-ability, only flexible accommodation—until even this becomes less and less accommodating, less and less flexible, and increasingly violent. Piper has the flexibility to tolerate black, brown, and queer differences, as well as to tolerate queer desire in herself, even to act on it, but her accountability to those impli-cated by her desire is suspect at best.

Piper may be read as a bisexual or even queer character. However we read her sexuality, we must note the entitlement that is highlighted several times in conversation between Piper and Larry, and between Larry and other characters, that has to do with the suppression of her queer desires. Larry's denial and Piper's own denial of queerness as it is subsumed by their hetero coupling must be addressed in any read of her as bi or queer. That said, the intersections of privileged and marginalized identities are present in the *prac-tices* of the new flexible subjectivity. And here I am most concerned with what we can learn from the representation of the entitlements of whiteness, cisgender, middle class status and Global North—New York City for that matter habitation and habituation. For my purposes, the accommodation of queer or bi desire, is another way we might read her flexibility.

Perhaps the best example of flexible accommodation as managing crisis comes in the Season One episode "Bora Bora Bora." Firstly, the addition of the third "Bora" here is a joke meant to highlight the working class character Morello's (Yael Stone) distance—epistemologically more than geographi-cally—from the Central South Pacific Island where she dreams of having her honeymoon. On the subject of (the effects of) imperialism, Bora Bora is still a French territory in 2015, though it shares its tourist destination role with many *post*colonial islands of the Global South Pacific and Atlantic. Within this broader context of working class white dreams of a colonial island vaca-tion, the episode also *hommages* the *Scared Straight* and *Beyond Scared Straight* documentaries, setting the scene for the disciplining of difference, and for Piper's flexible accommodation. A young woman of color and wheel chair user named Dina is the only youth brought to the prison who remains, for the most part, "scary not scared." All of the other youth pretty quickly lose whatever sense of confidence/swagger they come with, as eventually happens in the two documentaries the episode is riffing. Dina is positioned as a figure who makes the inmates uncomfortable—Poussey in particular—even though they are tasked with being scary in order to scare the youth "straight." This discomfort is in contradistinction to Piper's entitlement as the one who will do the scaring. An attenuated abled privilege is uncomfortably felt by Poussey, but not so by Piper. Nor is her whiteness of any consequence (to her, in her own sense of herself) in her patronizing orientation to Dina; she can manage what would otherwise be a crisis of her privilege when confronted by someone different from her.

Ultimately, Piper is the only one who "successfully" scares Dina. In this scene we literally look over Dina's shoulder at Piper, who is apparently conveying a truth to this young woman. We know a truth is about to be laid down because of the camera angles as they switch between Dina and Piper, but given similar moments when Piper thinks she is telling it like it is, we have plenty of good reasons to question her perspective. This truth she asserts is projection; this is Piper's truth and it doesn't need to be Dina's. After their own ableist fear of/pity for Dina makes it impossible for the other inmates to muster whatever it takes to scare her, they position Piper as the scary butch rapist by "warning" Dina about her. Piper metaphorizes "the truth" by inhabiting this role: "in here, … it's the truth that's gonna make you her bitch" (*Orange*, 2013, Season One, Episode Ten, 45:56). This comes just after another "truth" has been delivered: "I'm scared that I'm not myself in here and I'm scared that I am" (*Orange*, 2013, Season One, Episode Ten). Being down with difference is set in opposition to being scared of it, which then licenses the one who is *down* to accommodate that difference in order to appropriate what she needs: to speak her *own* truth as to her *own* fears. She claims the space and the occasion to do so by making Dina her sounding board and when the camera switches, we see Dina's face over Piper's shoulder: scared. Piper flexibly accommodates Dina's subject position by universalizing her own experience of prison—again. This move is imperialistic; she inhabits a colonizing orientation that flexibly accommodates difference. Just as she delivered the "telling it like it is" line to her mother, here again she reduces difference to sameness and makes it all about her. While we need the continuity of other scenes in which she is more explicitly called to task to inform a reading of the series at this moment, keeping in mind Suzanne's refusal of Piper's apology or Gloria chastising her after she accuses Flaca of stealing allows for a critical reading of the series. Piper's behavior in these scenes wherein she is *not* called to task, and in the particular scene wherein Dina looks scared after being lectured at, can be informed by other moments where she is called out. And if we read this continuity, we are led to critique Piper's flippancy about prison rape, her ableism and racism toward Dina, and her overall entitled flexible accommodation.

On my reading of Piper's devolving from flexibility to inflexibility, these earlier moments of flexible accommodation find one culmination in the end of the first season. Here she becomes inflexible when she goes for the kill with Tiffany. It may seem like her previous mode of flexibility was preferable. Inasmuch as it was less openly murderous, at least. The flexibility of normative subjects is exposed as all the more dangerous for its cunning protection of privilege. It doesn't look like more "blatant" or "obvious" oppression, so it is often allowed to go unchecked. In terms of audience perceptions of this blatant violence toward a character who we are most likely supposed to "love to hate," but also laugh at, I suggest that Piper's hatred of her is reflected back on us as witness to both Tiffany's bigotry and Piper's hatred. We can realize how dangerous it is to distance ourselves from Tiffany's bigotry in such a way that she becomes fair game for being subjected to violence, and to see that the logical conclusion to Piper's flexible accommodations of difference is her becoming completely inflexible. She is still trying to be down, but now it is through her violence toward a bigoted character, so she can "prove" how down she is. My analysis of Piper's violence toward Tiffany takes for granted that Tiffany, for all her racist, homophobic, transphobic misogyny, does not deserve to have this violence enacted on her body, and certainly not by Piper.

Another example of the unsustainability of flexible accommodation comes in a cafeteria speech she gives in Season 2, when she is criticized for receiving a furlough to be with her grandmother who is dying. The criticism is about how so many of the other inmates have applied for furloughs and never gotten them, and Piper's gain is attributed to her white middle class status (which seems indisputably true at the level of the show's portrayal of her white solidarity relationship with Officer Healy, who grants her the furlough). Her response may be satisfying for all the wrong reasons, if white audiences refuse to critically engage, but it can also show exactly how unsustainable her practices of flexibility are: "Yes, I am white! We have established that. And I got furlough, too. I guess white privilege wins again. And as a speaker for the entire white race, I would like to say I am sorry that you guys got the raw deal, but I love my fucking grandmother. And, yeah, she may be a whitey, too, but she's a fucking person and she's sick and she needs me! So shut the fuck up! It's not my problem" (Season 2, Episode 8). Piper cannot sustain the flexibility of being down with difference; when called to task at this later point in the show, she is entirely inflexible and reactionary. And rather than finding satisfaction in a white solidarity that appreciates her tirade, white audiences can instead be quite amused by what happens next: a huge, gooey piece of chocolate cake hits her on the back of the head as she turns on her heel, pleased with herself and her whiteness. As she turns around to see who threw it, we see none other than Suzanne, licking chocolate off her fingers and looking even more pleased with herself.

This essay has argued that new modes of flexibility have emerged as effects of imperialism and settler colonialism, and that Piper Chapman of *Orange Is the New Black* inhabits these modes in an interesting trajectory of becoming less and less flexible. Critically engaging with the show, we are invited to seek out forms of accountability, of being with, rather than being down, however specifically we are positioned in terms of majoritarian privilege. A critical engagement offers questions as to who and what we laugh at in *Orange*, and why, and opens us up to practices that can make new modes of relational politics possible.

Acknowledgments

A special thank you to the "Queer People, Places and Lives Conference" at The Ohio State University for the opportunity to give the first version of this work, and to the editors of this volume, April Kalogeropoulos Householder and Adrienne Trier-Bieniek. Clare Stuber provided invaluable help with feedback, as did Jana McAuliffe, Cynthia Medrano, Claudia García Rojas and Emily García. Thanks also to my former student, Sam, who pointed out the possible reading of Piper Chapman in comparison to Melvin Udall when I asked my class for a contemporary pop cultural example. And to Marie Draz, who suggested to me that what's interesting about *Orange* is that the show maybe doesn't want us to like Piper.

References

Alexander, M. Jacqui. 2006. *Pedagogies of Crossing: Meditations on Feminism, Sexual Politics, Memory, and the Sacred.* Durham: Duke University Press.

Ben-Moshe, Liat. 2013. "The Institution Yet to Come: Analyzing Incarceration Through a Disability Lens." *The Disability Studies Reader* 4:132–143.

Berlant, Lauren. 2011. *Cruel Optimism.* Durham: Duke University Press.

Berlatsky, Noah, Megan Comfort, Laurent DuBois, Kaveh Landsverk, Heather Love, Rebecca McLennan, Eric A. Stanley, and Mecca Jamilah Sullivan. 2014. *Virtual Roundtable on Orange Is the New Black.* Public Books. http://www.publicbooks.org/artmedia/virtual-roundtable-on-orange-is-the-new-black.

Davis, Angela Y. 2003. *Are Prisons Obsolete?* New York: Seven Stories Press.

Erevelles, Nirmala. 2011. *Disability and Difference in Global Contexts: Enabling a Transformative Body Politic.* New York: Palgrave.

Harvey, David. 1989. *The Condition of Postmodernity: An Enquiry into the Origins of Cultural Change.* Cambridge: Basil Blackwell.

Hong, Grace Kyungwon. 2006. *The Ruptures of American Capital: Women of Color Feminism and the Culture of Immigrant Labor.* Minneapolis: University of Minnesota Press.

Lorde, Audre. 1984. "Age, Race, Class and Sex: Women Redefining Difference." *Sister Outsider: Essays and Speeches.* Berkeley: Crossing Press:114–123.

Lugones, Maria. 2003. *Pilgrimages/ Peregrinajes: Theorizing Resistance to Multiple Oppressions.* Lanham, MD: Rowman & Littlefield.

Martin, Emily. 1994. *Flexible Bodies: The Role of Immunity in American Culture from the Days of Polio to the Age of AIDS.* Boston: Beacon Press.

McRuer, Robert. 2006. *Crip Theory: Cultural Signs of Queerness and Disability.* New York: New York University Press.

Mingus, Mia. 2011. "Changing the Frame: Disability Justice." *Leaving Evidence* (blog). https://leavingevidence.wordpress.com/2011/02/12/changing-the-framework-disability-justice/.

Miranda, Deborah. 2010. "Extermination of the Joyas: Gendercide in Spanish California." *GLQ: A Journal of Lesbian and Gay Studies* 16 (1–2):253–284.

Mogul, Joey, Andrea Ritchie, and Kay Whitlock, eds. 2011. *Queer (In)Justice: The Criminalization of LGBT People in the United States.* Boston: Beacon Press.

Muñoz, José Esteban. 1999. *Disidentifications: Queers of Color and the Performance of Politics.* Minneapolis: University of Minnesota Press.

Ogden, Stormy. 2006. "Pomo Woman, Ex-Prisoner, Speaks Out." *Color of Violence: The INCITE! Anthology.* Brooklyn: South End Press.

Price, Margaret. 2011. *Mad At School: Rhetorics of Disability and Academic life.* Ann Arbor: University of Michigan Press.

Spade, Dean. 2011. *Normal Life: Administrative Violence, Critical Trans Politics, and the Limits of the Law.* Brooklyn: South End Press.

Stanley, Eric, and Nat Smith, eds. 2011. *Captive Genders: Trans Embodiment and the Prison Industrial Complex.* Oakland: AK Press.

"Can't fix crazy"
Confronting Able-Mindedness

SARAH GIBBONS

"I am surrounded by crazy, and I am trying to climb Everest in flip-flops but I am not going crazy, okay?"—Piper Chapman, S1:13

"However, I argue that, while remaining skeptical of the motivations that have brought the enormous DSM into being, we might also take this proliferation of stories as evidence of two important truths about disorderly minds. First, such minds show up all the time, in obvious and not-so-obvious ways; and second, recognizing their appearance is not a yes-no proposition, but rather a confusing and contextually dependent process that calls into question what we mean by the 'normal' mind"
—Price 2011, 3–4

The finale of Season 1 of *Orange Is the New Black*, entitled "Can't Fix Crazy," concludes with protagonist Piper Chapman's violent confrontation with Tiffany "Pennsatucky" Doggett, who has threatened to take her life for disrespecting her religious beliefs. At this point in the series, Piper has saved Pennsatucky from her incarceration in the psychiatry ward by admitting that she tricked her into believing that she possessed miraculous healing powers. Yet in response to a new threat from Tiffany, Piper responds, "You do not wanna fight with me right now, crazy" (S1:13). Yet Piper does fight, and clearly crosses her own line of what she considers normal, acceptable behavior as she defends herself. Although she is quick to label Pennsatucky crazy, as she reflects on this fight at the beginning of Season 2, she becomes more confused about the line that demarcates what is normal from what is "crazy," as well as which side of the line she finds herself on. Piper and the other women serving time in Litchfield penitentiary often label others as crazy, confront perceptions that they are crazy, and fear that they themselves are slowly going crazy. While the anxious discourse of the characters is admittedly problematic and ableist in its expression, at the same time, the imperfect representation of these anxieties and vulnerabilities allows for interpretations that challenge dominant perceptions about what it means to be intelligent, agentive, and in control. Although the title "Can't Fix Crazy" may be cited as another example of a harmful word that is used quite liberally in the series, in this essay, I use an intersectional approach to explore how *Orange Is the New Black* represents pervasive anxieties surrounding able-mindedness. Bridging disability studies and intersectional feminist theory, I argue that the series paradoxically moves away from reifying the labels that it includes by allowing for a greater recognition of the validity and importance of a broad spectrum of human emotion, cognition, behavior, and intelligence.

As Rosemarie Garland-Thomson (2001) contends, disability studies and feminist theory can be strong allies. She argues for developing greater intersections between feminist theory and disability studies because "Western thought has long conflated femaleness and disability, understanding both as defective departures from a valued standard" (18). Just as feminist theory questions mistaken beliefs surrounding the inferiority of women, disability studies questions the belief that disabled individuals are somehow inferior to non-disabled, or temporarily able-bodied, people. Disability studies interrogates cultural understandings of ability, positioning itself against a medical model that understands disability as an individual problem, deficit, or pathology. Research within disability studies often works within the social model, an alternative to the medical model of disability. The social model distinguishes between impairment as a bodily state, and disability as a social and political experience of marginalization. This model emphasizes the disabling impact of built environments and attitudes (Pfeiffer 2002). Other scholars, however, are critical of how the social model retains the suggestion that impairment is automatically negative. Philosopher Shelley Tremain (2002), for example, points to examples of the how intersex bodies are pathologized even though individuals do not necessarily experience physical pain. She argues that our definitions of impairment are not neutral, but clearly change based on historical and cultural context (34). The example of the pathologization of intersex bodies that do not fit into clearly demarcated categories of male and female points to how definitions of disability are often particularly gendered.

However, while scholars like Garland-Thomson emphasize the centrality of connections between disability studies and feminist theory, historically, efforts to combat the assumption that female bodies are defective have, at times, led feminists to distance themselves from disability. American historian Douglas Baynton (2001) points out that in response to early opponents of women's rights, who conflated gender and disability by characterizing women as incapable, suffragists "rarely challenged the notion that disability justified political inequality and instead disputed the claim that women characteristically suffered from these disabilities" (43). As Baynton notes, suffragists assured a critical public that women were more entitled to political representation and legal rights than disabled people, which left cultural assumptions about disability and citizenship unquestioned. This example illustrates the difficulties that feminists and other marginalized groups have confronted and continue to confront when working toward the inclusion of disabled people in their movements; strategically, marginalized groups who are forced to confront assumptions that they are incapable may feel the need to distance themselves from disability to emphasize how social identities related to race, gender, class, and sexual orientation do not affect intelligence and rationality. Even within disability studies, early scholarship predominantly focuses on individuals with physical disabilities, as opposed to individuals whose disability identities complicate cultural understandings of intelligence and agency (Garden 2015, 73; Jones and Brown 2013; Murray 2006, 24–25). Increasingly, however, scholars are examining intellectual, invisible, and psychological disabilities. As I investigate the representation of anxieties surrounding able-mindedness in *Orange Is the New Black*, I primarily use the term "mental disability," as outlined by Cynthia Lewiecki-Wilson (2003) and Margaret Price (2011). Preferences surrounding the language of disability vary extensively, but I opt for mental disability following their suggestion that this term gestures toward coalition between neurodiversity advocates and psychiatric survivors, both of whom society often designates incapable of speaking authoritatively and truthfully about their own experiences because their disabilities are understood as located in the mind rather than the body (Price 2011, 17).

For the purpose of analyzing *Orange Is the New Black*'s fictional representation of disability, I bracket off certain important material questions, such as the inclusion of disabled people in casting, which merit greater attention in further analyses of the series that explore disability. My analysis in this essay is based on the insights of disability studies, which are grounded in Foucauldian understandings of how social institutions define and police deviance. Drawing on the insights of feminist scholar Susan Bordo (1993) I argue that the show offers insight into how deviance is not marked by a specific line, or a definitive pathology; instead, normalcy and deviance appear throughout a continuum, which creates anxiety for characters in *Orange Is the New Black* that want to distinguish themselves from disability because their daily survival often depends on an appearance of intelligence, rationality, and competence. Their anxiety allows for a disruption of the set of assumptions and negative connotations that Tobin Siebers (2008) defines as the ideology of ability, an ideology that, while pervasive, often remains unseen (9). My approach to examining the multiple narratives about disability generated through *Orange Is the New Black* as a cultural text borrows from disability studies scholar and rhetorician Jay Dolmage's use of *mētis* methodology as a tool for analysis (2014). Dolmage explains that unlike logic, which always implies forward movement, the rhetorical concept of *mētis* emphasizes cunning, creativity, and embodied thinking, and encourages thinking sideways and backwards (5). Rather than defining the meaning of disability in *Orange Is the New Black*, I seek to show how we can see this series performing the deconstruction of the binaries that divide normalcy and deviance through its imperfect representations, its disruptions in meaning, its showcasing of anxieties, and its complication of established categories as I trace the usage of the term "crazy" and its gendered associations.

Rather than distancing itself from disability, *Orange Is the New Black*, in multiple storylines, manages to challenge gendered assumptions about rationality and intelligence, even as it features a cast of female characters that would appear to have diagnoses for disabilities such as mood disorders and personality disorders. In order to illustrate the way in which these representations allow us to complicate a medical model that understands disability through pathology, I focus on the representation of four characters that others believe to be irrational and unstable: Blanca Flores, Suzanne Warren, Lorna Morello, and Brook Soso. Blanca Flores, whose physical appearance and animated conversations in the washroom stall lead others to question her sanity, deliberately cultivates these impressions so that she can make calls on a contraband phone without drawing any unwanted attention. Her efforts demonstrate how perceptions about behavior and appearance lead to erroneous assumptions about a person's motivations and agency. Yet even characters that would appear to have diagnoses trouble assumptions about ability, the complex characterization of Suzanne Warren, who is similarly pronounced "crazy," complicates her initial introduction to the show as a threat to the protagonist. While the other inmates circulate cruel rumors and nicknames like "Crazy Eyes," male characters also make problematic judgments about the sanity of women. Lorna Morello dreams of a wedding to a fiancé who continually rejects her, believing that she is delusional. Using the continuum model that Susan Bordo (2003) uses to discuss the relationship between female disorder and normal female practice with respect to anorexia, I borrow Nicky Nichols's critique of "the wedding industrial complex and society's bullshit need to infantilize grown women" to argue for an alternative reading of Lorna's beliefs about love and romance that suggests that they are not a departure from conventional practices so much as they are a representation of the perfect internalization of them (S2:03). It is to the social aspects of mental health that I turn to again with Brook Soso, as I argue that her struggles with depression in Litchfield bring into focus the social determinants of mental health.

Cultivating Madness and Challenging Ableism

While appearing composed, capable, and rational is important for individuals who must navigate the disempowering and dehumanizing environment of prison, the representation of Blanca Flores suggests that there are some instances in which cultivating an appearance of madness and taking advantage of ableiest beliefs can actually be useful. A relatively minor character with few lines of dialogue, by the end of Season 3, Flores's back story and the reason for her incarceration at Litchfield have not been revealed. However, while her appearance in the series is limited, Piper's encounter with Blanca marks a significant moment in the course of the series in which she is forced to confront that her initial judgments about sanity may be incorrect. Blanca's first appearance in the series is mediated through Piper's reactions to her; when Piper first arrives in Litchfield and encounters Blanca, who is exiting the only washroom stall with a door, she lets out a gasp of fear when Blanca, reveling in the trepidation that she inspires, lets out a single "Boo" (S1:01). Blanca appears to have near permanent occupancy of the only bathroom stall with a door because she talks to herself, a practice that the women with whom she shares a bathroom clearly associate with madness. Although the women in Litchfield simultaneously fear and pity Blanca, her behavior affords her a luxury that is in high demand in a confined space: privacy, in the form of a washroom stall of her own.

Piper learns of Blanca's strategic use of this washroom stall in an episode entitled "WAC Pack," in which Counselor Healy tasks her with locating a contraband phone. When Piper enters the washroom in this episode and joyfully discovers that the one stall with a door is finally available, she learns that Blanca has been secretly storing a phone in the washroom so that she can keep in touch with partner, Diablo. As the name Diablo means devil in Spanish, people had assumed that Blanca believed she was speaking with the devil when she was actually conversing with someone from outside, and sending him private photos. Marveling at the ingenuity of her fellow inmate's deception, Piper animatedly explains to Larry, "everybody thinks that she's crazy and that she's talking to herself in there, but she's not! She's talking on the phone. To Diablo!" (S1:06). Other inmates had made assumptions about Blanca based on her behavior, her appearance and her apparent conversations with the devil, perhaps influenced by dominant stereotypes of Latin American women as irrational and crazy for supposedly being "hot-blooded" or "fiery" (Arrizón 2008). Scholar Jennifer Esposito, in her critical narrative on living with chronic pain (2014), notes that other people interpret her reactions to her own embodiment as crazy in ways that are both gendered and racialized. She proclaims in "Power of the Mind," a poem about her experience of pain and how it affected her relationships and perceptions of her competence, "I am the stereotype of the crazy Latina" (1187). While Blanca would appear to fulfill such stereotypes, her detachment from the other inmates was actually deliberate and controlled. Blanca's use of her own semblance of madness allows for the cunning of *mētis*, and a movement sideways and backwards into spaces that other inmates are unable to occupy. The revelation that Blanca is not hearing voices or experiencing hallucinations illustrates how ordinary ableism operates. Individuals make assumptions about the degree to which people are competent and in control of their own actions based on conventions of behavior, personal appearances, and stereotypes associated with gender and ethnicity.

Piper's discovery of Blanca's secret coincides with her own need to defend herself against accusations that she is losing her sanity, which indicates her vulnerability to stigma. During a visit to the prison, Piper's mother asks her if she is "losing it" and reminds her that medications are available should she need them. In response to the claim that she is going crazy, Piper responds, "I am surrounded by crazy, and I am trying to climb Everest in flip-flops, but I am not going crazy, okay" (S1:06). I would argue that Piper's use of the term "crazy" to distinguish herself from the other inmates with whom she lives is unquestionably ableist. However, while one could argue that ableism is the predominant lens for speaking about disability in the series, I contend that we can see *Orange Is the New Black* challenging rather than reinforcing Piper's ableism through its illustration of how her initial beliefs about the distinction between sanity and insanity break down. Following her discussion with her mother, Piper discovers that Blanca, whom she has internally cast as other and defined in opposition to herself, is cultivating an air of madness so as to ensure her own privacy and protect her connection to the outside world. While some individuals, like Piper, may fear being perceived as crazy, Blanca fosters these impressions. Whether Blanca actually holds a diagnosis, and whether that diagnosis accurately describes her experiences, are difficult questions to answer; Blanca appears in the psychiatry ward at the end of Season 1, yet it is unclear whether Blanca clearly stands to benefit from a more benevolent form of assistance and behavior than she will find in the prison, or whether she is simply performing disability for the staff. The important insight here, however, is not the nature of Blanca's diagnosis, but rather the way in which individuals are forced to contend with the pressure to behave normally in extremely abnormal conditions. In an environment in which individuals lack control over almost every aspect of their lives, maintaining self control and the appearance of it becomes central to navigating everyday life.

Surviving the Psychiatry Ward and Its Accompanying Stigma

Although Piper is nervous around Blanca, whose behavior she judges abnormal and unpredictable, she does not appear to fear for her personal safety in her presence. The same cannot be said of Piper's initial feelings toward Suzanne Warren, known to the rest of the prison population by the cruel nickname "Crazy Eyes." Suzanne, one of the only people to show kindness to Piper when she first arrives in Litchfield, showers her new object of affection with romantic attention. When Piper describes her unwanted prison wife to Polly and her best friend asks what she means by "crazy eyes," she responds, "They're just crazy. They're just full of crazy. It's terrifying" (S1:03). The early episodes of Season 1 focus on Piper's discomfort at the persistent advances of Suzanne, who will not take her response that she has a fiancé seriously. As with other characters that I discuss in this chapter, the nature of Suzanne's disability is never fully disclosed. However, her difficulty understanding many social cues and her allusions to time spent in the psychiatry ward suggest that the character may have an official diagnosis or diagnoses, even if they are not revealed to the viewer. As a black woman, a lesbian, and a disabled person, Suzanne's character navigates multiple forms of stigma and oppression. While Suzanne's characterization fulfills some popular myths about disability, including the idea that people with disabilities are childlike, her increasing complexity throughout the series demands attention, as she develops into an interesting, multi-faceted disabled character and a talented storyteller, who incites feelings aside from pity or admiration.

Suzanne's characterization challenges the perception that individuals who experience mental disability present a great danger to other people. This claim may seem unusual, given that Suzanne admittedly approaches conflict with violence on more than one occasion throughout the series. Her initial characterization would seem to fulfill, rather than challenge, stereotypes. In addition to relatively harmless displays of aggression like throwing pies in the dining hall, Suzanne attacks Piper following a traumatic moment during the Christmas pageant in Season 1, and violently overpowers Poussey Washington to send a warning from Vee Parker in Season 2. However, while Suzanne may turn to aggression on occasion, she faces greater danger from the supposed care of institution than its residents face from her. Price, in her monograph (2011), addresses stereotypes that madness is dangerous, pointing out that while disabled people "do move in an aura of constant violence within institutions," they are more often victims of violence than perpetrators of it (2). Part of the violence that Suzanne experiences at Litchfield consists of the actual psychiatric care that she receives from the prison institution. In a candid conversation with Piper, she attests that the psych ward, which is worse than solitary confinement, is like the Bermuda Triangle of the prison, as inmates sent for psychiatric care typically do not return to the general prison population. When Piper asks for assurance that inmates in psychiatric care at least have access to consultation with a therapist, Suzanne responds, "Nope. I mean, they give me medication and make me calm. But that just makes me sleepy. Sometimes when I'm real upset, they tie me down. Like a balloon. So I don't fly away" (S1:11). Suzanne's description of the psychiatric ward reveals the extent to which violence is not only a means to which she occasionally resorts, but is also characteristic of the care that she receives, which is designed to control and manage deviance, as opposed to relieve any suffering that she might experience in the prison environment. Suzanne and Piper's conversation marks a turn away from the representation of Suzanne's character as a threat to Piper, and toward that of an individual struggling to receive basic human dignity from an prison population that calls her "Crazy Eyes," and an institution that attempts to reify this label at every turn.

Critics may compare stereotypes and challenges to them in order to debate whether the representation of Suzanne Warren is ultimately a positive or a negative representation of disability. However viewers choose to interpret her, her storyline draws attention to the inadequacy of care that individuals receive within the institution. Visual depictions of Tiffany's treatment within the psychiatry ward corroborate Suzanne's description of its operation. Her indictment of psychiatric care at Litchfield is persuasive enough to prompt Piper to defend Tiffany's sanity and plead for her release. Suzanne's description of the absence of counselors and the use of medication as a controlling force also gestures toward a critique of the medical model of disability, which understands impairment as an individual defect or pathology. As the medical model understands disability on an individual level, treatment takes the form of medical interventions like prescriptions. One of the important insights of disability studies is that disability is not an absolute state; the field shows how social attitudes and environments shape processes of disablement. A recurrent omission on the part of prison guards and other staff throughout the series is the lack of acknowledgment that prison itself is a disabling space, in which many women find their own mental states moving sideways and backwards along a continuum of mental health and mental illness. Rather than addressing the ways in which the prison environment itself is disabling for an individual's well-being, and working to change the conditions itself, interventions take place on an individual level through the administration of medication that leaves individuals sleepy, docile, and manageable. The psychiatry ward is not a place that relieves individuals of their suffering, but is instead a site of institutional control.

A Continuum of Vulnerability
and the "Wedding Industrial Complex"

While the Litchfield inmates circulate harmful rumors and ableist nicknames about one another as they police definitions of sanity, male characters also make problematic judgments about the sanity of women. Lorna Morello dreams of a wedding to an involuntary fiancé who continually rejects her, believing that she is delusional. As revealed through flashbacks, Lorna's absolute loyalty to Christopher is the reason for her incarceration, as she continued to telephone him, message him, and follow him long after he rejected her advances. Throughout the first season, Lorna remains faithful to her vision of Christopher, and carefully plans a wedding to take place following her release from prison. After she breaks into Christopher's home when left unsupervised in the prison's transport vehicle, he confronts her in Litchfield's visiting room. In a display of verbal aggression so violent that a guard escorts him out, Christopher calls Lorna "a mental case," "a fucking stalker," and "a psycho bitch," and asks her why she attempts to "keep up this lunatic charade" (S2:10). Christopher's accusations and Lorna's inability to accept his rejection appear to suggest that she has lost touch with her own reality and with the social codes that govern acceptance behavior. However, I would argue that an intersectional feminist reading of Lorna's one-sided relationship with Christopher reveals more about the gendered expectations of behavior than it does about Lorna's psychological state.

Lorna, after all, is very traditional in her beliefs about romantic partnerships, despite her affair with Nicky Nichols. Her bedroom in her family's home is a shrine to teen romance, featuring posters of celebrities and wedding collages that emphasize her faith in marriage as the path to true happiness. Lorna clearly fulfills the cultural stereotype of the woman who has been dreaming of her wedding day since she was a young child. The marriage of advanced capitalism and patriarchal doctrine that reinforces such childlike fantasies of weddings is the subject of critique for Lorna's good friend and occasional lover, Nicky. Nicky, who witnesses Lorna's outrage that Christopher's new fiancé has stolen her wedding date, responds with clear derision of what she calls "the wedding industrial complex and society's bullshit need to infantilize grown women" (S2:03). While some viewers and critics might diagnose Lorna's character with a clear disorder, Nicky's identification of the infantilizing, gendered aspects of marriage offers an alternative lens for understanding Lorna's unwavering devotion to Christopher. Feminist disability studies scholar Susan Bordo (2003) argues that examining disorders to which women have been vulnerable reveals that there exists a "continuum between female disorder and 'normal' feminine practice" (168). Examining the body as a text of femininity, Bordo connects her theory to Susie Orbach's insights on gender and anorexia. She notes that for Orbach, "anorexia represents one extreme on a continuum on which all women today find themselves, insofar as they are vulnerable, to one degree or another, to the requirements of the cultural construction of femininity" (47). Although Bordo's work primarily concerns gender and embodiment, I would argue that the application of her continuum model to Lorna's predicament draws attention to "crazy" as a term that is particularly gendered.

Here, I borrow Bordo's discussion of the continuum model and Nicky's critique of the "wedding industrial complex" to argue that Lorna's heteronormative beliefs about love are not a departure from conventional practices so much as they are a representation of the perfect internalization of them. As women in a patriarchal society are vulnerable to cultural constructions of feminine beauty, so women are vulnerable to cultural beliefs about the centrality of weddings, marriage, and romance. When understood through a continuum model, Lorna's commitment to her fantasy of a perfect wedding appears less like an attempt to illustrate a particular pathology and more like an illustration of the gendered constructions of rationality and able-mindedness.

Lorna receives her happy ending in Season 3, but I would argue that the show does not present her marriage to Vince Muccio and the end of her fascination with Christopher MacLaren as a narrative of overcoming disability. After Christopher confronts her in the visitation room at Litchfield and Nicky witnesses his outrage, Lorna confesses to her friend, "there is something really wrong with me," and admits that she took the van to Christopher's house. Nicky, at this point, does not attempt to relieve any anxiety Lorna might have about her sanity; instead, she calls her friend "bat-shit crazy," and tells her that she loves her (S2.10). Her terminology is blunt and offensive, but the message that Nicky does not care about whether Lorna fits into a particular template of normalcy is clear. While Lorna's recognition that her devotion to Christopher is unhealthy might appear to signal a movement toward recovery and normalcy, instead, Lorna finds a partner who shares her interest in tradition and is not dissuaded by her incarceration. In their vows to one another during a makeshift ceremony in the visitation room, Vince proclaims that they may be crazy, but they are crazy together; a statement that bears particular weight given how Christopher has often characterized Lorna. As Vince identifies himself as equally crazy for their decision to marry while Lorna finishes her sentence, Lorna's storyline at the end of the third season culminates not with an overcoming or with a clear diagnosis to manage, but with the celebration of her own particular way of being in the world that she is able to share and celebrate given the right partner.

Social Determinants of Health
and the Depathologization of Depression

While Lorna's story ends happily, *Orange Is the New Black* features other storylines that clearly demonstrate the importance of having access to services like appropriate counseling. Social, cultural, and environmental influences on mental health feature prominently in the representation of depression in the series. A disability studies approach, which mounts a critique of how the medical model identifies disability as an individual problem, defect, or pathology, emphasizes how mental health is not only a matter of individual responsibility and care, but also an issue of accessibility. Litchfield inmate Brook Soso, a young woman imprisoned for her political activism, draws attention to issues of health, access, and emotional well-being within the prison environment. From her entrance in Season 2, she dedicates her time in prison to protesting Litchfield's conditions and advocating for the rights of inmates to fair and humane treatment. In the second season of the series, Brook leads a peaceful hunger strike to raise awareness of the horrible conditions in the prison. Brook's characterization, from her gregarious personality, to her refusals to shower, to her friendships with bakers who sell "anti-authoritarian cupcakes," establishes her as a comedic figure on the show (S2:11). Yet while the series initially encourages laughter at Brook's naiveté, in the third season, her storyline takes a more sinister turn that illustrates the need for improving the conditions of the prison more strongly than her own efforts at resistance manage to convey. Brook's attempted suicide through an overdose following a lack of appropriate counseling draws attention to the social determinants of mental health that are overlooked in prison and society at large.

Brook's unsuccessful suicide attempt illustrates the perils of a lack of compassionate care and guidance within the institutional setting of prison. Sam Healy, Brook's counselor, brings many misogynist and ableist beliefs and anxieties into the workplace. He offers to write a recommendation for her to receive medication that will improve her mood, advising her that people do not enjoy being friends with sad people. When she refuses, he undermines the reality of her experiences by telling her that the secret to understanding depression is recognizing that, "it's all in your head" (S3:08). Berdie Rogers, Litchfield's other professional counselor, criticizes Sam's approach, assuring Brook that experiencing depression is an appropriate response to contending with the realities of prison life (S3:10). However, Berdie's dismissal from Litchfield leaves Brook transferred back to Counselor Healy, who believes that the strong can overcome depression through individual will, and the weak can overcome it through medical intervention. Healy's understanding of depression manifests one of the tenets of what Tobin Siebers (2008) calls the ideology of ability. The ideology of ability holds that "disability can be overcome through will power or acts of the imagination" because "it is not real but imaginary" (280). Individuals who experience individual disabilities such as depression are particularly vulnerable to accusations that their experiences are not real, or that they are inventing their own problems. While Sam's job places him in a position to assess the rationality of women, Season 3's provision of increased insight into his past and that of male staff members like Joe Caputo and John Bennett emphasizes that they are also given to feelings of depression and outbursts of rage that they associate with the women in their care. When Sam himself attends a counselor in Season 2, he leaves in a rage, convinced that he does not need help, but is instead appropriately tasked with providing help to others (S2:10). When transferred back into the care of Healy, who upholds an ideology of ability, Brook resigns herself to accepting a prescription.

The discovery of Brook's unconscious body in the prison library further highlights the grim realities of psychological care within the institution. Once Poussey and her friends determine that Brook is still alive, they discuss how imperative it is for them to conceal her actions from the prison administration. While covering up evidence of a suicide attempt may sound as though it would place Brook in further danger, character discussions reveal that the reality of incarceration in Litchfield is that knowledge of Brook's attempt to take her life will ensure that she is transferred back to the psychiatry ward, which Suzanne and other inmates acknowledge to be worse than solitary confinement. Suzanne insists, "Psych's so bad. I wouldn't even wish it on the people running it. Although that would be poetic in its own way" (S3:13). As Brook had acknowledged her own feelings of depression to be connected to a lack of companionship within the environment of prison, the actions of Poussey, Taystee, and Suzanne are consistent with her wishes, without her having to articulate them. Brook's well-being is not dependent upon medication and surveillance, but upon care and compassion from Poussey and her friends, who welcome her into their circle in the finale of Season 3.

Although mental health and its accompanying stigma is an increasing topic in mainstream contemporary media, I would argue that Brook's story gestures toward a disability and mad studies politics that push for acknowledging the social determinants of mental health. Discussions of stigma may be increasing, but such discussions often stop short of questioning distinctions between ability and disability with respect to mental health. Instead, mainstream discourse often advocates for further medicalization and comparisons between mental disability to physical disability or to illness to counter voices like that of the fictional Sam Healy, who do not believe depression is real. However, I would argue that the continuum model that Bordo proposes is also instructive for thinking about the representation of mental health and depression in *Orange Is the New Black*. Recognizing the reality of experiences of depression and the reality of other mental disabilities does not necessarily require elucidating a new kind of pathology. Instead, we can advocate for greater recognition of how experiences such as poverty, racism, incarceration, and lack of access to health care are contributing factors for depression. As Counselor Rogers points out, depression does not need to be understood as an aberration, but as an appropriate response to difficult circumstances. This approach is particularly important for understanding depression in prison, as it places responsibility for access to mental health care and services on prison administrators and counselors, whose role in disabling processes is clearly acknowledged in this series.

Conclusion

As the editors and contributors of this volume show, *Orange Is the New Black* pushes the boundaries for how women are represented on television, and fosters critical dialogue on the prison system in the United States. It would be difficult and perhaps unfair to argue that the series represents disability positively in all cases; after all, the characteristics of what constitutes a positive representation of disability can be personal and subjective, even when based on a critical disability studies perspective. In this analysis, rather than attempting to pin down the representation of disability in the series, I have turned to the methodology of *mētis* developed by Jay Dolmage to offer four examples of how we can read disability in non-traditional ways that question the binaries that divide ability and disability. While I would not argue that all representations of disability in the series appear positive or generative at first glance, I would argue that the show's inclusion of a variety of disabled characters, from multiple ethnic backgrounds and social classes, reflects the reality that many women in prison are disabled, or experience struggles with mental health even if they do not overtly identify as disabled. As a television series that engages with intersectional feminist ideas, *Orange Is the New Black* troubles the perception that women are inherently less rational, more emotional, and "crazier" than men. However, rather than avoiding the representation of characters with mental disabilities in order to strengthen the argument that women are capable and intelligent, *Orange Is the New Black* offers a cast of multiple characters experiencing disability to celebrate non-normative forms of identity, cognition, and embodiment. The repetition of eugenic terms such as crazy, lunatic, and moron, which exist in tension with this celebration, demonstrates the reality of the presence of ableism in our vocabularies and in our judgments of other people. Piper's gradually decentralized storyline shows her confronting the realities of prison life, which involves confronting the deconstruction of an ideology of able-mindedness that places normalcy and deviance in binary categories. The show's chronicling of pervasive efforts to appear normal, maintain self-control, and defend oneself against any accusations of being crazy illustrate the pervasiveness of ableism as an ideology that often goes unquestioned. Further, *Orange Is the New Black* shows how this ideology governs beliefs about care and access to services, highlighting how most characters do not receive any relief from the disabling environment of the institution. Its representation of disability, and responses to disability within the institution, shatters any perceptions that prison naturally rehabilitates or otherwise helps the vulnerable women who are incarcerated within it.

REFERENCES

Arrizón, Alicia. 2008. "Latina Subjectivity, Sexuality and Sensuality." *Women & Performance: A Journal of Feminist Theory* 18(3):189–198.

Baynton, Douglas. 2001. "Disability and the Justification of Inequality in American History." *The New Disability History: American Perspectives*, edited by Paul K. Longmore and Lauri Umansky. New York: New York University Press.

Bordo, Susan. 1993. *Unbearable Weight: Feminism, Western Culture, and the Body*. Berkeley: University of California Press.

Dolmage, Jay. 2014. *Disability Rhetoric*. Syracuse: Syracuse University Press.

Esposito, Jennifer. 2014. "Pain Is a Social Construction Until It Hurts: Living Theory on My Body." *Qualitative Inquiry* 20(10):1179–1190.

Garden, Rebecca. "Ethics." *Keywords for Disability Studies*, edited by Rachel Adams, Benjamin Ross, and David Serlin, 70–74. New York: New York University Press.

Garland-Thomson, Rosemarie. 2011. "Integrating Disability, Transforming Feminist Theory." *Feminist Disability Studies*, edited by Kim Q. Hall, 13–47. Indiana: Indiana University Press.

Jones, Nev, and Robyn Lewis Brown. 2013. "The Absence of Psychiatric C/S/X Perspectives In Academic Discourse: Consequences and Implications." *Disability Studies Quarterly* 33(1). Accessed October 17, 2015. http://dsq-sds.org/article/view/3433

Lewiecki-Wilson, Cynthia. 2003. "Rethinking Rhetoric through Mental Disabilities." *Rhetoric Review* 22(2):156–157.

Murray, Stuart. 2006. "Autism and the Contemporary Sentimental." *Literature and Medicine*. 25(1):24–45.

Pfeiffer, David. 2002. "The Philosophical Foundations of Disability Studies." *Disability Studies Quarterly*. 22(2):3–23. Accessed October 17, 2013.

Price, Margaret. 2011. *Mad at School: Rhetorics of Mental Disability and Academic Life*. Ann Arbor: University of Michigan Press.

Siebers, Tobin. 2008. *Disability Theory*. Ann Arbor: University of Michigan Press.

Tremain, Shelley. 2002. "On the Subject of Impairment." *Disability/Postmodernity: Embodying Disability Theory*, edited by Mairian Corker and Tom Shakespeare, 32–47. London: Continuum.

About the Contributors

Katie Sullivan **Barak** is an independent scholar in Denver, Colorado. Her research focusses on the intersection of media representation, identity and meaning-making. She has deconstructed the way female athletes are represented in the media, explored the ways rednecks, hillbillies and white trash characters function in horror and comedy films, and built a nuanced history of the cat lady trope.

Lydia **Brown** is a queer and East Asian autistic activist, writer and speaker whose work has largely focused on violence against people with disabilities who have multiple marginalized identities and experiences. She is co-president of TASH New England, chairperson of the Massachusetts Developmental Disabilities Council and an executive board member of the Autism Women's Network.

Sarah E. **Fryett** is a visiting assistant professor in the Department of English and Writing at the University of Tampa. Her work revolves around feminist and queer theory as well as philosophy, pedagogy and media studies. Her recent publications include an analysis of female comedians.

Sarah **Gibbons** is a Ph.D. candidate in the Department of English Language and Literature at the University of Waterloo. She is the assistant editor and social media coordinator of the *Canadian Journal of Disability Studies.* Her research explores the intersections and tensions among disability studies, material feminism and the environmental humanities.

Yvonne Swartz **Hammond** teaches courses in American literature and Native American studies at West Virginia University. She served as president of the Appalachian Prison Book Project, a not-for-profit that sends books to imprisoned peoples. Recent research includes the perspective of children's experiences of trauma as written through adult perspectives in various forms of life writing.

April Kalogeropoulos **Householder** is a media scholar and adjunct faculty member in the Gender and Women's Studies Department at the University of Maryland, Baltimore County. She also serves as the assistant director of the Ronald E. McNair Post-Baccalaureate Achievement Program. She is an award-winning documentary filmmaker and the author of several articles on intersectional feminist history and theory.

Kyra **Hunting** is an assistant professor of media arts and studies at the University

225

of Kentucky. Her research looks at genre, narrative form and minority representations in entertainment media, with special attention given to LGBTQ representation and teen and children's media. She also studies methodological approaches to large-scale content and textual analysis.

Zoey K. **Jones** is a Ph.D. candidate at Carleton University. Her research focuses on television shows about women in prison. She is particularly interested in representations of sexuality and necropolitics in these shows, along with other topics including sex workers' rights, critical criminology, penology and criminal justice policy.

Minjeong **Kim** is an assistant professor of sociology at San Diego State University. She is interested in gender and race in the media, with focus on Asian American representations. She also studies gender relations in immigrant families.

Hilary **Malatino** is the assistant director of the women's studies program at East Tennessee State University. She writes regularly in the fields of intersex and trans studies, affect theory, decolonial feminisms and medical humanities.

Anne **Moore** is a fellowship advisor in the Department of Undergraduate Education at Tufts University. She has contributed to the mediacommons project *In Media Res*, worked as a television critic for the blogs *Parabasis* and *Hooded Utilitarian* and has contributed to *Points: The Blog of the Alcohol and Drugs Society*.

H. **Rakes** is a visiting assistant professor at DePaul University in women's, gender and LGBTQ studies. Rakes' research interests include queer theory, gender studies, disability studies, women of color feminisms and transnational feminisms. Research interests trace the practices of neoliberal flexibility inhabited by majoritarian subjects to maintain centrality and privilege.

Susan **Sered** is a professor of sociology and senior researcher at the Center for Women's Health and Human Rights at Suffolk University. Her research interests include gender, religion, health and illness, and mass incarceration. She has conducted fieldwork in Israel, Okinawa and the United States.

Adrienne **Trier-Bieniek** is the department chair and professor of sociology at Valencia College in Orlando, Florida. Her research interests include music, gender and pop culture. She has published in the journals *Qualitative Research* and *Humanity and Society*, is a contributor to numerous books and has been a guest columnist for *The Orlando Sentinel*.

Kalima Y. **Young** is a Ph.D. candidate and instructor at the University of Maryland, and she also lectures in LGBT and film studies at Towson University. Her research focuses on the impact of race and gender-based trauma on black American identity and cultural production.

Index

Abbott, Traci 101, 102
abortion 52, 89, 128
Abu Ghraib 82
activism 71
adoption 188
AfterEllen 113
Alba, Richard 65
Alexander, Elizabeth 35
Alexander, Jeffery 33
Alexander, Michelle 3, 4
All American Girl 10
Althusser, Louis 11, 129
Americans with Disabilities Act 187, 202
Amish 39
Anderson, Michelle 82
Andreeva, Nellie 113
Appalachia 131, 133
Arend, Patricia 5
asexuality 28
assimilable epiphany 72
assimilation 65
autism 176

Bad Girls 11, 112, 114, 115
Bandele, Asha 38
Bechdel Test 6
Becker, Ron 117
Deirne, Rebecca 112, 115
Bettcher, Talia Mae 99, 100
Bhabha 24
"binge-watching" 1, 158
Boddy, Janice 129
bodies 9, 12, 16, 23, 25, 27, 36, 40, 68, 78, 142, 158, 163, 174, 177, 179, 183, 185, 212
Bonilla-Silva, Edwardo 65
Bradshaw, Peter 61
Brownmiller, Susan 40
Bureau of Justice 87
Burns, Kellie 29
Butler, Judith 5, 119, 141

capitalism 218
Capsuto, Stephen 16, 17
Carlin, Stella 28
Cecil, Dawn 79, 113
Central Park jogger 39
childbirth 163
Cho, Margaret 10
Ciasullo, Ann 16, 114, 119
Clowers, Marsha 79
Colbert, Steven 67
cotton ceiling 103
Cox, Laverne 1, 6, 10, 95–97, 105
Crash 61, 62
Crenshaw, Kimberly 6, 42
criminal justice system 1; *see also* law enforcement; prison system
Cronan, John 84
Cusac, Anne Marie 82
Cutler, David 130
cycle of poverty 38–40

Davies, Cristyn 29
Davis, Angel 3
Davis, Angela 142, 143
Davis, Glyn 115
Debord, Guy 36
Degeneres, Ellen 9
Degrouit, Nathalie 26
DeVeaux, Drew 103
Dillon, Stephen 108
Dines, Gail 26
diversity in television 45, 46
double jeopardy 49
Dow, Bonnie J. 18, 117, 119
Dragon Lady 62, 63, 66, 73
drugs 122, 136, 163; and drug crimes 4, 39, 163; and race 4; and sentencing guidelines 3, 38; and sex 87; and trauma 39, 131, 132
Duggan, Lisa 65

Elbert, Roger 61
The Eleventh Hour 18
Ellen 9, 18
Emmy's 157
erotica 153, 160
Exes & Ohs 11, 112

Fanon, Franz 11, 130, 132
Farr, Daniel 26
Federal Bureau of Prisons 63
feminist theory 211
Figeroa, Natalie 3
flashbacks 54, 68, 143, 148, 160, 162, 165, 166, 171
foster children 163
Foucault, Michel 11, 80, 185
Fratini, Dawn 111
Fresh Air 45
Freud, Sigmund 33
Friedman, Susan S. 49
Frost, Robert 57

Gay and Lesbian Alliance Against Defamation (GLAAD) 63, 96
gender identity 101
Gittel, Noah 104
Gordon, Avery 43
Gross, Terry 45

Haggis, Paul 61
Hall, Stuart 32
harassment 134
Hartman, Saidiya 36
Haslam, Nick 37
Heathaffairs.org 132
hegemony 16, 25, 183
Herman, Judith 35, 111, 116–118, 123–124
heteronormativity 22, 27, 51, 55, 83, 125, 219
heterosexuality 28, 124, 146, 189, 190
Hill Collins, Patricia 37, 49
holocaust 33
Homer's *Odyssey* 46
homonormative 111, 117
homophobia 121, 134
hooks, bell 2, 16, 23, 24, 28, 105
Hsu, Hsuan 61
Human Rights Project 42
Human Rights Watch 3

Imitation of Life 23
impoverished 77
incarceration rates 132
institutionalization 177
intersectionality 5, 8, 13, 28, 49, 211, 218
invisible knapsack 47
Irwin, Amos 79

Jezebel 67
John 54
Judaism 164, 165
juvenile justice system 42

Kellber, Douglas 36
Kerman, Piper 62, 63, 80, 100, 101, 106, 161
Kim, Minjeong 72
Kinsey Scale 51
Kohan, Jenji 6, 9, 45–47, 50, 58, 77, 78, 79, 81, 84, 160, 167, 199
Ku Klux Klan 49
Kuan Chung, Sheng 20

The L-Word 9, 11, 15, 18, 19, 20, 28, 29, 114, 115, 117
Lauzen, Martha 114
Leavy, Patricia 4, 5
Levine-Rasky, Cynthia 49
LGBT 6, 7, 9, 19, 20, 27, 68, 83, 86, 88, 101, 113, 125, 185, 216; and stereotypes 9; and television 17; and youth 7
Lip Service 11, 112, 114
Lotus Blossom 62
Lugones, Maria 197

madness 178
male gaze 4, 27, 174
Man, Christopher 84
mania 25
Marchetti, Gina 72
Marxism 129
masturbation 147
McCarthy, Anna 18
McClelland, Mac 6
McHugh, Kathleen 80
McIntosh, Peggy 47, 48
McNair, Brian 26
McRuer, Robert 72
Medhurst, Andy 115
media 20, 84; and gender 4, 157; and oppression 6; and society 5
melancholia 34
men's prison 129
mental health 12, 13, 24, 33, 38, 52, 161, 175–177, 182, 189, 203, 214, 215, 217, 218, 221
Meyer, Anneke 5
Meyer, Michaela D.E. 50
Mikvah 165
Millbank, Jenni 113
Milstone, Katie 5
Miss Gay Black America 101
Mittel, Jason 111
Mock, Janet 105
model minority 65

Modleski, Tania 24
Morgan, Ellen 9
Mulvey, Laura 4, 9, 16, 26

Najumi, Modhadesa 8, 16
natal alienation 106
National Center for Transgender Equality 98, 103
National Inmate Survey 7
Nee, Victor 65
Needham, Gary 115
Nichola, Nicky 16
Noton-Hawk, Maureen 129
NPR 45

Orientalist 64–66
the Other 22, 25, 28, 100, 144, 164, 166, 171, 199
overdose 186
Oz 10, 78

Patterson, Orlando 95
pedagogy 90
Pennsylvania Coalition Against Rape 131
Pennsylvania Office of Children, Youth and Families 131
physical violence 33, 34, 107, 163
police woman 18
pornification 26
pornography 181, 182
poverty 7
Pratt, Marnie 113–114
pregnancy 40, 89, 150, 171, 187
Prepon, Laura 2
Price, Joshua 106
Prison: Cell Block H 11, 112
prison family 124
prison-industrial complex 77, 95, 107, 185, 195, 196, 198, 216
prison system 3, 34, 91, 111, 120, 142, 180, and abuse 150 ;and Department of Corrections 3; and incarceration rates 3; and punishment 11; and sex 83, 86, 87; and surveillance 11; and the United States 3, 7
privilege 1, 46–48, 57, 91, 167, 196, 198, 201, 202, 206
promiscuity 21, 22, 26

queer identity 6, 12, 16, 51, 55, 72, 85, 90, 103, 111–115, 126, 205; *see also* bodies

Radish, Christina 47
Raine Sweet, Candi 108
rape 42, 49, 81, 82, 84, 86, 90, 91, 92, 121, 134, 145, 184, 187
rape culture 41

Reed, Natalie 103
Reeder, Constance 19
Regan, Ronald 3, 17
Richie, Beth 107
Rolling Stone 2
Russo, Vito 9, 17, 22, 113
Ryan, Michael 36

Said, Edward 64
Samuels, Allison 99
Santeria 164
Schilling, Taylor 2, 51
scopophelia 26, 27
Sedgwick, Eve Kosofksy 19
Sered, Susan 129, 131
sex 78, 81, 88, 122
sex work 136
sexual ambiguity 71
sexual power 140
sexual violence 33, 34, 39, 42, 53, 81, 87, 185, 187
sexuality 8, 38, 143; assertiveness 24, 83; and identity 15; and lesbianism 22; and women of color 8, 16, 154
sexually transmitted disease 119
Shai, Oren 111
Sherry, Mark 65
Shome, Raka 49
Skidmore, Emily 104
Smith, Anna Marie 79
social construction of gender 4
solitary 98
solitary housing unit (SHU) 35, 145, 186
Soules, Conor 38
Spade, Dean 95
spectacle 36, 37
Spektor, Regina 54, 166
Stern, Marlow 62
stereotypes 20, 24, 164
Streitmatter, Rodger 16, 19
suffrage 212
Sugar Rush 11, 112, 114
surveillance 85, 98

Tajima, Renee E. 62
television 1, 17, 103
Thanksgiving 144, 145
therapists 33
Tiger Mother 70, 73
A Time to Kill 48
Top of the Lake 80
transfeminine 105
transgender *see* LGBT
transphobic 98, 100, 121
trauma 6, 12, 32–35, 175, 184, 185, 187; *see also* physical violence; sexual violence
Trier-Bieniek, Adrienne 4, 5

Trojan Horse 45, 50, 53, 59, 79, 158, 167, 200
tropes 111
Tropiano, Stephen 16, 18
Tu, Irene 62

UCLA sociology 2
unions 201
University of Minnesota 2
unwanted pregnancies 134

Valiente, Alexa 68
Victoria's Secret 56, 200

Wallace, Michelle 98–99
Walters, Suzanna Danuta 17

war on drugs 3, 39
Washington Redskins 67
Weeds 45
Wentworth 112, 114
Weston, Kath 123
White Angelo-Saxon Protestant (WASP) 51
Within These Walls 112
Wong, Anna May 63
Wright, Erik Olin 130
Writer's Guild of America 160
women in prison 112–114, 121
women of color 15, 21, 147, 175, 182, 195, 198, 200

Zia, Helen 66